AF324193

DEFUNCT FEDERALISMS

Federalism Studies
Series Editor: Søren Dosenrode

The end of the Cold War profoundly altered the dynamics between and within the various states in Europe and the rest of the World, resulting in a resurgence of interest in the concept of federalism. This shift in balance has been further fuelled by the increase in the number of conflicts arising from the disaffection of the diverse ethnic or religious minorities residing within these states (e.g. Sudan, Iraq). Furthermore, globalization is forcing governments not only to work together, but also to reconsider their internal roles as guarantors of economic growth, with regions playing the major part.

It is the aim of the series to look at federal or federated states in historical, theoretical and comparative contexts. Thus it will be possible to build a common framework for the constructive analysis of federalism on the meta-level, and this in turn will enable us to identify and define federal tradition traditions, and develop the theoretical.

This unique and ground-breaking new series aims to promote a complete and indepth understanding of federalism by collectively bringing together the work of political scientists, lawyers, historians, economists, sociologists and anthropologists, and with this in mind, contributions are welcomed from authors in all of these disciplines. But whereas the federal approach is the crank of the series, it does not mean that contributions must adhere to the federal approach; critical contributions are welcome too.

Also in the series

Constitutionalising Europe
Michael Longo
ISBN 978 0 7546 4698 3

Approaching the EUropean Federation?
Edited by Søren Dosenrode
ISBN 978 0 7546 4244 2

Defunct Federalisms
Critical Perspectives on Federal Failure

Edited by

EMILIAN KAVALSKI
University of Western Sydney, Australia

MAGDALENA ZOLKOS
University of Alberta, Canada

ASHGATE

Published by
Ashgate Publishing Limited
Gower House
Croft Road
Aldershot
Hampshire GU11 3HR
England

Ashgate Publishing Company
Suite 420
101 Cherry Street
Burlington, VT 05401-4405
USA

www.ashgate.com

British Library Cataloguing in Publication Data
Defunct federalisms : critical perspectives on federal
    failure. - (Federalism studies)
    1. Federal government - Case studies 2. Comparative
    government
    I. Kavalski, Emilian II. Zolkos, Magdalena
    320.4'049

Library of Congress Cataloging-in-Publication Data
Defunct federalisms : critical perspectives on federal failure / [edited] by Emilian Kavalski and Magdalena Zolkos.
        p. cm. -- (Federalism studies)
    Includes bibliographical references and index.
    ISBN 978-0-7546-4984-7 (hardback) 1. Federal government--Case studies. 2. Comparative government. I. Kavalski, Emilian. II. Zolkos, Magdalena.

    JC355.D385 2008
    320.4'049--dc22

2008020167

ISBN 978 0 7546 4984 7

Printed and bound in Great Britain by
MPG Books Ltd, Bodmin, Cornwall.

Contents

Acknowledgements   *vii*
List of Abbreviations   *ix*
Notes on Contributors   *xi*

1   Approaching the Phenomenon of Federal Failure   1
     Emilian Kavalski and Magdalena Zolkos

2   Dwelling Separately: The Federation of the West Indies and the
     Challenge of Insularity   17
     Amanda Sives

3   The Pyrrhic Victory of Unitary Statehood: A Comparative Analysis
     of the Failed Federal Experiments in Ethiopia and Indonesia   31
     Thomas Goumenos

4   Partnership and Paternalism: The Federation of Rhodesia and
     Nyasaland (1953–1963)   47
     Tony King

5   The Games Elites Play: Notes towards an Elite-Focused Understanding
     of the Failure of the Federal Republic of Cameroon (1961–1972)   59
     Cyril Fegue

6   The Failed Experiment with Federalism in Pakistan (1947–1971)   71
     Farhan Hanif Siddiqi

7   The Demonization of Federalism in Republican China   87
     Steven Phillips

8   The Strategic Roots of Arab Federalism and Its Failure: Transnational
     Sovereign Power Issues, Military Rule, and Arab Identity   103
     Corri Zoli

9   The Failure of the Socialist Federal Republic of Yugoslavia (1945–1991):
     A Story of Contradictions, Weaknesses and Tensions   115
     Matt McCullock and Silvia Susnjic

10   From the Second Best Option to Dissolution: Instrumentality and
      Identity in Czechoslovak Federalism   129
      Jan Ruzicka and Kamila Stullerova

11   The Soviet People: The Rise and Fall of an Ideological Federalism   145
      Ivan Gololobov

12   Conclusions: Whither Defunct Federalisms   157
      Emilian Kavalski and Magdalena Zolkos

Bibliography   *173*
Index   *201*

Acknowledgements

The editors wish to express their gratitude to the contributors and the reviewers of the different chapters included in this volume. Personal thanks for their prompt 'response' to requests at different stages of this project also go to Rob Aitken, Angel Angelov, Justin Corfield, Jose Augusto Fontouro Costa, Søren Dosenrode, Joseph Heim, Mojtaba Mahdavi, Mohammed Nuruzzaman, and Margaret Younger. Financial assistance by the Izaak Walton Killam Memorial Fund is gratefully acknowledged.

List of Abbreviations

AAC—the Anglo-American Commission
AL—the Awami League (of Pakistan)
AVNOJ—the Anti-Fascist Council of the People's Liberation of Yugoslavia
BGWIL—the British Guiana and West Indian Labor conferences
CABPC—the Constituent Assembly Basic Principles Committee
CABWIC—the Closer Association of the British West Indian Colonies
CAP—the Constituent Assembly of Pakistan
CCP—the Chinese Communist Party
CzCP—the Czechoslovak Communist Party
CDP—the Civic Democratic Party
CDWO—the Colonial Development and Welfare Organization
CLC—the Caribbean Labor Congress
CNF—the Cameroon National Federation
CO—the (British) Colonial Office
CPNC—the Cameroon People's National Convention
CPSU—the Communist Party of the Soviet Union
CUC—the Cameroon United Congress
CYL—the Cameroon Youth League
DL—the Democratic League (of China)
ELF—the Eritrean Liberation Front
ESEP—the Economic Survey of East Pakistan
FCC—the Foumban Constitutional Conference (on Cameroon)
FCWU—the French Cameroonian Welfare Union
GIA—the Government of India Act in 1935
JEUCAFRA—the *Jeunesse Camerounaise Française* movement
JLP—the Jamaican Labor Party
KNC—the Kamerun National Congress
KNDP—the Kamerun National Democratic Party
KNIL—the Royal Netherlands Indies Army
LNM—the League of Nations Mandates in Eastern, Southern, and Northern
    Cameroons
LCY—the League of Communists of Yugoslavia
LRC—*La Republique du Cameroun*
MDS—Movement for Democratic Slovakia
ML—Muslim League
PKM—the Pan-Kamerun Movement
PNM—the (Trinidad and Tobago) People's National Movement
PNP—the (Jamaican) People's National Party

RACAM—the *Rassemblement Camerounais* party
RF—Rhodesian Front
Rs.—Rupee
RUSI—the Republic of the United States of Indonesia
SANU—the Serbian Academy of Sciences
SCP—the Slovak Communist Party
SNC—the (anti-Nazi) Slovak National Council
SCAC—the Standing Closer Association Committee
SFRY—the Socialist Federal Republic of Yugoslavia
TPPA—the Taiwan Provincial Provisional Assembly
TPLF—the Tigrayan People's Liberation Front
UAR—the United Arab Republic of Egypt and Syria
UAS—the United Arab States
UC—the *Union Camerounaise* party
UDI—(South Rhodesia's) Unilateral Declaration of Independence
UN—the United Nations
UNC—the *Union Nationale du Cameroun*
UNEF—the United Nations Emergency Force
UNTT—the United Nations Trusteeship Territories (in Cameroon)
UPC—the *Union des Populations du Cameroun* party
USA—the United States of America
USSR—the Union of Soviet Socialist Republics
WIFLP—the West Indies Federal Labor Party
WIRC—the West Indies Royal Commission
YPA—the Yugoslav People's Army

Notes on Contributors

Cyril Fegue (MUP, New York University) is the ILO-ITC Fellow in the Management of Development Programs at the University of Turin (Italy) and at the United Nations International Training Center. His research focuses on decentralized sustainable development planning, distributive justice, local development, the sociology and geopolitics of African international relations. He has published in the *International Journal of Sustainable Development and Planning* and is also the co-author of *Handbook of the Foreign Policy of African States*.

Ivan Gololobov (PhD, University of Essex) is a visiting lecturer at the Faculty of Humanities, Languages, and Social Sciences at the University of the West of England, Bristol (UK) as well as at the Institute for International Law of Peace and Armed Conflict at the Ruhr Universität–Bochum (Germany). He has published in a number of Russian academic journals and collected volumes as well as in *Ab Imperio*, *Logos*, *Journal of Sociology and Social Anthropology* and the working papers series of the Norwegian Institute of International Affairs (NUPI). His research interests include the discourses of regionalization in Russia, the political articulations of Russian identity as well as the formulation of national identity in contemporary Russian pop culture, discourses on patriotism and terrorism, the advances in discourse theory and critical discourse analysis.

Thomas Goumenos (MA, University of Essex) is a fellow of the Greek State Scholarships Foundation and a doctoral candidate at the Department of Political Science and History, Panteion University (Athens). His research focuses on the comparative analysis of the mobilization of separatist movements, as well as the interaction between national identity and foreign policy, constructivist theories of ethnicity and international relations, and contentious politics.

Emilian Kavalski (PhD, Loughborough University) is Lecturer of Politics and International Relations at the University of Western Sydney (Australia). His research focuses on the security governance of complexity and the interactions between China, India, and the European Union in Central Asia. He is the author of *Extending the European Security Community: Constructing Peace in the Balkans* (2008). He has published articles in journals such as *Cambridge Review of International Affairs*, *China Report*, *European Law Journal*, *Journal of Contemporary European Studies*, *Mediterranean Quarterly*, *Review of International Affairs*, etc. as well as chapters in volumes on security studies and international relations.

Tony King (DPhil, University of Oxford) is the Visiting Research Fellow in the Department of Politics, University of the West of England, Bristol (UK). His current research in collaboration with Dr Kate Flynn examines the redevelopment of former prison sites in South Africa and Northern Ireland as instances of post-conflict development and public policy. He has published and co-authored articles on Zimbabwe and South Africa in *Zambezia, International Journal of Heritage Studies*, *Journal of Southern African Studies*, *African Affairs*, *History in Africa*, as well as chapters in a number of edited volumes on diaspora communities, colonial history, nationalism, post-conflict reparations, etc.

Matthew McCullock (PhD, Loughborough University) is a tutor in Nationalism at the Department of Politics, International Relations and European Studies, Loughborough University. His broad field of interest is political thought, specifically the development of political Calvinism, nationalism as an ideational canon, the work of Johannes Althusius, and Yugoslav federal constitutionalism. He has published articles on aspects of Johannes Althusius' work in *European Legacy*, *Atlantic Journal of World Affairs*, *Studies in World Affairs*, etc. His current research focuses on 'polyvalent federalism' and its intersection with the conjectures made by political thinkers from Johannes Althusius to Edvard Kardelj as well as its intrication with the ideology of Titoism in former Yugoslavia.

Steven Phillips (PhD, Georgetown University) is Associate Professor in History and Director of Asian Studies at Towson University. Before coming to Towson, he was an historian with the Department of State, where he compiled the *Foreign Relations of the United States* volume on Sino-American relations during the Nixon years. Stanford University Press published his book, *Between Independence and Assimilation: The Taiwanese Elite Confront Nationalist China, 1945–1950*, in 2003. He has also written on the Taiwanese independence movement and intelligence reform in Taiwan.

Jan Ruzicka (MA, Brandeis; MA, Central European University) is a doctoral candidate in the Department of International Politics at the University of Wales, Aberystwyth. He was researcher at the Institute of International Relations (Prague) and a Fellow of the International Policy Program (Budapest). Since 2004 he has been an advisor to a member on the Foreign, Defence, and Security Committee of the Senate of the Czech Republic.

Farhan Hanif Siddiqi (MSc, London School of Economics) is a lecturer at the Department of International Relations, the University of Karachi. He is currently completing his PhD thesis on the Baloch, Sindhi, and Mohajir ethnonationalisms in post-1971 Pakistan at the London School of Economics and Political Science. He is interested in the processes of state building and the politics of ethnicity in Pakistan as well as conflict resolution and security dynamics in South Asia. He is co-editor of *The Challenges of Conflict Resolution and Security in 21st Century: Problems and Prospects* (2001). He has published book chapters and journal articles dealing with different aspects of South Asian affairs.

Amanda Sives (PhD, University of Bradford) is a lecturer in politics at the School of Politics and Communications Studies, University of Liverpool. She has recently completed a book *Political Parties and Violence in Jamaica* (due to be published in 2008). In addition, she has co-authored a report entitled *Teacher Migration, 'Brain Drain', Labour Markets and Educational Resources in the Commonwealth* (2006) and has published articles in *Commonwealth and Comparative Politics, The Round Table, Latin American Perspectives, Journal of International Development, Globalisation, Societies and Education* and the *Caribbean Journal of Education*.

Silvia Susnjic (MA, George Mason University) is a doctoral candidate at the Institute for Conflict Analysis and Resolution, George Mason University. Her research interests include the processes sustaining polarization in divided societies, collective historical memory and the psychological causes of intractable conflicts. Her regional areas of research include the nation states of the former Yugoslavia. She has recently co-authored a book chapter with Ho-Won Jeong published in the *Encyclopedia of Violence, Peace and Conflict* and has previously published in *Peace and Conflict: Journal of Peace Psychology*.

Kamila Stullerova (PhD, Central European University) is a post-doctoral research fellow at the University of Alberta. Her research interests include liberal political thought and its responses to emergency approaches to politics; the relationship of history and politics; and the issue of nation-formation as aspiration for just political order. She is currently finishing a book manuscript on the political thought of Judith Shklar.

Corri Zoli (PhD, Syracuse University) is a Postdoctoral Research Fellow at Syracuse University's Women in Science and Engineering (WISE) Program at the L.C. Smith College of Engineering and Computer Science and affiliated with the Institute for National Security and Counterterrorism (INSCT). Her current research focuses on global security issues at the intersection of cultural studies and security policy, with additional interests in gender and identity, terrorism, critical theory, and globalization. She is the author of *The Modern Invention of 'Culture': Empire, Globalism and the Persistence of History, 1776–1876* (2004) and has published articles on topics in historiography, education, and women and technology in journals such as *Victorian Literature & Culture*, as well as online monographs for Morgan & Claypool.

Magdalena Zolkos (PhD, University of Copenhagen) is the Izaak Walton Killam Postdoctoral Fellow at the Department of Political Science, University of Alberta and the Irmgard Coninx Research Fellow at the Social Science Research Center Berlin (WZB). She is also the *H-Ideas* Book Review Editor. Her research focuses on the critical appraisal of the transitional justice project with special emphasis on the politics of time, justice, and home in a global context. She is the author of *Conceptual Analysis of the Human Rights and Democracy Nexus* (2005) and co-editor of *The Challenge of Mobility in the Baltic Sea Region* (2005). She has published articles in journals such as *European Legacy, Journal of Communist Studies and Transition Politics, Journal of Transitional Justice, Nordic Journal of Human Rights, Slovo, Studies in Social and Political Thought*, as well as chapters in volumes on human rights, feminism, and political theory.

'We Have Worlds Inside Us'
Edvard Munch

Chapter 1

Approaching the Phenomenon of Federal Failure

Emilian Kavalski and Magdalena Zolkos

> State sovereignty, in its most basic sense, is being redefined … [There is a movement] from states' [to] individual sovereignty—by which I mean the fundamental freedom of each individual.
>
> Kofi Annan (Annan 1997)

Introduction

Why study federal failure and how to conceptualize its instances? These are the queries that have spurred this investigation. One of the pioneers of the comparative study of defunct federalisms, Thomas Franck noted the difficulty in establishing a 'common terminology' in assessing the phenomenon of federal failure (Franck 1968, 168). In such setting, the contention would be that federalism belongs to the family of 'essentially contested concepts' (Gallie 1964; Garver 1990). Therefore, the purpose of this introduction is to clear the conceptual minefield of the literature on federalism and define the dominant terms involved in the study of defunct federalisms. At the same time, this introduction also outlines the methodological and theoretical research agenda for the study of federal failure that steer the interpretation of the particular contexts of defunct federalisms in this volume.

It has to be acknowledged from the outset, however, that it is impossible to capture the complex normative web of several—often contending, rather than complementary—rationalities and sensibilities animating the study and implementation of federalism (Gaudreault-DesBiens and Gélinas 2005, 94). Therefore, it is not the objective of this opening chapter to offer an exhaustive and complete account of the debates on federalism. Rather, it intends to provide a reference map (charting the conceptual points of departure) for the explorations of the case studies through the neglected ruins of federal failure. This opening chapter, thereby, tackles some of the issues concerning the definition and operationalization of federal failure. It examines the concept of federalism, laying out the underlying conjectures about the processes and conditions that are assumed to provoke its failure. Subsequently, it addresses the relationship between federalism and identity. Concerns regarding the interaction between the practice and notion of these concepts underwrite the critical assessment of the meaning of failure. On this background, the chapter advances the main propositions of the theory on federal failure implicit in the literature on federalism.

The Meaning of Federalism

Tracing its roots to the Latin word *foedus*, meaning 'covenant' or 'pact' (Heywood 2000, 240), federalism does not have a universal form or definition. In fact, Daniel Elazar has asserted that the definitional ambiguities of federalism 'testify to the richness of the term and its importance in the real world of politics as well as political discourse' (Elazar 1985, 20). Despite the lack of an objective definition there seems to be, however, a broad agreement that federalism identifies a particular pattern of political order based on the territorial distribution of power and premised on the principle of shared sovereignty between two levels of government. In this respect, it is distinct from the territorial extension of state authority based on the principles of subordination—i.e., devolution; redistribution of decision-making—i.e., decentralization; and sovereignty dissociation—i.e., confederation (Esberey and Johnston 1994, 242; Hueglin and Fenna 2006, 35–37). Friedrich (1968, 7), therefore, defines federalism as an *interactive process* of 'federalizing a political community, that is to say, the process by which a number of separate political communities enter into arrangements for working out solutions, adopting joint policies, and making joint decisions on joint problems, and conversely, also the process by which a unitary political community becomes differentiated into a federally organized whole'. In this respect, the notion of federalizing implies a framework of constitutionally-established balance between self-rule and shared-rule (Elazar 1987, 5).

Following Kymlicka (1998, 127), we distinguish between two dominant interactive processes of federalism: territorial federalism and multinational federalism—sometimes referred to as 'plural federalism' (see Requejo 2004, 260). The former provides a means by which 'a single national community' can divide and diffuse power, while the latter indicates a conscious intention to accommodate the desire of national minorities for self-government. Although these are ideal types, our concern in this volume is with multinational federalism, as territorial federalism is a conceptual category which tends to sideline issues of identity and does not guarantee that different 'ethnocultural groups' would be accommodated, let alone empowered within a given federal unit (Kymlicka 1998, 127; Simeon and Conway 2001, 338). As Bishai (2004, 86) insists, the smelting of sovereignty and territoriality apparent in the practices of territorial federalism hinders problematizations of the 'identity of "outsiders" inside the state'.

Such attention to multinational federalism reflects the increased emphasis on the 'politics of identity' since the end of the Cold War (Agnew 1995, 294). In its most general form, multinational federalism can be conceived as an 'ideology which holds that the ideal organization of human affairs is best reflected in the celebration of diversity through unity' (Smith 1995, 4). The collapse of the bi-polar world at the beginning of the 1990s and the expanding dynamics of globalization are just two of the processes that seemed to challenge perceived wisdoms about international life. In an attempt to frame the emergent global complexity, James Rosenau (2003, 14) has suggested that the dynamic of world affairs have moved beyond the condition of being 'post' its predecessor. In this context, he coins the term 'fragmegration' in order to abridge the pervasive (and simultaneous) interaction between fragmenting and integrating practices. The fragmegration label intends to capture 'in a single word the large degree to which these rhythms consist of localizing, decentralizing, or fragmenting dynamics that are interactively and causally linked to globalizing, centralizing, and integrating dynamics' (Rosenau 2003, 11). In this respect, on the one hand the violence attendant in the collapse of former Yugoslavia and the Soviet Union seemed to challenge the relevance of federalism in an increasingly fragmegrative world. On the other hand, the experience of post-Dayton Bosnia and post-Saddam Iraq has urged some commentators to assert the relevance of federalism as a strategy for state-building in fragmegrative contexts (Burgess 2006, 251–268; Hueglin and Fenna 2006, 16–18; von Beyme 2005, 432–447).

The challenges for federalism from the nascent dynamics of globalization seem to be illustrated by the increasing contestation of the 'classic' model of American federalism as the yardstick for measuring other federal arrangements (Kull 1992). Already Franck (1968, 186) has hinted that the success of American federalism benefited from a unique constellation of events, which prevented 'ethnic, racial, and economic differences to come to the fore'. Alluding to the inherent lack of identity accommodation in the US territorial federalism, Johnson (1973, 119) declares that it is 'one of history's little ironies that no polyglot empire of the old world has dared to be so ruthless in imposing a single language upon its whole population as was the liberal republic "dedicated to the proposition that all men are created equal"'. In this respect, despite the 'classic' position of American federalism, this investigation concurs with the suggestion that owing to its unique history and content, it does not provide a useful blueprint for multinational states (Amoretti 2004, 20; Kymlicka 1998, 127). In fact, Agnew (1995, 298–299) suggests the 'danger' in proposing (let alone imposing) the American model of federalism as a strategy for managing ethnic or other group disputes because of its 'powerful cultural-assimilationist element'. Such sentiment echoes Patrick Riley's assertion on the irrelevance of the instances of 'the United States, Canada, Switzerland, and Australia' as benchmarks for federalism, because they are 'governed according to principles of national statehood' (Riley 1973).

Thus, the studies in this volume perceive federalism not as a fixed formula but as a process of evolving multinational interactions for the territorial division of power. At the same time, such arrangement has also an important symbolic quality as it reflects a definition of the political practices between diverse political communities according to their identity. In a multinational federation, therefore, in contrast to a nation-state (or a territorial federation), the state's power and control (ideally) are not exerted by a *self* (i.e. a dominant national/territorial identity) against *others* (i.e. minorities), but by an arrangement (covenant) between designated selves (i.e. constitutionally defined identity groups/identity communities).

Therefore, paraphrasing Watts (1999), *federalism* is treated in this volume as a normative (and not only a descriptive) term that refers to *the practice of multi-tiered government combining elements of shared-rule and regional self-rule for the purposes of maintaining the tensions between distinct identities. It is based on the presumed value and validity of combining unity and diversity, and of accommodating, preserving, and promoting distinct identities within a larger political union.*

Federalism and National Identity

In federal systems, the 'we'-concept consists of layered constellations, which condition the interplay between several identity-dimensions. The objective of this volume is to map and analyze these identity-constellations in specific cases of defunct federalisms, and, thus, link them to the moment of federal failure. The contention here is that the incidence of federal failure is closely related to the inability to accommodate distinct identities within a federal entity. The suggestion is therefore that while the study of federalism traditionally tends to focus on the distribution of powers, legislative and executive governance, as well as the fiscal and foreign relations (Kincaid and Tarr 2005), it needs to be recognized that federalism is also a *metaphor* that facilitates the understanding of how individuals structure their relationships with each other, how they realize their aspirations, and how they *conceive and configure their multiple identities* (Gaudreault-DesBiens and Gélinas 2005, 66). In other words, federalism is not only about the deduction, division, and allocation of power and about multiple and competing sources of authority, but it is also about the complex and overlapping configuration and negotiation of identities (Macdonald 2005, 253).

The relationship between federalism and nationalism has long been integral to the study of federal arrangements (Friedrich 1968, 30–41). Thus, most commentators insist that federalism is underwritten by the simultaneity of centrifugal and centripetal forces, which Albert Venn Dicey has captured in his classic formulation as 'desiring union and not desiring unity' (quoted in Burgess 2001, 20). The suggestion is that such intertwining of the ideational potential of federalism and nationalism has contributed to the occlusion of the random nature of political borders and, thereby, of territorial governance (Weinstock 2005, 210). This implicit contingency of federalism, as well as the contradiction within its dynamics, points to the tension between the (allegedly) 'artificial' identity of federalism and the 'natural'/'inherent' identity of national attachment. This volume, however, distances itself from such a distinction. Instead, its contributions share the assumption that any institutionalized collective sense of belonging is animated by political constructions that are historically contingent (Albert et al. 2001; Wenger 1998; Mason 2000; Íñigo-Mora 2004). This suggestion is in agreement with Brendan O'Leary's assertion that federalism and nationalism are 'congruent' and 'compatible political philosophies' (O'Leary 2001, 278); and, at the same time, it proposes that too often research into the intrication between the two has been shut off by the tendency to mistake the causes of national unification for the causes of federalism (Gibson and Falleti 2004; Ziblatt 2004).

In order to indicate the analytical relevance of identity tensions to the examination of federal failure, this volume adopts the approach of 'nested nationalities' (Miller 1999; 2001). While not developed for the study of identities within federal polities, the notions of 'nested nationality', 'nested citizenship', and 'nested membership' have been applied before in the study (and advocacy) of federalism, primarily in the European context (Faist 2001; Delanei and Barani 2003; Bauböck 2007). These notions capture the split between identities and loyalties resulting from an individual's belonging to two distinct political spaces, of which one is enclosed within (and subordinate) to the other. Such understanding acknowledges the 'identities-within-a-federation' situation implicit in federalism, which allows the individual contributions to this volume to capture the multiplicity, complexity and historical particularity of the identity mosaic within their specific cases (see Sarup 1996, 1–27).

At the same time, in an attempt to overcome the methodological homogenizing tendencies underwriting the umbrella terms of the 'federal failure' and 'national identity', the contributions to this volume investigate the patterns of failure in different *contexts*. The reference to context here is not coincidental. Following Gary Goertz, its conceptual ramifications confirm that human action is unfathomable outside of its sociological, cultural, and (eco)historical nexus of reference. The notion of context, therefore, stresses the 'variability—if not capriciousness—of human behavior [and] attempts to "de-universalize" knowledge and meaning' (Goertz 1994, 1). In recognition both of the contingency embedded in the federal contexts of identity accommodation and of the contested processes of identification, this investigation concurs with Michael Sheehan's observation that 'identity communities are self-constructed "imagined communities"'. In other words, while factors such as language or location might be involved in the construction of 'identity communities', it 'nevertheless remains a personal and political choice to identify with some community by emphasizing some factor or factors in contrast to others, particularly when more than one option is available, or when there are political pressures *not* to identify with a particular group' (Sheehan 2005, 84. Emphasis original; Bially-Mattern 2000).

Reaffirming this proposition, some commentators have even suggested that 'people's *need* for identity in social relations … [is] so strong that they will invent in-group and out-group identities and differences even when there is no rational basis for doing so' (Kowert and Legro 1996, 2004. Emphasis original). Thus, to borrow from a different context, identity interdependence is the context within which federal institutions operate—that is, the discord/social differentiation generated by the interdependence among human beings prompts the need for federal institutions; it, however, also stresses that these institutions can be oppressive (Keohane 2002, 10). Federal failure, thereby, gains its meaning by reference to the contextual contingency of normative, institutional, and discursive settings of identity accommodation.

In this respect, this volume operationalizes the notions of *national identity* and *federal identity* in the following way. *Federal identity* refers to *the larger overarching identity signified by the institutions, symbols, and practices of the federal state. National identity* refers to *the specific cultural, historic, and emotional features that reflect an individual's belonging to a group.* In a federal context, the notion of national identity is (occasionally) further elaborated through the membership of a group which is 'situated in a more or less clear territory and display a will to maintain their distinctiveness in the political sphere' (Requejo 2004, 260).

Being part of the dynamics of state building, the failure of federalism to accommodate the tension between federal and national identities tends to jeopardize state making and the viability of federal arrangements. In other words, the study of defunct federalisms is parallel—if not coterminous—to the analysis of state failure. As Hicks (1978, 178) has argued 'differences in human endowment may mar the harmonious operation of a federation [and] lead to an impossible situation'. Bøås (2000, 309) describes this situation succinctly in his observation that 'people are killing each other because of who they are and the identities they represent'. In this respect, the recognition of separate identity communities embedded in the distinction between national and federal identity is intended to avoid the simplification inherent in the traditional differentiation between minority and majority groups within a federation. The insistence on national identity not only suggests a reversal of the conventional view that it is the allegedly subversive (secessionist) proclivities of minority groups that 'do federalism in', but also allows for the problematization of the split-level identities of both majority and minority groups within a federal unit. In this setting, it is the creation of social practices and intersubjective meanings that leads to the formation of collectives with identities differentiated from other collectives (Sterling-Folker 2005, 19–21).

At the same time, the emphasis on national and federal identities suggests that the relationship between the overarching federal identity and the national identities does not have to be antagonistic and/or a mutually exclusive one (as is usually implied in the discussions of majority-minority relations). Rather, the federal and national identities can overlap and intertwine as they 'exist at more than one level' (Miller 2001, 306). This indicates that the interplay between federal identities and national identities manifests diverse identity constellations and understandings, which become conspicuous at different times, in different contexts and for different purposes. The issue then is to *identify* whether (and in what way) the federal and national identities construe themselves as different to the extent that they were no longer able to maintain accommodation within the arrangements of now defunct federalisms.

The Meaning of Failure

Since this volume undertakes a critical assessment of defunct federalisms it is necessary to delineate the meaning of their failure. The tendency in the literature on federalism has been to consider the instances of federal failure as exceptions, aberrations, or deviations from the general model of federal success. Instead, the attention to defunct federalisms in this volume suggests the theory-building and policy-making advantages from approaching federal failure as the 'norm' and federal success as the 'exception'. In particular, the focus on failure acknowledges 'the inherently unstable character' of federal arrangements—that is, 'the very things which make federalism desirable and occasionally possible also make it unstable and occasionally perishable' (Riley 1973, 120). The contingency of federal structures suggests that 'even when actors are ready to learn and not just adapt and survive, even when intentionality drives them, the contours of their imagined institutional change cannot prefigure, save happenstance, a distant outcome that possibly has never before been practiced' (Di Palma 2004, 250–251).

Initial inquiries into the issue of federal failure have focused exclusively on functional definitions. For instance, Franck (1968, 169) maintains that in the case of federalism failure reveals an invocation of a historical fact—the 'non-achievement of the necessary conditions for survival of a federation'. In a similar fashion, Hicks (1978, 9) posits that if the objective of federalism is 'to establish and maintain a polity where government by the people produces at one and the same time a strong self-conscious national organization and also keeps intact the rights and cultures of the units as enshrined in the constitution, then *any* deviation from such a polity must be accounted failure'. Although exposing the bearing of 'failure' on the study of federalism, such definitions fall short of delineating its relevance to the critical appraisal of defunct federalisms. There is a two-fold reason for this: firstly, the failure to distinguish between federation and federalism, and, secondly, the focus on functional explanations.

The notion of 'federalism' is regarded by this volume as conceptually distinct from 'federation'. The reason is that while the latter refers to the actual historical arrangement of state institutions, the former constitutes a much more multifaceted understanding, which indicates different aspects (political, economic, cultural, etc.) of the endorsement of a federal system (Burgess 2006, 2). As such, federalism combines normative and descriptive perspectives on federations (federation as politically superior organizational option and a locus of specific political values *versus* federation as an 'actually existing' historical entity).

While placing an emphasis on the distinction between the notions of federalism and federation, understanding the failure of federalism requires immersing the prevalent functional explanations in arguments on the management of identity-based conflicts. In this respect, the breakup of specific federations does not necessarily translate into a failure of federalism; nor is the opposite true as the continued existence of a federation does not always indicate a success for federalism (Heinemann-Grüder 2002; Webber 2002). The absence of explanations for the effects of identity on the assessment of federalism's failure is striking, in particular as Franck (1968, 189) asserts that 'ethnic, racial, and other historical distinctions are likely to assert themselves at the expense of unity'.

In addressing such lacuna, this volume claims that the success of federalism hinges, *inter alia*, on its ability to *manage* tensions between 'multiple and overlapping communities of identity' (Smith 1995, 3). Such a context reasserts the need to address the idea of federalism as a metaphor 'for imagining the manner in which citizens conceive who they are and how they organize the relationships through which they pursue their purposes and ambitions in concert with others across the entire range of human interactions' (Macdonald 2005, 261). Hence, the failure of federalism points to its abortive accommodation of diversity (Simeon and Conway 2001)—that is, its inability to engage creatively the 'ideologies of resentment' (Gaudreault-DesBiens and Gélinas 2005, 57).

Following Amoretti (2004, 2), by the term 'accommodation' we understand the capacity to manage identity-based conflicts through the mechanisms and procedures embedded in existing institutional arrangements of federal states. Accommodation has three dimensions: (i) minimizing violence and extra-institutional mobilization; (ii) diminishing hostility towards the state by minority groups; and (iii) respecting the political and civil rights of minority groups by the state. In this respect, the reference to the *failure of federalism points to its malfunctioning on any of those three aspects of identity accommodation. Defunct federalism*, therefore, reflects *the failure of federalism as a normative principle to maintain the accommodation of unity and diversity and to negotiate the perpetuation of their coexistence.*

The Theory of Defunct Federalisms

An overview of the literature addressing the concept, content, context, concerns, and practices of federalism and its failure has generated the hypotheses outlined in the remainder of this section. Their summation here is indicative of a latent *theory of defunct federalism* that seems to (in)form the subtext of much of the ongoing discussions on federalism. Such pulling together of the dominant assertions of this theory is intended to facilitate the critical endeavor of the cases included in this volume and ensure their coherence by providing them with a generalizable framework of reference.

The articulation of the following hypotheses of such theory of federal failure is intended to assist in *constructing the comparable* between the distinct contexts of the different cases of defunct federalisms—that is, this volume asserts the possibility of comparing the allegedly incomparable experiences of the implementation of the federal idea by attempting a 'reconciliation between the abstract unity of federalism and the concrete diversity of the federal phenomenon' (Gaudreault-DesBiens and Gélinas 2005, 53). At the same time, the use of a spectrum of approaches across the following chapters indicates that despite the articulation of the following hypotheses, there is no need for recourse to a single epistemology or methodology in exploring the phenomenon and instances of defunct federalism.

- Hypothesis 1: If federalism does not conform to the rules of liberal democracy it fails.

It has become a truism in the literature on federalism to emphasize that federal solutions are intrinsically linked to the practices of the liberal democratic polity. Thus, while some have declared that federalism is the 'handmaiden of democracy' (Smith 1995, 3), others have elaborated that 'only a system that is a constitutional democracy can provide credible guarantees and the institutionally embedded mechanisms that help ensure that the lawmaking prerogatives of the subunits will be respected' (Stepan 2001, 318). Occasionally such claims to the 'inherently democratic' nature of federalism have been validated in identity terms—on the one hand, it is asserted that federalism seeks 'to create and maintain a nation'; on the other, it attempts 'to preserve the integrity of the units, their identity, culture, and tradition' (Hicks 1978, 4). In this respect, the inability to conform to key liberal democratic values (such as representation, tolerance, pluralism, reciprocity, mutuality, etc.) would suggest the failure of federalism (Hueglin and Fenna 2006, 55–111; Burgess 2006, 162–191).

- Hypothesis 2: If federalism does not provide a just institutional setting for the accommodation of identity it fails.

The recent rash of attention to federalism tends to acknowledge that it is better to accommodate the desires of national groups to retain their identities, rather then suppress them (Kymlicka 1998, 122). Many authors insist that federalism offers a range of solutions and opportunities that make it an applicable device for managing identity-based conflicts in multinational contexts (Amoretti 2004, 11). It has been praised for providing the mechanisms that tend to secure the coexistence between federal and national identities and for implementing a strategy which offers sufficient institutional guarantees to enable an appropriate division of power (Smith 1995, 13). In this respect, the inability of federal arrangements to provide feasible mechanisms and procedures for the accommodation of federal and national identities would bespeak its failure.

This hypothesis has three further aspects:

- Hypothesis 2A: Asymmetrical institutional arrangements provide a better accommodation of diversity than symmetrical ones.

The notion of the asymmetrical federal arrangement implies 'the differential status and rights among the constituent units of federations and between the individuals and the federation as a whole' (Burgess 2001, 209). Recently, some commentators have argued that symmetrical models are 'ill-suited' to the management of identity conflicts (Requejo 2004, 272). The proposition in the literature, therefore, is that asymmetrical federalism contributes to the accommodation of national identities within federations owing to its flexibility and sensitivity to particular contexts. The task for the contributors is to find evidence that supports/disproves such claim in their study of the contexts of defunct federalism.

- Hypothesis 2B: Executive federal arrangements provide a better accommodation of diversity than administrative ones.

This hypothesis tests the *degree of federalism*. Although there has been some attention to the suspension of federal entities between the categories of nation-state and confederation, there is still some distance to go before the content of this tension is made relevant to the study of defunct federalisms. The difference between the institutional settings of executive federalism and administrative federalism is that while in the former 'the federal balance is largely determined by the relationship between the executives of each level of government', in the latter 'central government is the key policy-maker and provincial government is charged with the responsibility for the details of policy implementation' (Heywood 2000, 240–241; Smiley 1971, 91). Thus, in the instance of multinational federalism this would suggest that the accommodation of national identities within the executive federal model is intimately related to their political empowerment and their inclusion in the decision-making processes. Such assertion tends to be justified by the allegedly growing interdependence between the two levels of government in executive federalism, which makes it increasingly difficult for governments within the federation to fulfill their responsibilities in isolation from each other (Watts 1989, 439–456). In contrast, the administrative federal arrangement might be inclined to perceive the mechanisms of the territorial and/or functional diffusion of powers as only indirectly related to the issues of national identity accommodation. The query then is, to what extent such *degree of federalism* can be identified as a contributing factor to federal failure.

- Hypothesis 2C: The institutionalization of identity contributes to the failure of federalism.

The literature of federalism insists that conceding to the demands of national identity groups leads to a decline in their desire for independence (Bermeo 2004, 470). Such conclusion, however, largely rests on the study of *non-defunct* federalisms. Yet, even in this context some have pointed to the dilemma of federalism—its institutionalization (and, thereby, fixing into immutability) 'of what may be "temporary" or partial group identities' (Agnew 1995, 297). Thus, the territorial nature of the federal solution inscribes differences and ensures their reproduction through the recognition of the historic rights, territories and powers of self-government of national identities. In this way, federalism could (potentially) infuse a sense that national identities constitute 'separate people, whose participation in the larger federation are conditional and revocable' (Kymlicka 1998, 140).

Thus, the three dimensions of *Hypothesis 2* test the suggestion that owing to its institutional arrangement, federalism has a 'poor track record as a conflict-regulation device in multi-national and polyethnic states, even where it allows a degree of minority self-government' (McGarry and O'Leary 1994, 111–12). In this respect, the contributors are asked to assess in what way the institutional arrangements of federalism fulfill (and fail) the purpose of managing (and reconstituting) the relationship between federal and national identities.

- Hypothesis 3: If federalism is imposed (either externally or domestically, by a particular group) it fails.

This hypothesis presupposes that consensual politics and popular support are crucial for federalism's successful accommodation of the diversity of national identities. The obvious characteristic that the cases of defunct federalisms examined in this volume seem to share is that they were the product of particular post-colonial or post-communist environments. In the post-colonial cases, often the former imperial power 'encouraged' federalism, whereas in the post-communist cases federalism was perceived as the legacy of an imposed and authoritarian rule (Bermeo 2004, 471). Apart from the apparent binary opposition between coercion and compromise, this hypothesis also tests the relationship between *federalism as a means* and *federalism as an end*. For instance, if federalism is proposed as a *means* to achieving independence, economic development, the consolidation of power, etc., then once these objectives are achieved (or if it is confirmed that they cannot be achieved in this way) it appears that federalism is no longer needed and tends to be abandoned. However, as Franck (1968, 182–183) suggests, if federalism is conceptualized as an *end* in itself (i.e., beyond the immediate practical advantages) then it is less likely to fail (and less likely to be perceived as imposed).

Roadmap of the Book

The objective of this section is to offer a brief tour of the volume by sketching out the contentions of the individual chapters. It should be made clear from the outset that unlike other collective endeavors that feign the final word in their particular topic, this volume does not attempt a closure of the field. On the contrary, it hopes to open prospects for further discussions and interpretations. At the same time, this book results from contingent connections between scholars specializing in different and divergent areas, who took advantage of the opportunities offered by global(izing) communication technologies to come together and engage in a conversation around the phenomenon of defunct federalism. The following chapters are an outcome of these discussions.

In them, the contributors to this volume assess the relevance of the three hypotheses of the theory of defunct federalism. The chapters, thereby, depict the interplay between the specific content of the individual factors that led to the failure of the particular federalism. The submissions also investigate whether there are other context-specific reasons (not accounted for by the three hypotheses of the theory of defunct federalism) which reflect additional dynamic(s) revealing the juncture between federal failure and the intrication between federal and national identities. In this respect, the contributors were free to interpret the relevance of the hypotheses on defunct federalism. At the same time, the defunct federalisms examined here do not provide an exhaustive compendium of this phenomenon. Instead, the cases included in this volume merely suggest the variations across the experiences of federal failure; thereby, allowing for valid inferences to be drawn (King et al. 1994, 141–149).

Chapter 2, written by Amanda Sives, deals with the federation of the West Indies. This federation, which included the Greater Antilles, the Lesser Islands, the Windward Islands, the Bahamas Islands, as well as Trinidad and Tobago, existed from 1958 until 1962. The chapter outlines the development of the federal idea in the West Indies in the colonial period and offers a detailed account of its institutionalization during the transition of the West Indies from British rule to post-colonial sovereignty in 1950s. In her analysis of the causes and ramifications of the failure of the West Indian federation, Sives emphasizes the defunct institutional framework, as well as the disparities in the level of democratization among the West Indian islands and the conflicting interests regarding the conceptualization and political practice of federalism. While this chapter considers the hypothesis that the mode of establishing the West Indian federation by Britain (i.e. 'imposition') might have undermined the possibility of its success, it concludes by suggesting that much more critical was the treatment of federalism as a means to different political ends both by the former colonial ruler and the political elites of the West Indian states, rather than as an end in itself.

Subsequently, in Chapter 3, Thomas Goumenos offers a comparative perspective on two failed federal experiments: in Ethiopia (1952–1962) and in Indonesia (1949–1950). While this chapter offers an exhaustive analysis of each of these federal attempts (and failures) in the context of their historical (post-) colonial idiosyncrasies, it also suggests one underlying commonality. Namely that both in Ethiopia and Indonesia federalism failed because of its construction by the new political elites as antithetical to their post-colonial projects of asserting national sovereignty vis-à-vis the former colonial powers. Consequently, federalism was considered (and rejected) in separation from the debates on the democratic empowerment of post-colonial populations and, thus, became associated with reactionary and conservative political forces that aimed at subverting national unity. In addition, the case of the Ethiopia–Eritrea federation suggests that asymmetrical federal arrangements can be highly problematic if they are not accompanied by more nuanced recognition of various political vulnerabilities of minority groups. The instance of the Indonesian federation casts doubts on whether its particular arrangement of state organization should even be recognized as a functioning federation because of its institutional deficiencies and undemocratic tendencies (especially during the 'New Order' period of Sukarno's presidency).

In Chapter 4, Tony King tackles the case of the failed Federation of Rhodesia and Nyasaland. His analysis suggests that the failure of federal structures to negotiate between the black and white identity communities—each adopting distinct interests and normative convictions—precipitated the dissolution of the federation. At the same time, the federal shortcoming was also a reflection of the awkwardness of the federal state, which was neither a self-governing sovereign entity, nor an outright British dependency. According to King, the complexities of the federal origins and structure prevented the Federation of Rhodesia and Nyasaland to even attempt the promotion of a shared federal identity. Thus, in the vacuum provided by the absence of federal symbolism, racial differentiation became a potent feature of political attachment. In this setting, while the white community continued to derive its legitimacy (predominantly) from the British imperial project, the identities of the black population related increasingly to the decolonization discourse of African nationalism. King suggests that the incompatibility of these distinct forms of identification undermined the cohabitation assumed by the Federation of Rhodesia and Nyasaland.

Although geographically somewhat proximate, the experience of the Federal Republic of Cameroon discussed in Chapter 5 details a peculiar instance, when the end of federal statehood after a popular referendum did not provoke the dissolution of the country, but only its transformation into a unitary state. As Cyril Fegue explains, the convoluted legacy of colonialism in Cameroon has been a central feature both of the emergence of federalism and then of its disappearance. In particular, the formation of separate Anglophone and Francophone elites as a result of the colonial experience played a significant role in the dynamics of state-building. Federalism, in this context, became one of the pieces in the post-colonial 'games' that Cameroonian elites played for the achievement of their distinct political objectives.

Next, in Chapter 6, Farhan Hanif Siddiqi analyzes the unsuccessful federal experiment in Pakistan in the period between the partition of colonial British India in 1947 and the 1971 Bangladesh Liberation War. It focuses on the One Unit policy (introduced in 1955), which merged four Pakistani provinces into West Pakistan in an attempt to strengthen its ethnic and linguistic homogeneity. The federal failure of

Pakistan is explained in the context of centralizing dynamics among the post-colonial state elites. This chapter suggests therefore that in the case of Pakistan there was a strong correlation between centralization, the federal failure, and the undemocratic tendencies of governance. In this context, it also proposes that the federal malfunction is understood as a political and a constitutional failure to accommodate the plurality of ethnic identities, in particular as regards the (numerically dominant) Bengali group. Siddiqi's chapter also considers additional factors that 'assisted' the federal failure, such as the economic disparities among the federal units.

The issue of devolution—especially, the perceived dangers of decentralization—dominates the analysis by Steven Phillips in Chapter 7. Although his investigation concentrates primarily on the 'demonization' of federalism during the period of Republican China, the chapter offers poignant insights into the post-war sidelining of federalism in Chiang Kai-Shek's Taiwan and Mao Zedong's China. In a noteworthy addition to the other studies included in this volume, Phillips suggests that the project of federalism in China failed not only because of the inconsistencies and dissatisfactions with any actual or proposed federal arrangements, but also because the Chinese term for regional autonomy/devolution also designates 'feudal' practices. Federalism was, thereby, constructed by nationalist elites of all colors and affiliations as an obstruction on the road to 'national progress' that threatens a return to a pre-modern and oppressive past (see Waldron 1990).

In the following Chapter 8, Corri Zoli engages with the experience of pan-Arab federalism, and suggests that its failure was related to its treatment as a framework for political opportunism, whose 'utility' evaporated as soon as its expediency failed to deliver on the expectations invested in it. The analysis suggests that the controversial legacy of such federal attempts underwrites many of the current Middle Eastern posers. Thus, by focusing on the 'sovereignty power issues' elicited by such schemes for unification, Zoli interprets the origins and subsequent failure of pan-Arabism through the idisyncracies of civil-military relations in the region. In this regard, the discursive constellations of Arab identity become subject to the instrumental stratagem of particular leaders—most notably, Gamal Abd al-Nasser of Egypt. Such exploration of the persistent contestations of transnational sovereign power issues in the Middle East emphasizes the strategic (in very material terms) rationale behind the project of Arab federalism, especially in providing an organizational platform for a diverse set of regional actors.

In Chapter 9, Matthew McCullock and Silvia Susnjic analyze the experience of the Socialist Federal Republic of Yugoslavia (1943/1945–1991) from the perspective of its, ultimately, violent breakup. This chapter sketches the conflicting dynamics of the Yugoslav federal experience, which was torn between two rather different (if not contradictory) political visions of federalism. On the one hand, the federation has been structured along the idea of 'organic federalism' which was endorsed by President Tito and which, in short, reflected a South Slavic variant of the broader Pan-Slavic nationalism. On the other hand, there was the more 'civic' vision of federalism promoted by Edvard Kardelj, which evolved around the project of 'workers' self-management'. McCullock and Susnjic depict the complex mosaic of institutional and political practices of Yugoslav federalism(s). At the same time they also indicate a whole plethora of problems emanating mostly from the spiraling tensions between 'civic' and 'organic' federalism, which contributed to the gradual unraveling of the federation. The chapter, nevertheless, concludes by suggesting that while the violent dissolution of the former Yugoslavia was indicative of its failure as a *federation*, the almost half-a-century-long Yugoslav federal experience evidences an innovative engagement with the political ideas of *federalism*.

Similar issues animate the explorations of Jan Ruzicka and Kamila Stullerova in Chapter 10. Their analysis focuses on the experience of Czechoslovakia, tracing its state organization from 1918 until its peaceful dissolution in 1992/1993 (although it was a formal federation only from 1969). This chapter provides a historical outline of the formative process of the Czechoslovak federation and describes the institutional and political dynamics that led to the 'Velvet Divorce' between Czechs and Slovaks. The focus of Ruzicka and Stullerova's investigation is both institutional and conceptual. In the explanatory section, they argue that in the post-communist period a political consensus transpired which claimed that the Czechoslovak federation had exhausted its potential and its relevance. At the same time, the argument is that any attempt to conceptualize the Czechoslovak federalism as 'defunct' must include the problematic (insufficient and ultimately defective) accommodation of the diverse ethnic and national identities encompassed within its space.

In Chapter 11, Ivan Gololobov offers an innovative discourse critical approach to the study of the federal failure in the former Soviet Union (1922–1991). This chapter is preoccupied with the study of the identity/ideology nexus in the discourses of Soviet federalism, and with its dysfunctional character not at the level of constitutional politics, but rather as an inconsistent accommodation of Marxist theorizing within the (so-called) 'political realities' of the post-revolutionary Soviet federation. Consequently, Gololobov suggests that the crisis of federal identity and the rise of new nationalisms during the 1980s (which ultimately contributed to the demise of the Soviet Union) were modalities of the 'cognitive gap opened by the explanatory inconsistencies of Soviet Marxism'. The conclusion is that the failure of Soviet federalism was not due to the political and discursive *antagonisms* between the federal, state, and ethnic identities. Rather, Gololobov asserts that this failure needs to be understood in the light of the formative discursive moment of the 1918 October Revolution, which brought together into the hybrid of Soviet statehood the insistence on federal belonging, a seditious political project of the working class, and deferential attitude to political leadership.

Finally, in the concluding Chapter 12, the editors bring together the suggestions of the contributions and assess the relevance of the conceptual map provided by the theory of defunct federalism. While this chapter is focused on mapping out the specificities of the analyzed federal arrangements, at the same time it also tries to avoid ahistorical and decontextualized generalizations. It contends that if there is any commonality shared by the analyses included in this volume (apart from the analytical prism of their 'defunctness') it is the tentativeness and (institutional and ideational) fragility of their federal arrangements. Thus, in the vacuum effected by the lack of identity-interaction, federalist structures become not only party to, but also tools for the suppression of identity difference. The suggestion therefore is that for a federalism to be considered successful it (among other criteria) will have to facilitate, on the one hand, the resilience of social agreements and political practices, and, on the other hand, it will have to open up for the radical unexpectedness and uncertainty of democratic politics.

Chapter 12 contends that federal failure is a constitutive dimension of the larger continuum of state building and state collapse—i.e., the breakdown of federations is an instance of state dissolution. Said otherwise, the focus on defunct federalism draws attention to important parallels between the occurrence of federal failure and the ongoing study of weak statehood. Such proposition reengages with the somewhat sidelined (yet, long-standing) challenge of the literature on federal theory to the dominant conviction of political science that states are functionally similar and differ only in regards to their capabilities. In this respect, the experience of defunct federalisms illuminates the intellectual paradox of federalism—i.e., it moved from an alternative (if not antithetical) framework to state sovereignty to one that gradually adopted its systemic practices and ideological principles. As it would be explained in the following chapters, such identification of federal structures with the theory and practice of statism indicates not only the 'organized hypocrisy' (Krasner 1999) of Westphalian sovereignty, but also its 'self-incurred immaturity' (Booth 2007, 84). Thus, the appropriation of the 'Westphalian straitjacket' (Buzan and Little 2001, 25) by federal arrangements has tended to hinder the imagination of federalism—despite its changing epistemologies—to query the underlying assumptions of its state-centric perspective. Such sovereignty-based approach usually frames the interpretation of state building—(i) where its 'adoption' has not been successful, 'the talk is of "weak" or "failed" states on the margins of the international society/system'; (ii) where its localization seems successfully institutionalized 'ideas of sovereignty, territoriality, and nationalism with their attendant understandings of what defines "inside" and "outside" are indigenized' (Acharya and Buzan 2007, 301). According to Richard Falk, this policy attitude indicates that within its dominant Westphalian understanding 'the state is … both inhumanly large in its bureaucratic dimension and inhumanly small in its territorial and exclusionary dimensions'. Nevertheless, he has portended that the 'globalization of societal life' may undermine state-centrism and could permit 'cooperative organizational forms to flourish', leading to 'a fusion between universal confederation and organic societal forms of a communal character' (Falk 1978, 63–87).

More importantly, however, the proposition of this volume is that bringing together the analyses of defunct federalism with that of state failure would help emphasize the centrality of identity politics to the projects of both federalism and state formation. In other words, the identity-based conflicts that precipitated the unraveling of both failing states and federations did not occur in a vacuum. Thus, what to make of difference and diversity—whether they are securitized or engaged in a dialogue—depends on the dynamics of change and continuity characterizing the pervasive turbulence of international life. At the same time, the contributions to this volume take into account that 'our view of possible alternatives to the state system [and (we add) federalism] should take into account the limitations of our imagination and our own inabilit to transcend past experience' (Bull 1977, 256). The intrication between the reflections on defunct federalisms and failed statehood promises both to imagine and to critically reengage with the emancipatory potential underlying federal arrangements. Such reengagement should therefore begin from the underlying ideational feature of federalism—its assertion that states are defined not only by territorial boundaries and divisions of power, nor are they (as is so often assumed) homogenous entities, but also (and more importantly) through the individuals that inhabit them and who have multiple bases for both shared and different identities.

We believe that it is in this context that the statement of the then UN Secretary General, Kofi Annan (in the epigraph to this chapter) should be read—the inherent promise of 'individual sovereignty' underwriting the project of federalism is in its emphasis on the former (i.e., facilitating cohabitation and communities of destiny) rather than the latter (securitization of difference). This volume asserts, therefore, that the appropriation of federalist principles without the structures and processes of federalism do not portend effective identity accommodation. Federalism, in these contexts, becomes a sham and a guise for the achievement of particularistic interests and not for the unprejudiced cohabitation of different identity groups. Thus, this voyage into the relics of federal failure suggests that just as ideas animate the sinews of human endeavors, the trajectory a federalism takes (success or failure) is also a product of design.

Chapter 2

Dwelling Separately:
The Federation of the West Indies and the Challenge of Insularity

Amanda Sives

Introduction

The Federation of the West Indies was formally launched in January 1958, following eleven years of discussions between the ten islands (Antigua, Barbados, Dominica, Grenada, Jamaica, Montserrat, St. Kitts-Nevis-Anguilla, St. Lucia, St. Vincent and the Grenadines and Trinidad and Tobago) and British colonial officials. Despite the years of preparation and intergovernmental conferences, the federation lasted four years and was formally dissolved in May 1962. The main impetus driving federation originated from within the British colonial office, which had initially wanted to control the costs of administering the West Indian colonies and later sought to totally disengage as a colonial power from the region. For the West Indian colonies, the key motivation was independence from the colonial power. There was a consensus from both parties that the only way to achieve a viable economic and political separation was through a federation.

This chapter explores the reasons for the failure of the Federation of the West Indies. It begins with an overview of the development of the idea of federation (beginning in the late nineteenth century) and examines how it influenced political discourse within the region, particularly among those small, but influential groups that were seeking self-government. This is followed by a brief description of the stages in the construction and dismantling of the federal process. The third section of the chapter discusses the relevance of the three hypotheses to the failure of the West Indies Federation. While it argues that the lack of liberal democracy both within the islands and the federal government was a factor in its failure, it was not possible to reach a conclusion regarding the role of institutions and identity accommodation due to the fact that the nature of federal institutional arrangements remained a contentious issue throughout its short life-span. The extent to which federation was imposed by the British is recognized but it is also argued that both the West Indian governments and the British viewed Federation as a means to an end. Finally, the chapter examines a number of other issues which help explain why the process was so short-lived.

Background to the Federation of the West Indies

The genesis of federation in the British West Indies originated in the colonial office and it was primarily motivated by financial considerations (Munroe 1984). In 1882, for example, a Royal Commission was established to enquire into the financial situation of the British West Indian islands and suggested 'a closer union among all the British territories in the Caribbean and envisaged some form of ultimate federation' (Braithwaite 1957, 133). Financial and administrative factors were the drivers for the colonial office in the late nineteenth and early twentieth century. These were later reinforced in the post-World War II period when pressure was brought to bear on the colonial powers to pursue decolonization. The colonial office perspective was that independence (political and economic) could only feasibly occur within a federal framework.

Federation was a reality in the region prior to the agreed proposal to create the West Indies Federation. The Leeward Islands (Antigua, Montserrat, St. Kitts and Nevis, Anguilla and Dominica) had been federated since 1871. The Windward Islands (Grenada, St. Lucia, St. Vincent and the Grenadines), and Dominica (after 1939) had retained island autonomy but had shared a Governor. Attempts to federate the Leeward Islands, Windward Islands and Barbados in 1876 failed as Barbadians violently protested against the union in what became known as the confederation riots (Mordecai 1968). Later commissions continued to advocate a form of federation: a proposal to unite Barbados with the Windward Islands was suggested in the Royal Commission 1896–1897 and following his visit to the region in 1922, Major Wood recommended closer association between Trinidad and the Windward Islands. Neither of these recommendations was pursued. In his report, Wood noted not only the fundamental importance of island populations supporting federation but also the fact that there was little evidence that they did so:

> The establishment of West Indian political unity is likely to be a plant of slow and tender growth. If any advance in this direction is to be achieved, it can only be as the result of a deliberate demand of local opinion, springing from the realization of the advantages of cooperation under modern, world conditions … [At the current time] it is both inopportune and impracticable to attempt amalgamation of existing units of Government into anything approaching a general federal system (Wood quoted in Cmnd6607 1945, 324).

The 1938 riots in the Caribbean were followed by a major commission of enquiry led by Lord Moyne. The report, which was not published in full until 1945, provides a snapshot of opinions in the West Indies (albeit mediated by the colonial office) about the possible role and impact of federation in the late 1930s. It is worth quoting at length as it reinforces the absence of a general and genuine interest in federation among the citizens of the region:

> Our general impression, from the evidence which we have heard, is that while local opinion has made a considerable advance in the direction of political unity since 1932, it is doubtful whether the time is yet ripe for the introduction of any large scale federation. Local pride is a more important factor and recent experience has shown that efforts to secure cooperation for the common good from all the West Indian Colonies are still at

times frustrated by an insularity which is illustrated by the skepticism felt by even well informed people who freely express the view that nothing beneficial to their Colony could result from institutions established elsewhere in the West Indies (Cmnd6607 1945, 327).

That there should be an 'insularity' and strengthening of 'local pride' within the region in the late 1930s should not be surprising given that the islands (with the exception of the Leeward and Windward Islands) had been treated as separate entities by the colonial office. Coupled with this administrative division, the lack of inter-island transportation and communication hindered the creation of a sense of regionalism among both the leaders and the population groups. The report continued, however, to state that Federation should remain the ultimate policy goal of the colonial office. In that regard, it recommended the closer union of the Leeward Islands and Windward Islands arguing that the success of such an initiative would persuade the other islands about the merits of participating in a federation. An additional suggestion proposed by the Commission was that West Indian governments try and unify their colonial services and, it argued, while there were difficulties to overcome in achieving this, it would be a useful exercise 'if the West Indies are to work towards a federation which will have more than a nominal significance' (Cmnd6607 1945, 333). The key point is that there was a clear colonial policy agenda, which can be seen within the official reports of the period, to develop the idea of, and make practical steps towards, a federation of the West Indies.

Aside from colonial proposals advocating closer association, there were influential voices within the West Indies advocating federation. In 1929, a proposal was made to the colonial office by the unofficial members of the Antiguan Legislative and Executive Councils that Trinidad, the Windward Islands and Leeward islands be united under one Governor and Legislative Council (Cmnd6607 1945, 324). Key West Indian political figures, including member of the Grenada Legislature T.A. Marryshow, trade unionists Captain Cipriani (Trinidad) and Grantley Adams (Barbados), were involved in calling for federation during three British Guiana and West Indian Labour (BGWIL) conferences (held in 1926, 1938 and 1944). At the first conference, Cipriani declared that 'in the best interests of the people of British Guiana and the West Indies these colonies should be federated and granted some form of self government which will enable them to conduct their own affairs under a Colonial Parliament with dominion status (Braithwaite 1957, 297). Whilst the demand was vague, as Braithwaite (1957) has pointed out, it was significant that federation was being viewed as the channel through which greater self-government could be attained. During the second conference in 1938, Grantley Adams proposed a draft bill for federation which included self-government. Thus, the explicit connection between federation and self-government was both reinforced and given more substance. Finally, at the 1944 conference a resolution was put forward by Marryshow calling for federation with self-government and eventual dominion status. It was passed unanimously. Jamaican delegates had not been involved in these conferences, indeed as Hart points out, 'prior to 1944, the issue of federation had not been considered in Jamaica, the only Jamaican organizations with Caribbean wide connections being the cricketers and the sugar manufacturers' (Hart 2004, 22). However, Jamaica was represented at the two Caribbean Labor Congresses (CLC) in 1945 and 1947 when delegates were unanimous in calling for federal union with self-government.

Thus, there is evidence to highlight that debates about the merits of federation were being held within the region as well as among colonial officials, although evidently their motivations were different. The impetus of the colonial office was to reduce the costs of administration and to ultimately divest itself of the colonies. For political leaders and trade union activists within the Eastern Caribbean the goal was to attain self-government and political liberation via a federal framework. The fact that federation was seen as a method for the achievement of a political goal, rather than an opportunity to create a West Indian nation, was to prove increasingly problematic as the process developed. Allied with this, the discussions and meetings held prior to World War II did not involve Jamaican delegates. Hence, while a sense of common identity was emerging within the eastern Caribbean, this was not extended to Jamaica until 1945 when the CLC was established.

Concrete initiatives, from the colonial office and within the region, to develop a West Indies Federation gained prominence towards the close of World War II. Several developments during the war had a bearing on the renewed impetus towards federation. First, on the practical level, communication between the islands had improved, both in terms of transport links and via the media. In terms of transportation, the 1947 report from the Montego Bay conference stated that 'improvements in air-communications facilitated contact between representative leaders in the British Caribbean Colonies on a scale previously impossible' (Cmnd7291 1948, 3). The circulation of information between political elites and citizens of the islands was important in any attempt to develop a common identity across ten units geographically divided by 1,000 miles at the widest point. Second, the formation of a West Indian identity had strengthened during the wartime period as the 'war situation provided opportunities for united actions at many levels' (Springer 1962, 6–7; Bell 1960). Third, a number of region-wide bodies had developed during the early 1940s. In 1940 the Colonial Development and Welfare Organisation (CDWO) was established which for the 'first time was a West Indian wide administrative unit, dealing with every aspect of the islands' affairs, except political aspects' (Mordecai 1968, 31). Other associations, such as the Anglo-American Commission (1940) and the Caribbean Labour Congress (1945) provided evidence of emerging organizational unity in the region. At the same time, political and financial pressures in the post-World War II period accelerated the drive to decolonize.

Steps Towards the Federation of the West Indies

On 14 March 1945, the Secretary of State for the Colonies invited the legislatures of the islands to discuss the idea of a federation. Two years later, on 14 February 1947, a further memo was sent inviting each colony to send three representatives from their legislatures to attend a conference in Montego Bay, Jamaica, 11–19 September 1947 to 'consider the formulations of proposals for closer association' (Col218 1948, 4). The 1947 conference was the first time that leaders of all the territories had come together with the colonial office to formally discuss Federation. At this early stage in the process, there were three key issues which underlined the difficulties that would come to undermine the creation of a sustainable Federation: the strength of the federal government, the de-linking of political advancement from federal progression and the strength of division among the leaders of the various territories. These issues will be discussed in the next section of the chapter.

Aside from resolutions confirming agreement to move ahead with Federation, the Montego Bay Conference established the Standing Closer Association Committee (SCAC) to develop firm proposals on the creation of the Federal structure. The so-called Rance Report was presented in October 1949 and published in March 1950. It then took three years for the leaders to meet again to discuss the findings of the report. In all, there were three conferences in London (1953, 1956 and 1960) and three inter-governmental conferences in Trinidad (1959, 1960, and 1961) plus a conference on Freedom of Movement in Trinidad in 1955 (Bell 1960; Cheah 1997). Agreement was reached on a number of key issues during these conferences and in August 1956, enabling legislation was passed in the British parliament. This was followed by an Order in Council in July 1957 establishing the Federation of the West Indies and on January 3, 1958 the first Governor-General, Lord Hailes, was sworn in. Elections for the 45 seat Federal Parliament were held in March 1958 and the first (and only) Prime Minister, Grantley Adams, was appointed on April 18, 1958. Given that it had first been mooted over one hundred years previously (1840 is the first mention of federation), and in spite of the numerous conferences and discussions regarding the precise nature of the West Indies Federation, it only lasted four years. The federation effectively ended when the Jamaican population voted no to continued membership in September 1961.

In the following January, Dr Eric Williams, Prime Minister of Trinidad and Tobago signaled his intention to leave with the famous comment that 'one from ten leaves naught'. With the two largest islands having withdrawn from the process, the British Government formally dissolved the federation on 10 May 1962. While the other eight islands continued to debate the creation of a federation, by 1965 it was evident that it was not viable and alternative constitutional arrangements were agreed. In the next section of the chapter, the reasons for the failure of this short-lived federation are examined.

Accounting for the Failure of the Federation of the West Indies

The reasons for the failure of the West Indies Federation have been widely discussed in the literature. Issues such as a failure of leadership, delays in the implementation of legislation, the lack of commitment to the process by both the colonial power and key leaders within the West Indies, the existence of competing national identities, the elitist nature of the process and the inability to resolve the crucial issue of the role of the federal government vis-à-vis the units have been highlighted (Mordecai 1968; Springer 1962; Munroe 1984; Padmore 1999; Johnson 1999; Winks 1971). This section tests the hypotheses of the theory of federal failure and determines the extent to which they have relevance in explaining the demise of the West Indies Federation.

The role of liberal democracy

The individual units of the federation did not function as fully autonomous liberal democracies but remained, to different degrees, under colonial control. In addition, island representatives were continually negotiating their own internal political arrangements with the colonial power during the federal period. Indeed, West Indian leaders initially participated in Federation in order to attain political autonomy and an enhanced form of democratic politics. The continuation of colonial oversight of the internal political island administrations coupled with the desire of the colonial power to direct the political and economic process of decolonization had a number of repercussions on the formation and functioning of the Federation.

First, the constitution of the Federation was not liberal democratic. Although the original proposal of SCAC presented in 1949 had gone through a number of amendments prior to 1958, which reflected the growing level of self-government of the individual units, an element of colonial control remained. The differential political development of the individual islands also led to a lack of consensus about the federal constitution. For example, the proposals of the SCAC were accepted without question in Antigua, St Kitts, St. Vincent and Montserrat whereas in Barbados, Grantley Adams argued that the proposed constitution was no more than 'glorified crown colony' (Mordecai 1968, 41). There is little doubt that the constitution became more democratic and the balance of power changed as discussions continued. In 1949, for example, the Standing Closer Association Committee had recommended a bicameral legislature with a House of Assembly elected by universal suffrage and a Senate appointed by the Governor. Executive power rested in the hands of the Governor and a Council of State. This would consist of six members appointed by the Governor and seven Ministers appointed by the Prime Minister (Mordecai 1968, 39). By 1956, at the second London conference, it was agreed that the role of the Governor-General would be reduced and executive power would rest with Ministers.

Second, the fact that the islands were at different levels of democratic development proved to be a source of contention, one which would inadvertently undermine the federation. In 1945, when the Secretary of State for the Colonies first wrote to the leaders of the West Indies asking them to consider the issue of federation in their legislatures, only Jamaica and Trinidad operated under a system of universal adult suffrage (granted in 1944 and 1945 respectively). The issue of the discrepancy in levels of democratic governance between the colonies was raised at the 1947 Montego Bay conference when the Chief Minister for Jamaica, Alexander Bustamante, made the following analogy relating levels of political development to walking:

> Jamaica can walk. Trinidad is creeping. Barbados and Dominica are right behind Trinidad or almost the same. St. Kitts and St. Vincent are attempting to creep and only attempting. Antigua is creeping, and all of the other small islands, some can barely creep on the palm of their hands, and others on hands and feet, and others not at all, and yet you say to us "We want you to federate". How can the walking and the creeping and the babe who has not begun to creep yet, how can they walk in the same avenue? It cannot be done. All of us

have a different constitution so if all of us were to join together in a federation, instead of Jamaica who is walking, Trinidad who is really creeping, and creeping fast, progressing, we would have to make a retrograde step and try to help all these countries who cannot creep. (Cmnd7291 1948: 23)

Needless to say this comparison caused resentment among the smaller islands. Whilst Bustamante had chosen an insulting way to make the point, the issue itself was relevant. Not only did the different constitutional status of the islands lead to disagreements between them, it also led to one of the key reasons for the failure of the Federation of the West Indies. This was resolution No 2 agreed at the Montego Bay conference which stated:

> That this conference believes that an increasing measure of responsibility should be extended to the several units of the British Caribbean territories, whose political development must be pursued as an aim in itself, without prejudice and in no way subordinate to progress towards federation (Cmnd7291 1948, 7).

What this resolution effectively called for was a parallel process of political progression: greater powers of self-government could be granted outside of federal membership and would not rely on participation in the federal organization. The discussions held at the conference recorded differences of opinion between the delegates (unfortunately, the minutes do not record which units argued which position):

> During the discussion it was again argued that there could—and should—be no federation until responsible government had been attained by the separate units which would constitute it: conversely it was claimed that federation would prove the means of facilitating the progress of the component units towards full self-government within the Commonwealth, whereas self-government in isolation might result in economic domination by some other country (Cmnd7291 1948, 97).

The aim of self-government (and eventually independence) was a key driver propelling West Indian leaders towards federation. The discussion and the subsequent resolution which was agreed by all sides weakened the rationale for federation (Munroe 1984). It also created a scenario in which individual units could pursue their own constitutional advance independently of the federal process, thereby potentially further enhancing constitutional inequality between units within the Federation (Mordecai 1968, 38). However, given the disagreements between the units on how to proceed and the increasing demands from West Indian political organizations about greater powers of self-government, it is difficult to argue against the inclusion of this resolution. If the process of creating a federal organization had proceeded more rapidly, then the problem of attaining self-government independent of, or within, Federation would not have been so problematic. As it was, six years passed before the delegates participated in another conference and it was eleven years before the first federal elections were held. By this time, the individual units had gained more autonomy and control over their affairs and perceived 'without enthusiasm the loss of a measure of control of their own affairs to a Federal Government that is new

and inexperienced and with which they have not yet come to identify themselves'
(Springer 1962, 55).

Finally, the fact that individual units were not liberal democracies was problematic
for the creation and sustainability of the Federation. The lack of democratic political
will pushing federation from within each of the units meant that internal pressure was
not put on the leaders to reach compromises with each other. In addition, citizens of
the West Indies were not consulted about these new constitutional arrangements and
so political leaders were not obligated to persuade citizens of the merits of federation
as they would have been forced to do within a liberal democratic society. Munroe
(1984) has argued there was a politics of non-participation operating within Jamaica
and this 'found its extreme expression in the treatment of the federal issue in Jamaican
politics. It was therefore 'no accident that the Jamaican legislature committed the
colony to West Indian Federation without any attention to the formation of popular
opinion on the question' (Munroe 1984, 121). This failure to inform and engage the
populations of the islands led to a low level of understanding about the impact and
nature of federation amongst West Indian citizens.

The lack of liberal democratic norms governing the creation of the West Indies
Federation had a number of negative impacts. It led to a constitution which, when
finally implemented, had less democratic credentials than some of the individual
constituent units. The lack of political equality among the member states led to a
hierarchical positioning which intensified inter-island suspicions (particularly of
Jamaica by the Eastern Caribbean) which became increasingly difficult to resolve.
The desire of the individuals units to pursue self-government, and not to be hindered
from doing so by those that were less advanced, led to a crucial undermining of one
of the key purposes of the West Indies Federation and finally, the lack of a democratic
political culture within the islands stymied political debate about federation and
limited the creation of a vibrant regional identity. It is to this issue that we now turn.

Institutional arrangements and the accommodation of identity

The issue of identity was problematic within the West Indies, operating as it did on
a number of competing levels at a crucial moment in the process of decolonization.
On the one hand, island identities were beginning to assert themselves in the context
of the decolonization process. At the same time, Federation required the creation of a
West Indian identity in order to successfully establish and consolidate itself. Writing
in 1961, Lowenthal commented that the 'difficulty is that the people who inhabit
these scattered islands are just beginning to become a nation; they are, as yet, hardly
West Indian at all' (Lowenthal 1961, 67). The growing strength of island identities,
particularly in Jamaica, and the failure to actively pursue and develop a West Indian
identity was a key component in the failure of the Federation. The extent to which
the creation of institutional arrangements could have managed the process of dual
identity formation is questionable.

The problem with the nature of the institutional arrangements was that they were
continually contested prior to, and after, the Federal constitution was created. The
key issue was how much power should be vested in the centre as compared to the
individual units. Initially, delegates had agreed that the Australian model should

be followed where the balance of power should lie with the individual units. As discussions continued through the 1950s, two fundamentally opposed positions emerged. In May 1959, the Jamaican government, under the leadership of pro-federation Norman Manley's People's National Party (PNP), released *Ministry Paper No.18* which called for a 'constitutional formula … which would enable such Units to entrust the Federal Government with a greater range of powers over their internal affairs, yet still leave a Unit like Jamaica free to have a looser association with the federal center and keep control over all matters which, in her view, she could take care of for herself' (Springer 1962, 16).

This proposal was in complete contrast to the position of the People's National Movement (PNM) government in Trinidad and Tobago which had advocated a strong, central federal government a few days before the Jamaican position was articulated. Such stance was reasserted in the *The Economics of Nationhood* released in September 1959. In this publication, the PNM government outlined its vision for the creation of 'a tightly-knit Unit Federation, adequately empowered at the Centre, to shape and direct the future of the Nation … the centre should have a far wider range of powers than at present it possesses' (Mordecai 1968, 161 quoting *The Economics of Nationhood*). Not only did the PNM government argue for a strong federal government but it also defined the federation as one nation, as opposed to the Jamaican proposal, which had advocated a loose association in which individual units would be free to choose the nature of the relationship with the centre. While compromises were made between the two largest members of the Federation during the conferences held in London and Trinidad and Tobago during the 1950s, the failure to reach agreement on the control that should be ceded to the federal government hampered its development and therefore, its effectiveness. Given that West Indian leaders were unable to reach agreement about the institutional arrangements of federation, it is difficult to state how the institutional accommodation of identity could have contributed to its demise.

The second issue, whether an executive federal arrangement would have provided a better accommodation of diversity than an administrative arrangement, is again difficult to argue in the case of the West Indies. What is clear is that the federal constitution created a set of governing institutions that were weak and this was a factor in federal failure. A stronger executive could have sustained the federation in two ways. First, a more powerful executive would have made the creation of a West Indian identity more likely as leaders and citizens would have seen the relevance of federation within their own lives and would have been more willing to construct a political identity which was regional as well as national. In effect, a West Indian identity could have been created alongside, rather than in competition with, emerging island identities. Second, if more power had been vested in the Executive it would have attracted a higher caliber of politician leading to stronger leadership and more political investment in the process. Instead, with the exception of Grantley Adams, the well-known, experienced West Indian political actors took the decision to remain in their island legislatures. A prime example is Norman Washington Manley, leader of the Jamaican PNP and the regional West Indies Federal Labour Party (WIFLP), who decided not to contest the 1958 federal elections. If he had become federal prime minister it would have led to the Jamaican population being more engaged with the process and it would have reassured the islands in the Eastern Caribbean that Jamaica was committed to federation. Mordecai (1968) has argued that in withdrawing and deciding not to send senior members of his party, Norman Manley 'condemned the federation to having a government located a thousand miles from its most populous unit [the capital of the federation was in Trinidad], carrying in its cabinet nobody from that unit who commanded wide support at home (Mordecai 1968, 82).

The third factor, whether the institutionalization of identity contributed to the failure of federalism, raises the question of how the West Indies sought to address the issue of regional versus island identities. Whilst all federations struggle to accommodate potentially competing identities, the West Indies presents an interesting case due to its colonial experience. It could be argued that, unlike other countries involved in federal arrangements, the West Indies was an ideal candidate for federation because the individual islands had been colonized since the fifteenth century, did not have an indigenous population (aside from a small Carib population in Dominica) or a strongly defined national identity. Rather, the islands were in the process of constructing a national identity at the same time as federal proposals were being discussed and debated at inter-island conferences. If attention had been paid to the creation (and institutionalization) of a regional identity at the point at which the islands were debating the finer points of the federal constitution, it could be argued that the process may well have proceeded more successfully. As it was, accommodating competing identities within specific institutional formats did not arise in the discussions held by inter-island and colonial officials and representatives.

It is evident in assessing the role of the institutions devised and established under the 1958 federal constitution that they were ill-equipped to manage the dual process of identity formation occurring in the West Indies during the 1950s. There were two potentially contradictory processes occurring at the same time: one which attempted to pull the islands together under the banner of a West Indian regional identity and the other which reinforced separate national identities, economic and political development processes. The policy of the British Government, in line with West Indian leaders requests, to pursue a twin-track approach to constitutional developments (via the Federation and as individual units as outlined at the 1947 Montego Bay conference) undermined the development of a regional political identity and political process. The weak nature of the initial federal structure exacerbated the situation as it served to enhance division rather than draw island leaders together. Rather than formulating a feasible form of constitutional development within a federal framework, plans were negotiated separately between each island and the colonial power. A stronger Federal Executive would have assisted the development of a regional focus in both political and economic development planning as well as engage the leaders and citizens in the concept of federation as a viable method of government. Providing stronger, central institutions that functioned effectively would have had positive repercussions for the creation of a West Indian regional identity.

The impact of the imposition of federalism

Colonial office reports and enquiries, as argued at the beginning of the chapter, mentioned the possibility of federation as early as the nineteenth century. The view of the British government as outlined in June 1949 was 'that Federation and only Federation affords a reasonable prospect of achieving economic stability and through it political independence which is our constant object' (CO 318/487/2, No. 1 quoted in Ashton and Killingray 1999, 10). For the British, the key issue was to ensure the decolonized territories were financially viable before granting political independence and the only way to achieve this was via the federal route. This was not crudely 'imposed' on the West Indies, in fact there was recognition within early colonial reports (i.e., the Wood report quoted at the beginning of the chapter) that trying to push ahead with federation without support within the region would be a futile exercise. Although federation was not strictly imposed, it is clear that federation was presented as the only alternative through which the individual territories could gain independence. It is therefore not surprising that this perspective was shared in the region as there was no discussion about the other routes through which the individual territories could gain independence: the only viable path presented was federation.

Aside from the consensus on the need for federation, it was also evident it was a means to an end for both parties. For the British, a Federation of the West Indies would allow them to withdraw from the region. As a colonial office memorandum stated in April 1961 'In fact the Caribbean is an area of the world where there are no vital United Kingdom interests and few strategic considerations, and where our fundamental aim in the area since 1945 has been political disengagement' (CO1031/4274, No. 5 quoted in Ashton and Killingray 1999, 400). The Colonial Office records of the period are preoccupied with financial questions, particularly with regard to the increase in the money made available to the region. In February 1956, the Secretary of State for the Colonies made it clear in conversation with West Indian delegates that 'more money was made available to the Caribbean than to any other comparable area administered by the Colonial Office' (CO1031/1754, No. 9 BCF (56)7 quoted in Ashton and Killingray 1999, 133). Federation would bring financial independence to the region and relieve them of their 'burden'. When the Jamaicans voted against continuing federal membership in 1961, further discussions were held within the Colonial Office about the possibility of continuing with a federation composed of Trinidad and Tobago and the smaller islands of the Eastern Caribbean which would 'relieve us of the prospect of having the smaller islands indefinitely on our hands' (CO1031/3270, No 43A quoted in Ashton and Killingray 1999, 439).

For the leaders within the West Indies, the aim of federation was to achieve greater self-government and ultimately independence (political and economic). This is clear from the original resolution put forward by the Trinidadian delegate Captain Cipriani at the first British Guiana and West Indian Labor conference in 1926 (mentioned at the beginning of the chapter). The link between federation, self-government and independence was a constant theme prior to the 1947 Montego Bay conference. As we have seen this link was undermined at the conference and therefore the role of federation as the only means to achieve greater political autonomy and ultimately independence was weakened at the start of the federal process. Mordecai (1968) indicates the centrality of this decision as 'this "free for all" policy could not but set a rocky path for the Federation leaving the way invitingly open to uneven constitutional advances by the units' (Mordecai 1968, 38).

Given discussions formally began in 1947 and elections were not held until March 1958, it is clear that attitudes towards federation shifted during the intervening period. While negotiations about the nature of the federal constitution were debated in inter-island conferences, individual island leaders were negotiating increasing powers of self-government. The changing perspective of Norman Manley, who had been one of the key advocates of federation, is an excellent illustration of the way in which the meaning of federation changed as the decade of the 1950s progressed. First, Manley, as we have seen, decided not to stand in the Federal elections of 1958 arguing that it was more important for him to remain in Jamaica and present the case for federation against growing opposition to it within the country (Sherlock 1980, 178). However, more importantly, his party had won the general election of 1955 and as Mordecai (1968, 62) pointed out 'not many leaders would be willing to leave their powerful home governments to take on this weak and penniless federation'. Second, it was the Manley government which called the referendum on whether Jamaican should remain in federation. He only did so having first met with colonial officials on a visit to London in May 1960 to ask whether they would be prepared to grant independence to Jamaica if she decided against federal participation. Whilst Manley was under political pressure from the opposition Jamaica Labour Party, it was also evident by 1958 that the Jamaican economy could survive independently of federation (Springer 1962, 19). For the larger colonies, federation no longer functioned as the means to an end: it was clear that political and economic independence could be achieved outside of the federal structure and indeed it might be more successful if attempted alone. With the withdrawal of the largest territory, the federation could have continued but the PNM government of Trinidad and Tobago was reluctant to shoulder the financial responsibility of federation as the largest, most prosperous economy and in January 1962 withdrew.

Whilst it is not accurate to argue that the British Government imposed federation on the West Indies, it is evident that they did not entertain or discuss alternative proposals. For the West Indian political leaders and activists, the goal was independence and, if federation was the route to achieve this, then it was the route to follow. The fragility of the island economies was also a strategic consideration. If the desire to create a regional identity had been stronger and if there had been a greater commitment to create a strong federal government, the West Indies Federation could have been more successful. Viewing the federation as a means to achieving political and economic independence became increasingly irrelevant for the larger islands, particularly Jamaica, as the decade of the 1950s progressed.

Reflections on Failure: Other Factors

There are a number of other factors which explain the short-lived nature of the West Indies Federation. I will focus on: the lack of a West Indian identity, the role of internal political processes in the context of a rapidly changing external environment and the lack of strong leadership within a weak federal structure.

In the previous discussion I have argued that the lack of a West Indian identity was a crucial impediment to the survival of a federal government (Springer 1953;

Lowenthal 1961; Gonsalves 1998; Kavalski 2005). A major difficulty, aside from the inability to recognize the need to educate West Indian citizens about federation, was the geographical separation between Jamaica and the islands of the Eastern Caribbean which led to a lack of common identity and experience—apart from a tenuous (if not generic) 'West Indianness' among part of the intelligentsia of the region (Samad 1990). As Lowenthal remarked 'physical insularity not only aggravates inter-island differences: it also intensifies a sense of belonging within each island, whatever its size' (Lowenthal 1961, 68). Both Mordecai (1968) and Springer (1962) refer to the tensions between the Jamaican and Eastern Caribbean leaders which were evident throughout the process, particularly after Norman Manley took the decision not to contest the federal elections. The speech by the Jamaican Alexander Bustamante at the 1947 conference, and quoted earlier in the chapter, encapsulated the general view that Jamaica was far more advanced than its Eastern Caribbean neighbors and did not want to be 'burdened' by the economically weaker and 'politically backward' islands over a thousand miles away.

Linked to this fragmentation of identity as a result of geographical separation and relative size, Hugh Springer makes the important argument that there was a lack of common enemy which the islands could unite against. As he argues there was no 'compelling pressure or inducement of sufficient strength to enable the component units to overcome voluntarily their natural reluctance to accept the subordination to a central authority that political amalgamation entails' (Springer 1962, 55). The relationship between the individual islands and the British government was a relatively positive one and there were no other external forces attempting to subvert the political or economic processes in the islands. Contrast this with the increasing tensions and divisions which were developing between the individual islands and between certain islands and the federal government during the same period, and it is not difficult to see why regional unity failed to coalesce (Merrill 1961).

The lack of leadership of the federal government under Sir Grantley Adams was another factor which undermined the basis of the federation in the region. He made a number of key errors at crucial moments which increased tensions between pro-federalists and which gave ammunition to anti-federalists: the Chaguaramas affair and the retrospective taxation comment on a visit to Jamaica are good examples. However, it is also important to recognize that he was in a very difficult position. He did not have an experienced team of ministers and the federal government was poorly funded; in fact, one of the key problems had been a failure to agree on how the federal government would be funded over the long term. As a colonial office report stated in January 1960 'it was decided to give the Federal Government very limited powers and tightly restricted financial resources and this has made it hard for the Federal Government to make its mark' (CAB134/1630 quoted in Ashton and Killingray 1999, 308). It was an unenviable position for Adams who explained, in a broadcast, following the collapse of the federation that 'as the Federal Government took up the reins of government, it had to face the possibility that the whole basis of its existence was still under discussion in all the units of the Federation'. It was 'something like trying to build a house on shifting sand' (Hoyos 1974, 207). The decision to proceed when a number of fundamental issues, such as how federation would be financed, had not been resolved put a great deal of pressure on a weak Federal Government.

Conclusions

In any discussion of the failure of an organization comprised of a number of members at different stages of political and economic development, divided geographically and culturally, there will be a number of interlocking issues which will be worthy of analysis. In examining the Federation of the West Indies, it has become evident that one of the key issues was not the imposition of the federal process but the failure on behalf of all the participants (British and West Indian) to create a strong institutional federal framework. This weakness was compounded by a lack of commitment by the British and West Indian leaderships to focus attention on federation. The decision of experienced political leaders to remain in their home legislatures and executives rather than engage more directly in federal politics signaled a lack of commitment and undermined the importance of regional politics when compared to national.

This was allied with the lack of focus on constructing a regional identity, which was an important omission made apparent when the Jamaican population voted against continued membership in 1961. Without a strong positive presence in the region, it was difficult to continue to argue the case for federal membership, particularly for those islands that could envisage an economic and politically independent future. Ultimately, the central problem was that regional unity was not the main aim of all of the participants: the desire for independence and the consensus that federation was the only way to achieve it drove the process in the initial stages. Once it became clear that there were other routes to the end goal, the commitment to, and the need for, a viable federal structure collapsed.

Chapter 3

The Pyrrhic Victory of Unitary Statehood: A Comparative Analysis of the Failed Federal Experiments in Ethiopia and Indonesia

Thomas Goumenos

Introduction

This chapter argues that the post-war federal experiments in Ethiopia and Indonesia can be analyzed comparatively. In both countries the federal arrangements were accepted only reluctantly, since state-elites perceived them as externally imposed and as a threat to national unity. Although various social forces and actors consented to the demise of federalism, it was the central governments that subverted federal arrangements in order to establish a unitary state structure. Therefore, the Ethiopian and the Indonesian cases constitute two instances of a single phenomenon: the demise of federalism owing to the vested interests of state-elites in the centralization of ethnically diverse states.

The Ethiopian federal experiment is largely the story of Eritrea's integration into Haile Selassie's Ethiopia, which was realized after a UN proposal in 1952. Soon after the formation of the federation, the autocratic Ethiopian government gradually established direct control over Eritrea and formally dissolved the federal arrangement in 1962. Whereas in the early 1950s the Eritrean population seemed divided between the proponents of unification with Ethiopia and the supporters of independence, the policies of the 'federal' government resulted in a rapid decline of pro-Ethiopian feelings and the strengthening of Eritrean identity (reflected in the emergence of a separatist movement in the 1960s).

The Indonesian federation was a result of an internationally brokered agreement that ended the armed conflict between the Indonesian Republic and the colonial Dutch government. The Republican elite under Sukarno perceived the federal provisions as an instance of neo-colonial 'divide and rule' policy, aimed at weakening the political and territorial unity of Indonesia. In August 1950, only nine months after the creation of a federal state, Indonesia was proclaimed a unitary Republic.

In this respect, the demise of federalism in Ethiopia and Indonesia tends to be interpreted as part of the state- and nation-building projects in these countries. Federalism, therefore, was not considered by Ethiopian and Indonesian state-elites as a mode for accommodating different identities. On the contrary, the federal arrangement was perceived as an obstacle to the goal of nationalizing/centralizing the state and the construction/imposition of a prescribed identity.

The claim here is that the perceived victory of such unitary-state policies has been proved pyrrhic. First, in the short term, this led to the violent articulation of regional grievances and the emergence of various armed separatist movements in both countries. Second, the secessions of Eritrea from Ethiopia (in 1993) and East Timor from Indonesia (in 1999) demonstrated the limits of unitarian policies in multinational societies. In both states, these events forced the post-authoritarian governments to realize that more accommodative policies should be pursued.

The Ethiopia–Eritrea Federation

Historical overview

Eritrea was arbitrarily constituted as a distinct territorial unit in 1890, when Italy officially declared it as a colony. For centuries, the Eritrean highlands have been part of (or in close interaction with) the Abyssinian cultural and political space. Most Eritrean highlanders are Tigrai, ethnically and linguistically akin to the adjacent Tigrai of Ethiopia. Tigrai groups profess the Coptic Orthodox religion along with the Amhara, the dominant group of the modern Ethiopian state. Lowland Eritreans are predominantly Muslim; two-thirds are Tigre-speaking and belong to a number of ethnic groups. Parts of the lowlands have been conquered by the Ottomans and the Egyptians and have been in close interaction with the Arab world, rather than with the Abyssinian territories. Therefore, it was the colonial experience that for the first time brought together these disparate groups and initiated the construction of a distinct 'national' identity circumscribed by the territory of Eritrea (Haile 1988, 14–15; Heraclides 1991, 179).

The Italian colonial rule lasted from 1890 until 1941, when the Great Britain occupied Eritrea as well as the adjacent Ethiopia (which had been subjected to Italian rule since 1936). The Ethiopian emperor Haile Selassie was restored to power, whereas Eritrea was placed under a British Administration. However, the question of the future status of Eritrea arose even before the Italian defeat (Negash 1987). Selassie had expressed to the British during 1940–1941 his aspiration to annex Eritrea owing to its cultural proximity (Ellingson 1977, 261; Trevaskis 1960, 58–59).

The period 1941–1952 was marked by the political mobilization of the Eritreans. This mobilization is usually portrayed as a polarizing process along the lines of religious identity—that is, while Christian groups tended to support the union with Ethiopia, the Muslims preferred independence. Support for the union among the Eritrean Christians has been usually linked to factors such as: the ethno-cultural affinity of the Christian highlanders with the Abyssinians in Ethiopia; the expectations of material benefits and access to state resources owing to the Abyssinians' dominant status in Ethiopia; and the widespread anti-colonial feelings, buttressed by the post-war economic corrosion (Araya 1990, 82; Ellingson 1977, 268; Markakis 1988, 52–53).

Muslim opposition to the union, although less coherent in terms of its organization, stemmed from (not unfounded) fears of their exclusion and subordination in a Christian-dominated state. Muslim political formations not only stressed the distinctiveness of the Eritrean identity, but also supported independence as well as the emancipation of the Eritrean serfs (consisting mainly of Muslims but also of a considerable number of Christians). Because of the latter factor, the Muslim peasant nobility tended to support the 'unionist' aspirations of Christian formations (see Ellingson 1977, 272–279; Gebre-Medhin 1989, 150–151; Trevaskis 1960; 72–74).

This sketch of Eritrean political mobilization helps understand some of the internal dynamics of the federal failure. However, both the emergence and the imposition of federalism were outcomes of the decisive involvement of external actors that paid little consideration to Eritrean popular aspirations. After World War II, the Eritrean question was internationalized as part of the broader question of the former Italian colonies. Three options for Eritrea's future were proposed: (1) union with Ethiopia, supported by the USA (Marcus 1994, 156; Sorenson 1991, 304); (2) partition of the territory, backed by Britain, in which Ethiopia would annex the Christian highlands, while the Muslim lowlands would be ceded to the Anglo-Egyptian Sudan (Negash 1997, 18–46); (3) independence, after a period of trusteeship, as proposed by Italy. Owing to the inability of several UN-sponsored commissions to adjudicate between the different options, federation seemed to offer a 'rational' compromise between independence and union (Araya 1990, 84; Ghebre-Ab 1993, 76; Zewde 1991, 183).

Thus, on 2 December 1950, Resolution 390 of the UN General Assembly recommended that 'Eritrea should constitute an autonomous unit federated with Ethiopia under the sovereignty of the Ethiopian Crown' (quoted in Marein 1954, 355). The Preamble of the Resolution stated that the UN decision was informed, among other factors, by 'Ethiopia's legitimate need for adequate access to the sea' (quoted in Ghebre-Ab 1993, 195). Furthermore, a UN Commissioner was sent to Eritrea to draft an Eritrean Constitution in consultation with the Eritrean people, the Ethiopian government and the British Administration. The Eritrean Constitution, which contained the 'Federal Act', was approved by the Eritrean Assembly (formed by the vote of representatives of local communities, rather than by universal suffrage). The Ethiopian government was recognized as the Federal Government and the emperor was given the right to appoint a Representative in Eritrea. The Eritrean Executive would be in charge of a 'Chief Executive' elected by the Assembly. After the Eritrean Constitution had been ratified by the Ethiopian emperor, the Ethiopia–Eritrea Federation was formally created on 15 September 1952 (Haile 1988, 25; Longrigg 1974; Trevaskis 1960, 120–121; Marein 1954, 356–357).

Although the context of such emergence raises (well-founded) concerns about the process of democratic deliberation, as well as understandable doubts about the *federal* character of the Eritrean and Ethiopian arrangement that emerged in 1952, this does not mean that the federation was inherently bound to fail. The UN Resolution called for 'the fullest respect and safeguards [of the Eritrean] institutions, traditions, religions and languages' (Negash 1997, 184). Indeed, Eritrea had its own flag, official languages, and constitutional safeguards for the 'principles of democratic government', 'the enjoyment of human rights and fundamental freedoms' and 'periodic, free and fair elections' (Ghebre-Ab 1993, 205–206).

In practice, however, these provisions were ignored by the Ethiopian government which chose to disrespect the Federal Act and Eritrea's autonomy. Thus, by the end of 1953 the federation 'existed in name only' (Negash 1997, 90). The subsequent measures of the Ethiopian government not only resulted in the formal dissolution of the federation on 14 November 1962, but also reactivated the Eritrean desire for self-rule (Heraclides 1991, 181; Markakis 1988, 54–58; Zewde 1991, 219).

Hypotheses of defunct federalism

The Ethiopia–Eritrea federation failed to satisfy such federalist normative aspirations as the protection of 'minority interests against the tyranny of the majority' and the institutionalization of 'ethnoregional voices' (Smith 1995, 17). This failure was not an outcome of tensions between federal units or competing claims that eventually brought the federal collapse. In fact, federalism was not even tried in the Ethiopian–Eritrean case. Therefore, it was not 'federalism' as a normative principle that failed in Ethiopia; it was primarily the *unwillingness* of the Ethiopian state-elites to meaningfully *implement federalism* that defined the federal failure. This reluctance was informed by their preoccupation with the centralization of power and its concentration in their hands rather than in federal power-sharing bodies. Thus, it is not an overstatement to argue that the Ethiopian–Eritrean federal arrangement constituted a federation without federalism.

In order to understand federalism and federal failure and their relation with identity accommodation in the Ethiopian context, it is necessary to discuss the main features of the Ethiopian state and the Ethiopian identity. The core political project in Ethiopia since the end of nineteenth century and especially under Selassie's reign (1930–1974) was determined by the attempt to eliminate the power of local strongmen by creating a modern centralized state (Clapham 1988, 26–29). The Ethiopian state-elites—mostly members of the Amhara ethnic group—monopolized power and state resources underwriting their 'sense of proprietary control over the [state] … which [made] them generally *intolerant of non-centralist claims*' (Osaghae 2004, 174, emphasis added). Such process of 'opportunity hoarding' (Tilly, 2003, 10), was ensured through the repressive policies of authoritarian rule that prevented potential contenders from getting access to state resources. Despite the introduction of an Ethiopian constitution in 1931 and an elected lower house in 1955, the supreme power rested in the hands of the emperor and political parties never functioned (Clapham 1975, 72–73). Thus, power monopolization and authoritarianism contributed to the failure of the Ethiopia–Eritrea federation—a process common to other federal experiments in Africa (Thomas-Wooley and Keller 1994, 421–426; Osaghae 2004, 174).

It is reasonable to assume that the existence of *voluntary will to federate* constitutes a necessary condition of federal success (Kincaid 1995, 31–32). Therefore, the *unwillingness* of the state-elites to abide by the federal provisions, which was manifested as soon as the federation was formally established (Negash 1997, 92), indicates the failure of federalism as a normative principle in Ethiopia. The Ethiopian state-elites were negatively inclined in endorsing federalist values, such as power-sharing and cooperation in decision-making, since this could undermine their hegemonic position and their exclusionary rule. Indicative of their lack of adherence to federalist principles and their unwillingness to regard Eritrea as an equal federal partner is Selassie's view that there is 'little difference between federation and complete union' (Negash 1997, 90) or the statement of the emperor's Representative that 'federation is *only a form of decentralization* of authority which should be applied to *Ethiopia as a whole*' (quoted in Negash 1997, 106, emphasis added). Given that federations do not simply aim to limit central power, but constitute 'noncentralized' systems characterized by the 'dispersion of power' (Watts 1998, 124), the value incompatibility between authoritarian centralist policies and federal ideas is evident in the Ethiopian case.

Liberal democracy and federalism   Federalism in Ethiopia failed not only because of the reluctance of the Ethiopian (and the Eritrean 'unionist') elites to espouse its principles, but also because it did not gain critical popular support. This aspect of the federal failure is intimately linked to the lack of a democratic political culture in Ethiopia (Kincaid 1995, 37). Moreover, the autocratic political environment of Ethiopia stood in profound antithesis with the democratic Eritrean constitution. The claim of most analyses of the Ethiopia–Eritrea federation is that the failure of federalism in such context was to be expected unless the center democratized (Araya 1990, 99). However, the Ethiopian government indicated no such intention. On the contrary, by 1957 it had annulled most provisions of the Eritrean Constitution with regards to democratic government and human rights protection; trade unions and newspapers were banned, as well as all political parties (Thomas-Wooley and Keller 1994, 424). Thus, the legal and administrative systems of federalism provided little (if any) means to redress the grievances of disenfranchised groups (Cohen 1987; Paul 200). Therefore, the heavy-handed state rule hindered the socialization of federalist principles among the populations of Ethiopia and Eritrea.

Federal institutional setting   The failure of the Ethiopia–Eritrea federation was precipitated by its weak and flawed institutional design. This weakness consists in a number of constitutional deficiencies and in the inadequate accommodation of cultural and regional identities. With regards to the aspect of constitutional design, one could point out several failures. First, the lack of a *federal* constitution (since only an Eritrean one was drafted) and the absence of a separate federal government (Trevaskis 1960, 114). This promulgated the consolidation of an *asymmetrical* arrangement, which privileged the Ethiopian government with excessive power by granting it the responsibilities of a federal government. This resulted in a profound political disparity between Ethiopia and Eritrea, since '[i]n cases of dispute, the Eritrean government had no other power to resort to other than the Imperial Ethiopian government' (Negash 1997, 79). Second, the absence of the federal principle of shared sovereignty, since the sole sovereign was the Ethiopian Crown (Article 3), whereas Eritrea is vaguely defined by the same Article as an 'autonomous unit federated with Ethiopia' (Ghebre-Ab 1993, 202). Third, the 'semi-presidential' character of the Eritrean Executive—that is its lack of accountability to the Eritrean Assembly (Cummings 1954, 132)—rendered it more susceptible to the wishes of the imperial government. Thus, the lack of constitutional safeguards and the power asymmetry permitted the most powerful part to impose its will. Eventually, such constitutional deficiencies failed to bind all actors, and primarily the Ethiopian state–elite, in respecting the federal rules and in engaging with the values of federalism.

Identity accommodation   The Ethiopian federal government, furthermore, was reluctant to create an institutional framework that would accommodate regional and cultural identities (Iyob 1995). Despite its multiethnic character, Ethiopia never implemented any meaningful programme of decentralization (Ayenew 2003, 134). The institutional mechanisms through which regional claims could reach the central government were notably weak and, in general, peripheries were treated as administrative units to be controlled with minimal concessions (Clapham 1975, 75). This centralization of power largely coincided with (and was instrumental in sustaining) a system of cultural hierarchy. The state apparatus was dominated by the Amhara ethnic group, whereas most other groups, especially those in southern Ethiopia, were relegated to a subordinate status both in political and economic terms. Although in principle the Amhara culture was open to anyone speaking Amharic and professing Orthodoxy (Clapham 1994, 29–31), the predominantly Amhara state-elites actively implemented policies of amharization, especially through education (Abir 1970, 47). The Amharic language became official in Ethiopia—it was the prescribed language of governance and the legal system at levels of education and the media— whereas all other languages were banned from the public sphere. Such policy was justified through 'the need to establish a national identity' (Paul 2000, 184).

Thus, the central government began imposing an overarching 'state' identity over the numerous ethnocultural groups. The Ethiopian national narrative was overtly particularistic, since it employed myths of imperial continuity and emphasized 'Amhara cultural supremacy' (Abbay 2004, 597) and Orthodox Christianity. Thus, it lacked the inclusive symbolic codes with which a wide range of cultural communities, such as the various groups in southern Ethiopia or the Muslims in Eritrea, could identify. Although cultural diversity existed, it was not in all cases politically significant (at least not until the 1960s). This was partly due to the authoritarian rule and partly because of the 'traditional' social organization of most groups, which impeded the formation of *supra-local* identities and the sustained articulation of collective demands. The Ethiopian government, therefore, did not recognize any need for accommodating diverse identities; instead it was the '[h]omogeniz[ation] of] Ethiopian society [that] was perceived as a pre-requisite for the emergence of a unitary state. In this regard, language and history became 'crucial tools for diluting diversity' (Abbay 2004, 595). Ironically, it was the state modernizing project, illustrated by the assimilationist policies and the imposition of direct government control over the regions that often provoked resistance and mobilized communal identities. The assimilationist and centralizing Ethiopian policies left very few options available to the regional and communal groups apart from 'quietism, partial assimilation … or revolt' (Clapham 1975, 81). The last alternative manifested itself in dramatic ways through the regional rebellions in the 1960s and the subsequent nationalist and separatist movements by various ethnoregional groups, one of which was the Eritrean (Cohen 1987).

The Ethiopian imperial regime not only did not treat Eritrea differently from its other provinces (Negash 1997, 73), but its 'inability to construct linkages with regional political interests was most sharply demonstrated in Eritrea' (Clapham 1988, 36). Although a common Eritrean identity was rather weak until the 1950s, it was the repressive and assimilationist policies of the Ethiopian government (as well as the subsequent nationalist struggle) that forged Eritrean unity (Rich Dorman 2005, 205). The banning of the Eritrean flag and the substitution of the Eritrean languages with Amharic only a few years after the creation of the federation (Haile 1988, 28–29) transformed the Eritrean identity into the site of political resistance. This mobilization was manifested by the creation of clandestine Eritrean groups even before the formal dissolution of the federation (Markakis 1988, 55–56). The Eritrean self-determination movement, in alliance with other organizations within Ethiopia, overthrew the Ethiopian military regime in 1991. In 1993, over 95 per cent of the Eritrean population voted in favor of an independent Eritrean state (Killion 1998; Prouty and Rosenfeld 1994).

Federalism imposed　As argued above, the Ethiopian–Eritrean federation was neither a local initiative, nor a compromise between conflicting views within Eritrea or between Ethiopia and Eritrea; it was externally imposed as a 'convenient' compromise between the deviating interests of external actors—i.e., Britain, Italy and mainly the USA (Gebre-Medhin 1989, 150). There was no institutionalized method of popular consultation, nor was there any alternative option offered as in other cases of former colonies (Selassie 1989, 54). The federal arrangement was regarded with suspicion by the Ethiopian government and was accepted as a temporary concession in order to annex Eritrea. For instance, Selassie insisted that federation was 'a foreign concept introduced to divide the people' (Negash 1997, 106). Federation has not been the preferred option either for Christians, whose majority supported unification with Ethiopia without a federal arrangement at least until the late 1950s, or for the Muslims in Eritrea. As a result, federalism had never enjoyed substantial internal support (Negash 1997, 132–143). The fact that federalism was not a *'negotiated outcome'* between the federal partners underwrites its failure (Osaghae 2004, 170). Even after the federal imposition, the federal arrangements were never negotiated between central elites and 'state-challenging' (or 'non-centrist') actors (Osaghae 2004, 169–170). As suggested, this reflected the lack of pluralism and democratic deliberation in imperial Ethiopia.

Factors explaining federal failure

Assuming that (i) sustaining a balance between union and non-centralization and (ii) accommodating unity and diversity constitute crucial criteria of federal success (Kymlicka 1996; 1997), the failure of federalism in Ethiopia becomes apparent. The federation was abrogated by the 'federal' government in favor of a unitary system, whereas ethnoregional diversity was suppressed rather than politically acknowledged and legally and institutionally accommodated and empowered. The violation of democratic rights in Eritrea and the growth of anti-regime mobilization constituted further indicators of the federal failure.

In this respect, the Ethiopian-Eritrean case confirms the suggestion that the foreign imposition of federalism compounded by the lack of democratic institutions of governance and popular support for such institutions tends to underwrite the failure of federal arrangements. This analysis does not support the claim that asymmetrical institutional arrangements succeed in identity accommodation, since in the Ethiopian case asymmetries between the federal units only created more incentives for the imperial government to pursue its unitary and assimilationist policies.

There are also a number of context-specific factors explaining the Ethiopian–Eritrean federal failure. First, one needs to take under consideration the uncompromising centralizing policies of the Ethiopian government and its *political will* to dissolve the federation and assert its hegemonic nationalist narrative over Eritrea. Second, one need to recognize the distorted character of the federal arrangement, since core federal principles (shared sovereignty) and instruments (federal constitution and government) were absent. A third factor could be included here as well, namely the lack of an established Eritrean national identity during the period under examination (Iyob 1995). Although the common colonial experience of Eritrea had brought about a subtle sense of national belonging, Eritreans stood divided with regards to Eritrea's future and imagined *Eritreanness* in diverse ways (Abbay 1998, 28). Those favoring union with Ethiopia downplayed the characteristics of Eritrean national and cultural distinctiveness, while supporters of independence promoted a sharper boundary between the Ethiopian and the Eritrean identities. Due to this lack of a minimum consensus, the pressure towards the Ethiopian government for identity accommodation was weak and there was virtually no resistance against the imposition of the unitary rule (Killion 1998).

The Indonesian Federation

In contrast to the Ethiopian–Eritrean federation whose formal life-span lasted a decade, the Indonesia Federation existed for only nine months. Yet, the issue of federalism became a central facet of Indonesian politics in the period 1946–1950.

Historical Overview

Indonesia represents an intricate pattern of more than 3,000 islands, populated by over 100 ethnolinguistic groups, professing diverse religious denominations and beliefs (although Islam is the dominant one). The country emerged from the decolonization of the 'Dutch East Indies' (Drakeley 2005; Vickers 2005; Ricklets 2001). Owing to the complexities of the post-World War II environment, since 1946 the situation in Indonesia can be described as one of dual sovereignty. Towards the end of the Japanese occupation the nationalists declared independence and on 17 August 1945 founded the Indonesian Republic on the populous islands of Java, Sumatra and Madura (backed by a revolutionary nationalist movement and a loosely organized army). However, in the eastern part of the archipelago the Dutch managed to re-establish their rule (Kahin 1985, 6–8; Ricklefs 1993, 212–222).

It is in this specific late colonial context that federalism was promoted in Indonesia. The Dutch authorities acknowledged that they would eventually have to recognize Indonesia's independence, yet at the same time, they wanted to ensure their interests in the region. The Dutch objective was to transfer sovereignty to a federal state, thus preventing the Republic from dominating the country (Caldwell and Utrecht 1979). On 10 February 1946 the Dutch proposed the creation of a federal state of Indonesia. In the subsequent Linggajati Agreement (12 November 1946), they recognized the de facto authority of the Republic in Java and Sumatra (Friend 2003; Reid 1973). This agreement seemed to offer a promising compromise between the Republic and the Netherlands, since it called for the cooperation of the two governments in the formation of a federal United States of Indonesia, consisting of the Republic, Borneo (Kalimantan) and the Great East (Finkelstein 1951, 286; McMahon 1981, 217; Wolf 1948, 43–46).

However the Linggajati Agreement remained ineffective primarily due to Dutch subversion. On the one hand, between 1946 and 1948 (without any consultation with the Republic) the Dutch began establishing federal structures in the territories under their control. On the other hand, the Dutch army expanded its zone of control into the Republican territories and then proceeded with including them in the Dutch process of federalization. On 19 December 1948, the Dutch occupied the Republic's capital, Yogyakarta, which led to the surrender of the Republican cabinet to the Dutch troops. Such expansionist policy discredited the idea of federalism and portrayed it as a project for maintaining Dutch hegemony (Frey 2003, 95–96; Kahin 1949, 229–230; Ricklefs 1993, 226–230; Wolf 1948, 106–107).

After considerable external pressure (mainly from the side of the UN and the USA), the Dutch had to curb their expansionism. In the summer of 1949, representatives of the Republic and the fifteen federal areas (six states and nine autonomous constitutional units) met at an Inter-Indonesian Conference and agreed on the form of independent statehood. On 27 December 1949 sovereignty was transferred to the Republic of the United States of Indonesia (RUSI) (Frey 2003, 96; Schiller 1955, 61–62). However, the federation proved extremely short-lived. The outbreak of several rebellions reinforced the Republican elites' conviction that power should be centralized in order for the state to survive and their unwillingness to tolerate a federal arrangement. In the next two months, a process of 'voluntary' dissolution (Tønnesson and Antlöv 2001, 13) saw most of the fifteen federal states merging with the Republic, rather than with the RUSI government. Although the federal demise was opposed by regional revolts in East Indonesia, the RUSI was officially dissolved on 17 August 1950 and was replaced by the unitary Republic of Indonesia (Drakeley 2005; Friend 2003; Reid 1973).

Hypotheses of defunct federalism

Federalism in Indonesia failed (like in Ethiopia) due to the centralizing policies of state-elites and their perceptions that federal arrangements could severely undermine national unity. Whereas the political environment of the Ethiopian federation was that of an autocratic state, federalism in Indonesia emerged in the absence of embedded state structures. The political context was defined by the nascent Indonesian Republic and by the nationalist Indonesian revolution against the Dutch. Within this conflictual framework, federalism in Indonesia came to represent the ideological 'Other' to nationalism. Indonesian nationalism embodied 'radical perceptions of modernity, republicanism and anti-colonialism' (Tønnesson and Antlöv 2001, 50). Federalism was not only identified with the (former) colonial masters, but also with the old aristocratic elites, which embraced federalism out of opposition to nationalist revolutionaries and in order to retain their (pre-war) power and privileges (Kahin 2003, 351–352). Given that Republicans perceived federalism as 'part of the counter-revolution', Indonesian nationalism can be classified as 'Jacobin', since it held that 'nationalism and federalism [were] mutually exclusive' (O'Leary 2004, 160). Eventually, federalism and unitarianism (which was perceived in close juxtaposition with nationalism) were not understood as organizational principles, but denoted distinct political identities. The former was conceptualized as a conservative pro-Dutch and neo-colonial orientation; whereas the latter 'became an article of nationalist faith' (Legge 1961, 8).

Federalism imposed   The analysis conducted above indicates that federalism as a normative principle failed in Indonesia because it was politically discredited as a Dutch-imposed neo-colonial project. This perception, moreover, suggests the limited popular support for its arrangements (Kahin 1985, 11). No meaningful popular consultation took place in the Dutch-sponsored federal areas, although the Dutch had been pledged to conduct plebiscites in order for the local people to decide whether they wished to be governed by the Republic or by the Dutch federal government (Kahin 1985, 9; Schiller 1955, 27). Even before RUSI's formation there had been some negotiations conducted among the federal partners, for example in the Inter-Indonesian Conference (unlike the Ethiopian case). However, this was viewed by the Republic primarily as a necessary cost to pay in order to obtain state autonomy. As soon as Indonesia became independent, the Republican state-elites felt that there remained no factual obstacles for them to abolish the federal arrangement, and they acted on this opportunity almost instantaneously.

Liberal democracy and institutional setting   Since the Republic lacked a stable state apparatus during the period under examination; it is not possible assess here the actual federal policies. However, it can be asserted that the majority of Republican leaders, despite their internal differences and antagonisms, were committed to a unitary political system, as well as to the concept of a monistic popular sovereignty. Importantly, unitary statehood was promoted as the only appropriate constitutional form for safeguarding the territorial integrity of the vast Indonesian archipelago and the fledgling national identity of its ethnically, religiously and linguistically diverse populations.

Just before the creation of the unitary Indonesian Republic in August 1945, in a speech that set out the Indonesian national doctrine of *Pancasila*, Sukarno called for the 'establishment of a National State based on the entity of one Indonesian soil' (Soekarno 1952, 22). Although the cultural diversity of Indonesia was not muted in his speech, Sukarno emphasized the organic unity of the Indonesian nation (Soekarno 1952, 19–21). In addition, most Republican leaders disdained local cultures as 'feudal or primitive' (McVey 1996, 14). Thus, Republican elites were ideologically disinclined to espouse federalist values, such as the principle of shared sovereignty or the institutionalization of sub-national identities. This predisposition was strengthened by a number of important political occurrences. First, in 1948 the Republican government faced two internal challenges, the Darum Islam rebellion in Pasundan (West Java) and a communist revolt. Second, only one month after RUSI's formation, another rebellion (the so-called 'Westerling affair') aimed to overthrow the federal government. It broke out in Pasundan, with the participation of demobilized and active members of the Royal Netherlands Indies Army (KNIL) (Penders 2002, 185–190; Ricklefs 1993, 227–232). Although the Dutch government was not involved in this particular incident, the coup reinforced the Republican fears that the federal arrangement would facilitate Dutch aspirations of 'divide and rule', as well as provide various subversive actors with opportunities to undermine the unity of the Indonesian state. According to most analyses on this subject (i) the lack of popularity of the federal arrangement as a Dutch-imposed plan; (ii) the Republic's prestige as the leader of the Indonesian independence; and (iii) the overwhelming force of the nationalist tide, all signaled a significant level of the popular consent to the federal dissolution (Ferrazzi 2000, 66; Kahin 2003, 450).

However, there was no popular process—elections, referendum or public debate—through which to assess the actual popularity of federalism. The RUSI lacked an established democratic political system and an embedded pluralistic public culture, since Indonesia had no legacy of representative structures from the colonial era. Both the Republic and the Dutch-created federal states during 1945–1949 lacked *elected* bodies (Kahin 1947, 38–40; Schiller 1955, 44–48). With regards to RUSI's representative structures, the provisional constitution stipulated the formation of a House of Representatives, a body of 150 members, and a Senate, where each of the sixteen states was represented by two members. The delegates of each territorial unit were not elected, but appointed by the respective governments, and a clear majority of them approved the federal demise. Furthermore, elections for the legislature should have taken place within a year of independence, but instead these happened only in 1955. It was not party politics or constitutionalism that regulated the regime, but essentially Sukarno's ability to strike a balance between contending actors (Kahin 2003, 447–463; Schiller 1955, 63).

Certain deficiencies with regards to the federal constitution facilitated the federal demise, as in Ethiopia's case. The first one was the very lack of a permanent Constitution, which was expected to be drafted only after RUSI's formation. This, however, never occurred precisely because of the federal dissolution. By the summer of 1950 a new provisional constitution had been drafted and approved. It was essentially based on the unitary constitution of 1945 (Kahin 2003, 261). The second deficiency was the Government's entitlement to enact on its own initiative emergency laws 'on account of urgent circumstances' (Kahin 2003, 448). Importantly, it was through this instrument that the dissolution of the federal states was made legal (Kahin 2003, 446–8, 456; Schiller 1955, 65–6). Therefore, although the federal constitution did not contain severe inconsistencies with federalist principles (as the Ethiopian–Eritrean one), its provisional nature permitted the Republican elites to interpret it loosely and in conformity with their political goals of unitary statehood.

Asymmetrical relationships underwrote the status of the Republic *vis-à-vis* the other constituent units. This asymmetry was not derived from the constitution, but it was understood in political terms. The Republican elites were reluctant to share power in a state that they had created (as they believed). The Republican Prime Minister insisted that: '[we would find it difficult] to move to a small house while for some considerable time [we] had been used to living in a large house' (quoted in Penders 2002, 192). These perceptions certainly denote the 'narrow' interest of Republican elites to maintain tight control of power structures and state resources. A federal arrangement would, by definition, impede the accomplishment of this objective and could permit the emergence of powerful contenders. Therefore, the Republican elites were characterized by a 'proprietary' mentality with regard to state control (similarly to the Amhara elites in Ethiopia).

However, the Republicans enjoyed much more popular legitimacy due to the successful waging of the independence war and their egalitarian rhetoric. 'What counted in the national imagination was the Republic' (Tønnesson and Antlöv 2001, 12). Moreover, although the popular base of most Republican parties was in Java and Sumatra, the Republican aspirations for unitary statehood did not imply the imposition of a particularistic (ethnic) identity (a point analyzed in the following section). Rather, Republicans were promoting (at least in their own eyes) an all-encompassing national identity. A *unitary* state was perceived as the appropriate institutional embodiment of the Indonesian identity and their leadership was the only one to guarantee the Indonesian unity. The only group that was theoretically 'excluded' from the Republican unitary and nationalizing project was a small traditional pro-Dutch elite. Therefore, the decisive factor for inclusion or exclusion was political rather than cultural.

Furthermore, the Indonesian case confirms Hale's hypothesis that the existence of a disproportionately large administrative unit (in terms of the population) brings about the collapse of ethnofederations (an argument that is applicable to the Ethiopian case as well). This asymmetry creates incentives for the larger unit to overturn federal arrangements, which are perceived as overtly restricting, strengthen its separate political structures and pursue its own interests (Hale 2004, 167–179). Indeed, the Republic, apart from putting forward its centralizing goals, remained 'virtually autonomous' from the RUSI government (Kahin 2003, 450). Such an asymmetrical relationship assisted the goal of unitary statehood.

Identity accommodation   The question of identity accommodation necessitates also a brief discussion of issues such as the Indonesian identity, cultural diversity and center-periphery relations. Unlike the articulation of an exclusive Ethiopian identity, the official Indonesian national narrative was consciously crafted towards inclusion. For instance, Sukarno attempted to go beyond the 'problem' of numerous particularistic (ethnic, cultural, regional) identities by defining *Indonesianess* in territorial terms. He asserted that the 'Indonesian people are all human beings ... who live throughout the entity of the entire archipelago of Indonesia' (Soekarno 1952, 21–22). Analogously, the Indonesian language was not recognized as the language of any particular ethnic group. The five principles of *Pancasila* included such 'universalistic' principles as social justice, humanitarianism, democracy, Indonesian unity and belief in one God (Kingsbury 1998, 42–43). *Pancasila* represented a normative system that brought together a number of diverse cultural and ideological values that made it compatible with communal understandings, Islam as well as liberalism or even Marxism (Van der Kroef 1954, 226). Given not only the multiplicity of identities, but also the relative fuzziness of identity boundaries in the Indonesian society, this non-particularistic narrative was potentially suitable to provide an overarching national identity, and often it did.

At the same time, however, there are certain inconsistencies and failures with regards to the construction of an inclusive Indonesian identity. First of all, ethnic diversity was not explicitly recognized, celebrated or negotiated in the official Indonesian narrative. Although consciously universalistic in principle, this narrative remained the ideological construction of nationalist elites and was imposed by state institutions as the only acceptable version of *Indonesianess*. Instead of being the product of ideological osmosis between various identity claims, the official Indonesian discourse sought to impose cultural integration and identity accommodation from above. During the 1950s many revolts broke out. Although the boundaries of the national polity were not disputed, cultural considerations and regional discontent for central state policies did play some role, not least because of unfulfilled promises for broad local autonomy and anti-Javanese feelings (Anderson 1991, 132; Legge 1961, 11–12, 20; Mackie 1980, 672).

Next, the preoccupation of central elites with national unity and territorial cohesion acquired a stronger authoritarian dimension during Suharto's presidency (1965–1998). His 'New Order' regime sought to 'folklorize' all cultural and regional identities (Hellman 2003, 19). This means that it suppressed the articulations of political demands by different identity groups and depicted ethnocultural diversity as a mere local variation of a largely homogeneous Indonesian culture. This policy involved harsh suppression of separatist claims (in East Timor, Aceh and West Papua) that involved rejection of the imposed official discourse of a unitary Indonesian identity (Aspinall and Berger 2001, 1009). It was only after the fall of the New Order that a public debate concerning questions of national integration, regional identities or even federalism, has emerged, although support for the unitary state remains dominant (Ferrazzi 2000, 63–77).

Neither during the 1946–1949 period nor during RUSI's existence was there any conscious attempt to empower local *identities* and permit their institutional expression. The boundaries of the federal states and autonomous units rarely corresponded to distinct ethnic or cultural groups. They were essentially 'accidents of war' (Legge 1961, 8). Despite its multiethnic character, the RUSI was essentially a territorial federation. The extreme diversity of identities in Indonesia and their often vague boundaries rendered the task of creating viable federal territorial units difficult (Tønnesson and Antlöv 2001, 17). Thus, the existence of multiple, fragmented and politically weak identities urged the Republic to abrogate the federation. Although the Republican elites aimed at promoting the *Pancasila* version of Indonesian identity, there was little success, during this brief period, to institutionalize it in any substantive way. However, it is beyond doubt that one of the principal reasons for imposing a unitary government was the Republican elites' fear that federalism would result in endless identity fragmentations, thereby threatening the unity of Indonesia.

Factors explaining the federal failure

The failure of the Indonesian federation reflected the discrediting of federalism both as an organizational and as a normative principle, due to its promotion by the Dutch colonial elites. Therefore, it failed to secure the necessary support of the new state elites and the public. Federalism failed to inform Indonesian political preferences and gain considerable legitimation. In essence federalism never operated meaningfully in Indonesia, just like in the Ethiopian case. Also, the federal arrangement did not succeed in preventing regional violence, given the revolts in Pasundan and East Indonesia (South Sulawesi and South Moluccas) (Penders 2002, 195–199). Most of the participants and supporters of these revolts had cooperated or sided with the Dutch in the past, and consequently the Republic's hegemonic position in the new state posed a threat to their privileges. To a certain extent, these revolts reflected also the reluctance to accept the imposition of an overarching Indonesian identity, or at least its Republican version.

The Indonesian case supports the relevance of the hypotheses which claims that if federalism is externally imposed and lacks consolidated democratic institutions it is likely to fail. In the Indonesian case, failure was also assisted by the absence of a coherent constitutional framework and the power asymmetry between the Republic and the other federal units. Eventually, this facilitated the federal dissolution by the Republican forces. This analysis has also revealed the importance of several case-specific factors that led to the demise of federalism. First, it was the political will and the ideological commitment of the Republican elites to abrogate the federal arrangement due to its perceived colonial character. Second, it was the process of 'frame-bridging' (McAdam et al. 2001, 119), which made possible the ideological equation among anti-colonialism, Indonesian nationalism and the support for the unitary statehood. The fact that this discourse became hegemonic explains (at least to some extent) the discrediting of federalism and the limited popular support for the federal solution. A third factor rests with the fragmentation of local and ethno-cultural identities, an aspect that impeded their politicization and the articulation of a powerful alternative discourse to *Pancasila*. Such identity fragmentation, along with the largely territorial character of the federal units, rendered difficult the coincidence of federal states and identity boundaries in RUSI. Consequently, there was a very weak opposition to the Republican centralizing objectives.

Conclusions

This analysis demonstrates that there are a number of similarities between the federal failures of Ethiopia and Indonesia. The central assumption of this chapter is that the federal arrangements failed in Ethiopia and Indonesia as a result of the prevailing unitary policies, pursued by powerful centralizing (and explicitly anti-centralist) state elites. The comparative analysis of the two case studies indicates that the external imposition of federalism (in those two cases, primarily by the former colonial powers), compounded by the lack of popular consultation, discredited the federal organizational and its normative and practical advantages. The juxtaposition between these and other similarities indicated also that federalism was not genuinely pursued by key actors but rather was used as a means to specific political ends.

In the Ethiopia–Eritrea case the temporary federal arrangement facilitated the annexation of Eritrea by Ethiopia. In Indonesia it was through the federal project that (i) the Dutch authorities tried to maintain their interests after Indonesia gained independence in 1945. Also (ii) the Republic used it in the process of achieving independence and consolidation of their control over the entire expanse of the former Dutch colonies. In both cases the emergence of federalism was linked to decolonization and its demise was facilitated by institutional and constitutional deficiencies and power asymmetries among the federal units. Neither of the cases analyzed above seems to suggest the relevance of federal arrangements in accommodating diverse national identities, since the federal institutions barely functioned in Ethiopia and in Indonesia. In this sense, federalism as a normative regulative principle did not *become 'defunct'*, since it was never functioning in any meaningful way.

Finally, the dissolution of both federations was underwritten by specific perceptions of nationalism and the appropriate political and territorial organization of national unity. Assuming that multinational states can be legitimate and functional only by 'developing mechanisms for accommodating the interests of different ethnic groups and integrating them politically, economically and socially' (Mengisteab 1997, 117), Ethiopia and Indonesia have failed to address the problem of accommodating diverse loyalties within the project of national integration (Liddle 1970, 205). The multiple articulation of regional and ethnic demands in both states during, but also after the federal period, can be linked to the current attempts to rectify this shortcoming by the re-federalization of Ethiopia and the decentralization (with autonomy provisions) in Indonesia. Therefore, although *federations* in these two cases failed, *federalism* seems to have re-emerged as a domestic solution to the impasse provoked by the policies of unitary statehood.

Chapter 4

Partnership and Paternalism: The Federation of Rhodesia and Nyasaland (1953–1963)

Tony King

Introduction

Between 1953 and 1963 the British self-governing colony of Southern Rhodesia (now Zimbabwe) was joined with the colonies of Northern Rhodesia (Zambia) and Nyasaland (Malawi) in the Federation of Rhodesia and Nyasaland (also known as the Central African Federation). The federation was dissolved in 1963 with Zambia and Malawi gaining independence and the white-minority government of Southern Rhodesia (also known simply as Rhodesia) declaring an illegal and unrecognized Unilateral Declaration of Independence (UDI) from Britain in 1965. The character of the new Federation of Rhodesia and Nyasaland was determined by the presence of (at their peak) three hundred thousand white settlers, over three-quarters of whom were in Southern Rhodesia, who ruled over seven million black Africans. At the same time, the federal arrangement did not constitute an independent state, but were always considered as a step towards an eventual Dominion status.

This chapter examines the reasons for the failure of the Federation of Rhodesia and Nyasaland. As well as analyzing the background to the federation of the three territories, it examines the issue of the white elite's unsuccessful efforts to co-opt the black middle class as a way of controlling the pace of change in the Federation of Rhodesia and Nyasaland through the policy of 'multiracial partnership'. The federation's failure is analyzed through the prism of the three hypotheses of defunct federalism set out in the introduction to this volume. This chapter emphasizes that the Federation of Rhodesia and Nyasaland was not based on liberal democracy, but a limited (although widening) franchise, and the failure to establish adequate mechanisms for black representation contributed to its demise. Additionally, the institutions and identity of the federation were based on the notion and practices of white hegemony making them inflexible in dealing with the black majority. The imposition of Federation of Rhodesia and Nyasaland did not fully satisfy either racial group, making its legitimacy questionable and leaving the federal project open to challenges from both sides. In addition, this chapter examines the persistent issue of discrimination against black Africans as a factor which was distinct to the Federation of Rhodesia and Nyasaland as a central African colonial entity dominated by a white settler minority, and which contributed to its failure.

Background to the Federation of Rhodesia and Nyasaland

Talk of some form of amalgamation between the British territories in central Africa had been going on since the 1920s. Both the local white settlers and the British government believed that association could be beneficial, but this had come to nothing primarily because of the British government's reluctance, as reported by the 1939 Bledisloe Commission, to countenance the expansion of Southern Rhodesia's discriminatory practices to other territories (Windrich 1975, 20). The merger of a self-governing quasi-Dominion and two territories with an overwhelmingly black population ruled directly by the Colonial Office had not always been attractive to the Rhodesians either, but after 1945 a number of other factors came into play. The possibility of Southern Rhodesia's eventual union of one sort or another with South Africa had not entirely disappeared in 1923 when white Rhodesians had voted for self-government.

However, the growing ascendancy of Afrikaner nationalism had rendered that prospect distasteful, and so by 1948 when the Afrikaner-nationalist National Party won the South African whites-only election, such a union was extremely unlikely. At the same time, the expansion of the Northern Rhodesian copper industry during the war had made a union between the two loyally British Rhodesians more feasible, and Southern Rhodesia especially stood to gain much economically from adding the Northern Rhodesian copperbelt to its sphere of influence. The copper wealth and raw materials coming from Northern Rhodesia would complement the growing secondary industry sector in Southern Rhodesia, and so would provide extra resources with which to pay for the white Rhodesian way of life (which after 1945 was among the most affluent in the world). Added to this was the enormous increase in white immigration into the two territories as part of the outflow from post-war Europe that more than tripled the federation's white population in the space of ten years. These developments 'seemingly legitimated the vision of a modern European state being carved out in the Central African bush' (Holland 1985, 139).

Establishing the Federation of Rhodesia and Nyasaland

The establishment of the Federation of Rhodesia and Nyasaland has to be considered in the context of post-war decolonization. Especially, following the independence of India in 1947, the British were working to ensure the survival of the Empire elsewhere by co-opting local elites. Thus, under the banner of 'multiracial partnership', the prospect offered by the Federation of Rhodesia and Nyasaland promised to open up opportunities for the growing urban black middle class while safeguarding the dominant position of the local white Rhodesian elites. In addition, the Cold War emphasized the need to safeguard strategic resources—in this case Northern Rhodesian copper—for the West. Regionally, the Federation of Rhodesia and Nyasaland was construed as a bulwark against the southward spread of African nationalism and the northward encroachment of South African-style racial discrimination. In this setting, from the point of view of London, the Federation of

Rhodesia and Nyasaland had the additional advantage of constructing a loyal British bloc at a time when South Africa was becoming less reliable.

Despite the loss of India, British thinking about African decolonization worked in a timeframe of decades, not years or even months, even though independence would be the eventual outcome. The Federation of Rhodesia and Nyasaland was conceived before the speed and scale of European decolonization in Africa became apparent. It was neither an independent state, nor a colony. It had control over its defense, finance, and trade policies, reflecting substantial devolution of power from London to the white settlers in central Africa. At the same time, the federal setup reflected the paternalistic view of most European capitals suggesting that black Africans were not yet ready for self-government and would need several decades of tutelage. In 1953 Leo Amery, the former Secretary of State for India, proclaimed that 'no sane person would suggest that any of our West African colonies ... will be ready for such a status in any near future' (Amery 1953, 182). Yet within three years one of those colonies, Ghana (then named the Gold Coast), was independent and within ten years the bulk of British colonies in Africa also had their sovereignty recognized.

The Federation of Rhodesia and Nyasaland was officially established in 1953 after a series of conferences in Africa and London between the three territorial governments and the Colonial Office. The British government, in particular, blocked any form of amalgamation of its central African colonies which did not have the support of black elites; therefore, behind the scenes it exerted pressure for a deal on the establishment of a federation as a self-governing state with British oversight The need to hinder the spread of South African apartheid and African nationalism, and to minimize any possible diversion of British resources while Britain was re-arming against the Soviet Union dominated official thinking, and so agreement with the settler leaders had to be reached (Holland 1985, 140–42).

The proclaimed guiding principle of the Federation of Rhodesia and Nyasaland was 'multiracial partnership' (usually referred to simply as 'partnership'). It should be emphasized that it was never formalized as a legal principle, although it was mentioned in the Preamble to the Federation's constitution (Rhodesia and Nyasaland 1953, 15). The assumption was that despite the continuing prejudice against black Africans and the ongoing obstructions to their aspirations, the dominant white minority would lead the black majority to a gradual integration into the mainstream of the Federation's political, economic and institutional life (and, thereby, differentiating it from growing discrimination in neighbouring South Africa (Mason 1957, 155). However, 'partnership' did not manage to make substantial strides in the everyday life of the Federation of Rhodesia and Nyasaland. Indeed, the thorny issue of race relations and opportunities for black Africans in the new federation would dominate its ten-year life and contribute directly to its failure. The paternalistic political thinking informing the institutional makeup of the Federation of Rhodesia and Nyasaland assumed that blacks were not ready for full membership of the body politic, so it was incumbent on the white elite to 'educate' them and slowly bring them into the mainstream. Godfrey Huggins, the federal Prime Minister, revealingly (and unhelpfully) described it as the partnership between a rider and a horse (Keatley 1963, 224).

Thus, the development of any meaningful form of 'partnership' premised on close cooperation seemed stalled by the dominant white mindset informing the Federation of Rhodesia and Nyasaland. The ruling white minority had problems considering political accommodation of the black majority, largely due to its isolation from the daily lives of black Africans (except in strictly master-servant relationships). Emphasizing the gulf in comprehension, Edgar Whitehead, Southern Rhodesia Prime Minister from 1958 to 1962, confidently asserted 'I know my Africans and they are not interested in politics. They are interested only in things of immediate practical concern ... schools for their children, the improvement of their land, raising their standard of living, and things of that kind' (Keatley 1963, 219) as though these issues were not the stuff of politics everywhere else.

Accounting for the Failure of the Federation of Rhodesia and Nyasaland

The question of liberal democracy

The Federation of Rhodesia and Nyasaland, like instances of colonial rule elsewhere in Africa, was not based on liberal democratic norms and there were pressures within the white elite to limit the scope of democratization (mostly due to fears of 'swamping' by much greater numbers of black Africans). The concern of the white community of being outnumbered at the ballot box warranted the conviction that most black Africans were immature and irrational and, therefore, undeserving of the vote (Dvorin 1954, 378). Thomas Chegwidden, a leading Rhodesian industrialist, characterized full suffrage as 'the counting of heads most of which are empty of thought and intelligence, but full of desires and emotions' (quoted in King 2001, 205). The failure to develop adequate structures of representation and the anachronistic attempts to maintain discriminatory policies contributed directly to the failure of the Federation of Rhodesia and Nyasaland (especially, at a time when other colonies were achieving full and unconditional independence).

However, tentative moves to establishing a democratic structure of sorts were taken by making the franchise less restrictive with a view of enrolling a considerable number of black voters, although leaving the whites in firm control. The matter of who had the right to vote was central to the development of the Federation of Rhodesia and Nyasaland as an entity separate from the dominant pressures of apartheid South Africa, but was also in keeping with the familiar British pattern of slowly opening up the franchise. Unfortunately for the federal authorities, what had seemed sensible in late Victorian Britain was anachronistic and reactionary in the context of 1950s central Africa. While widening the franchise was just about acceptable, keeping the influence of the new (and invariably black) voters to a minimum was also essential.

The issue of trying to develop a structure of suffrage that did not look overtly racist was aided by the fact that the franchises of the constituent territories of the Federation of Rhodesia and Nyasaland had never been explicitly racial. Attainment was through literacy and income or property qualifications, and there had always been a small number of black voters. Most whites comfortably achieved the threshold while most blacks, who earned far less and often owned property in common, did not. In effect even if not in letter, therefore, the franchise operated on a racial basis. However, the Federation of Rhodesia and Nyasaland under partnership was embarking on a course to widen the franchise, lower the qualifications, and thus attract enough people away from African nationalism. Not offering universal suffrage was not immediately problematic, as even the black middle class was happy to be separated from the masses through recognition of its achievements, and nor was the question of differentiated citizenship controversial.

In fact, it is important to consider that the idea of gradations of citizenship was not necessarily illiberal in the Rhodesian or British contexts. Universal suffrage was only fully achieved in Britain in 1948 with the abolition of extra votes for holders of certain university degrees. All Britons and imperial subjects owed allegiance to the British monarch. Loyalty in Britain and the Empire was not horizontal between citizens and institutions, but vertical between subjects and the monarch. The very essence of British and imperial identity was indistinguishable from a very fundamental inequality. Therefore, it made sense in the context of the Federation of Rhodesia and Nyasaland to have a graded system of citizenship, and to keep, in amended form, a franchise that was based on levels of literacy and income or property. No universal suffrage, but a slightly outdated sense of the franchise being a privilege rather than a right, and moves, unlike in South Africa, to widen it rather than restrict it.

The three territories all had their own franchises, and Southern Rhodesia's was the most restrictive. It soon became apparent that it was anomalous to have a system where a person could qualify to vote in one territory but not another and these different stages of development for black representation on the electoral roll certainly caused tension. Black, and some white, opinion in Northern Rhodesia and Nyasaland were concerned that the high threshold explicit in the Southern Rhodesian qualifications would spread north, tempering the limited gains the black middle class had made. This fear was especially pronounced because the right to vote on a common roll had iconic status among middle class blacks. Because the franchise was technically non-racial, once one had fulfilled the conditions, every vote was equal, and one had passed the 'civilization test'. It was the only arena where blacks and whites could be judged on the same basis. In addition, addressing a supposedly non-racial issue could divert attention from the myriad examples of racial discrimination that all blacks suffered and that could scupper the federal project. In reality, however, so few black Africans attained those qualifications that the franchise was effectively closed to them. Southern Rhodesia was accused of following a 'civilization policy on paper and reducing it to a farce in practice' (Walker 1953, 94).

The 1956 Federal Franchise, equally applicable to all three territories, equalized the qualifications for federal elections, but the territorial franchises remained differentiated. In place of a single common roll on which all votes were equal, two rolls were created. The 'A roll' looked like the old franchise onto which most whites and a few blacks were enrolled, and it elected 44 members of parliament for the federal legislature. The new 'B roll' had lower qualifications, and elected nine MPs, thus leaving electoral power in the hands of the more affluent and overwhelmingly white 'A roll' voters (King 2001, 210). But this looked like raising the qualifications again and introducing racial representation through the back door, and far too few black voters registered to legitimize the system. Many commentators, both black and white, worried that not enough was done to attract the black middle class, many of whom still ended up on the 'B roll', and that the system simply emphasized the color bar. The British journalist, Cyril Dunn, summed up the frustratingly confusing formula:

> like so many other structures compounded of liberal thought in Africa, it was nobly proportioned at the foundations and then appeared, as they might say locally, a bit shack built. If above the base of its mighty pillars David's Temple had been finished off as a garden-party marquee, the effect would not have been dissimilar (Dunn 1959, 167).

Although in the context of the time and region the Federation of Rhodesia and Nyasaland was moving towards widening representation, it did not embrace liberal democracy or any other meaningful system of representation for the black middle class and indeed the masses beneath it. Because the route to gaining the vote was so tortuous for most people, it made the system look hypocritical, claiming to support greater democratic representation while maintaining the color bar. The lack of tangible progress in widening representation was a crucial factor in much of the black middle class turning to African nationalism that promised the vote without reservations. The lack of significant democratic accountability meant that there were few ways of expressing opposing opinions, and even fewer ways of effecting peaceful change, thus opening the way for the growth of African nationalism.

Identity and institutions—a just institutional setting?

Unlike other instances, the failure of the Federation of Rhodesia and Nyasaland was not necessarily due to tensions between federal and national identities within the federation, but rather the conflict between a white identity that looked outward to Britain and its empire, and a black identity that related increasingly to the liberation discourse of African nationalism rather than to its representation as imperial subjects. The lop-sided nature of power in the Federation of Rhodesia and Nyasaland, concentrated as it was in Southern Rhodesia, did little to assuage black anxieties that federal arrangements would not simply facilitate the spread of white domination to the other parts of the federation. During the 1950s, the coexistence of these two identities within the same federal setup was becoming increasingly incompatible. In addition, the asymmetric arrangements characterizing the Federation of Rhodesia and Nyasaland were not concentrated in some parts of its territory, but also tended to favor the whites at the expense of black Africans. Thus, a white person living anywhere in the federation had more rights than a black one, and black Northern Rhodesians in their home territory had more rights than black Southern Rhodesians did in theirs—which meant that black Africans who moved between territories experienced different levels of discrimination.

Moreover, the institutions of the Federation of Rhodesia and Nyasaland that were charged with guiding its development were based on the existing structures of self-government that the white settlers of Southern Rhodesia had developed (which were particularly exclusive). In fact, federal institutions were largely responsible for matters affecting whites, such as immigration and higher education, as well as infrastructure, transport, and so forth. The so-called 'African affairs' were left to the individual territories, lending an unfortunate racial dimension to the asymmetry underwriting federal responsibilities towards its inhabitants, giving some support to the claims that the Federation of Rhodesia and Nyasaland was for the whites' benefit alone (Holderness 1985, 97). Federal institutions, therefore, offered further formalization to the dominant Rhodesian idea of tutelage for black Africans, which denied them the recognition as equal participants in the political process. It is noteworthy, however, that despite the racial tensions implicit in such federal arrangements, in 1953 sufficient numbers of the black middle class accepted their legitimacy and so there was not an obvious imperative to reform or replace them.

The 'shared' identity on which the Federation of Rhodesia and Nyasaland was premised combined (i) white Southern Rhodesian identity that reified the symbolic figure of the mining magnate Cecil Rhodes (after whom the Rhodesians were named); and (ii) the British monarchy. Such construction was neither entirely far-fetched, nor illogical—both white Rhodesian identity and substantial aspects of black aspirations had already developed around the myth of Rhodes and loyalty to the British crown. Furthermore, the identity of the Federation of Rhodesia and Nyasaland revolved around the notion of 'partnership' as distinct from South African-style racism (which in many ways was perceived as *the other* of the federation). It was hoped that Rhodesian institutions—such as the qualified franchise—could accommodate partnership by leaving room for people to become 'civilized' and thus cross the threshold of full citizenship.

Indeed, the federal institutions were based around the sense that black Africans *could* be uplifted, under white guidance. The aphorism 'equal rights for all civilized men', credited to Rhodes, encapsulated this perspective, although the obstacles for blacks were considerable. This conviction was the cornerstone of white Rhodesians' self-image. In this respect, the figure of Rhodes and his importance to the development of white settler identity in central Africa is hard to exaggerate: the poet Kingsley Fairbridge observed that Rhodes 'was something more than human ... he was Rhodes, the Colossus' (King 2001, 37). Both whites and blacks frequently made a point of venerating his memory in public, the latter using his dictum as a retort to white attempts to limit black participation on the common roll (Rotberg 1988, 610). Thus, while to whites Rhodes symbolized imperial ambition and white supremacy, to blacks he represented trusteeship and a certain protection through the imperial government against South African-style discrimination. In this way the ideological and racial absolutes that characterized South African politics were arguably avoided in the Federation of Rhodesia and Nyasaland (King 2001, 38).

Virtually nothing has been written about the public symbols of the Federation of Rhodesia and Nyasaland, and for a good reason. Despite the uniqueness of the central African federal arrangement premised on the idea of 'multiracial partnership', the Federation of Rhodesia and Nyasaland was not founding a new 'decolonized' nation. Thus, the symbols of the old order remained, and there was no radical departure from the *status quo*. No grand public buildings were erected to announce the coming of a new political order, unlike, for example, the Union Buildings in Pretoria or Stormont in Northern Ireland. Despite the continuing oversight of the Colonial Office in the northern territories, the federal elites and the government were essentially the Southern Rhodesian version writ large. Not until the mid-1950s was there any hesitant talk of encouraging a federal national loyalty. There had been no change in terms of allegiance, no significant break with the past, and so there was no need for any declaration of a new nation or a nation-building project. In many ways it was business as usual. The ruling party, the Federal Party, was the Southern Rhodesian United Party transposed onto the federal scene. The new Prime Minister, Godfrey Huggins (newly ennobled as Lord Malvern), was previously Prime Minister of Southern Rhodesia. Despite the inclusion of Northern Rhodesia and Nyasaland, the federal political scene revolved around the federal legislature and civil service in Salisbury and so was little different from the Southern Rhodesian one. As a result, there was little emotional appeal to either whites or blacks. As far as whites were concerned, life would go on as normal, if not improve, as the economic benefits of the federal arrangements became apparent. Black Africans, despite partnership, were not going to be even equal partners for the foreseeable future, which validated their reservations. Since the Rhodesian political system had maintained white hegemony for so long without serious challenge, there was no reason, in white minds, why this state of affairs should not continue. In this setting, the creation of the Federation of Rhodesia and Nyasaland was treated as an improved political arrangement, not the birth of a new nation. As the historians Lewis Gann and Michael Gelfand wrote:

> The federal state lacked color. Victorian Englishmen like Malvern [Huggins], for all their good qualities, or perhaps precisely because of them, lacked the mind which could envisage a brilliant new banner floating from public buildings; few Europeans could in fact have correctly described the Federal flag, a blue ensign adorned with a heraldic hotchpotch. There was no stage management, no torchlight processions and no mass rallies; there was no name on the bread and there were no circuses. The Federal Party, an old-fashioned type of oligarchic organisation, lacked both the men and the money to set up branches in the villages, or to conduct popular propaganda; it maintained no more emotional contact with the people than did the Department of Income Tax (Gann and Gelfand 1966, 264).

The flag of the Federation of Rhodesia and Nyasaland, itself—a dark blue ensign with a new coat of arms that looked much like any other British colonial flag—did not have the visual resonance which flags acquire in other countries. The national flag which whites looked to was the British flag, cementing the close relationship with the metropolis. As the Rhodesian politician Frank Clements wrote, 'the lack of a personal royal presence created veneration for the 'Flag' not unlike that given to the Stars and Stripes in the United States of today' (Clements 1969, 42).

In examining the institutional set-up of the Federation of Rhodesia and Nyasaland, the role of the British government is critical because of its continuing oversight over federal legislation. The white elites were short of complete self-government, and the federal state did not have a course entirely independent of Britain. Originally London's reserve powers over discriminatory legislation applied to Southern Rhodesia, and acquired a somewhat iconic status for black Africans. Although they were never overtly used, these powers offered protection from excessive discrimination, and tended to encourage negotiations that usually watered down discriminatory policies. Importantly, their stature was exaggerated by the lack of British troops that in other colonies could enforce London's will. On the advent of federation, the reserve powers applied to Federal legislation.

In addition, the Federation of Rhodesia and Nyasaland ultimately owed its existence to an Act of the British Parliament, and although it had wide-ranging self-government, its legitimacy flowed from London. Importantly, the Colonial Office adopted a doctrine of 'African paramountcy' (Keatley 1963, 408) in Northern Rhodesia and Nyasaland, meaning that official policy was obliged to consider the needs of the black population as a first priority, something which clearly conflicted with white settler rule. Whether or not this was consistently followed on the ground is less important than the fact that Britain maintained structures of political authority independent (and overriding) those of the Federation of Rhodesia and Nyasaland. In the end, it was in London, not Salisbury, that the decision to break up the federation was taken by allowing the secession of Northern Rhodesia and Nyasaland. Therefore, the withdrawal of Britain's support for the Federation of Rhodesia and Nyasaland was crucial to its failure.

In this setting, it could be argued that the failure of the central African federal arrangements to imagine federal identity independent from that of white Southern Rhodesia is an important contributing factor to its failure. Thereby, the division between white and black communities in the Federation of Rhodesia and Nyasaland remained unbridged due to the inflexibility of white settler identity to allow the functioning of federal institutions that would meaningfully enfranchise the blacks. When the myth of Rhodes and attachment to the crown proved less powerful than African nationalism, the federal arrangement proved weak and lacked the legitimacy and flexibility to fashion an alternative political project.

Imposition of federation and rise of African nationalism

The Federation of Rhodesia and Nyasaland was a compromise, and its failure was partly because that compromise did not properly satisfy the political ambitions of either the dominant white or the emerging black elites. Ironically, both sides felt they had been pushed by the British into accepting an unsatisfactory arrangement. White settlers had originally wanted complete amalgamation that the British would not grant, which disgruntled many whites with the perceived lack of autonomy of federal arrangements. Most black leaders were also suspicious of the federal project even though much of the black middle class was not openly hostile at first. Such reticent support was underwritten by the implicit prospect that black elites would have political opportunities hitherto denied them, which would simultaneously recognize their status as more 'advanced' than the 'black masses'.

At the time of establishment of the Federation of Rhodesia and Nyasaland, many black politicians (especially in the northern territories) did not object to the continuation of British rule. However, what some feared was that the Colonial Office's protection from Southern Rhodesian-style discrimination would be weakened if local whites were given more autonomy. As a result, while most black politicians continued to voice support for their status as British subjects, they also expressed opposition to the federal project (King 2001, 179). Black elites were also more strident in their skepticism that the economic benefits of federation would flow north as well as south. Therefore, although the federal project offered a compromise, it was a compromise imposed by London. Owing to their dissatisfaction, by the early

1960s many in the white elites turned to the pro-independence Rhodesian Front that led Rhodesia into its illegal UDI in 1965.

However, the growing frustration with the slow pace of black advancement and the scale of white intransigence resulted in increasing instances of nationalist mobilization, civil disobedience and rioting. The draconian security measures accompanying the 1959 federation-wide Emergency and the ban on a number of nationalist parties in all three territories called the entire federal project into question. Thus, although the Federation of Rhodesia and Nyasaland as appeared an economically sound enterprise, politically it was increasingly unstable In Southern Rhodesia, in particular, the passing of increasingly repressive security legislation tended to undermine the prospects underwriting the federal arrangements. For instance, the use of white Southern Rhodesian troops to enforce the Emergency in the northern territories simply confirmed the fears of many nationalist leaders. In London too, the sight of a white minority administration deploying force to quell nationalist agitation made the settlers look like the obstacles to peaceful change rather than the nationalists. The Emergency and the slow progress on issues addressing everyday instances of racial discrimination effectively alienated a large swathe of the black middle class. It also shocked much of the business community that had supported partnership as a viable option.

This setting seemed to convince the British that plans for independence of the Federation of Rhodesia and Nyasaland within the Commonwealth should be shelved; the Devlin Commission that reported on the Emergency called Nyasaland a 'police state' (Keatley 1963, 445). At the same time, the black middle class throughout the Federation of Rhodesia and Nyasaland was turning away from seeking acceptance in a white-dominated system, and began to articulate desires that the political project of African nationalism seemed able to deliver. By 1962, the shortcomings of not taking into consideration black opposition to the federal setup were becoming all too apparent, especially as London was beginning to openly heed nationalist leaders and their growing demands for independence.

The issue of discrimination

The question of racial discrimination against black Africans is a constant and entrenched theme running through the history of the Federation of Rhodesia and Nyasaland, without whose acknowledgement the full spectrum of dynamics that contributed to federal failure would be incomplete. Discrimination affected virtually every aspect of daily life in the federation: from the petty segregation of post office queues and train carriages to residential segregation and job reservation (with much higher wages) for whites. With the establishment of the Federation of Rhodesia and Nyasaland, a public discourse around the issue of how to lessen and even abolish (rather than extend) discrimination, became fashionable in upper-middle and middle class circles of all colors. Liberal whites advocated aggressive moves towards recognizing the achievements of the growing urban black middle class as a bulwark against African nationalism. Rhodesian business organizations called for greater rights (and slightly higher wages) for Africans that could turn them into consumers that could boost Southern Rhodesia's blossoming secondary industry and commercial sectors.

In this setting, the proclamation of 'multiracial partnership' provided for some ways in which discrimination would be reduced. But progress towards lowering the color bar—radical by the standards of white southern Africa—was too slow, incomplete and outdated, and was a particular point of tension with the black middle class. The failure of the promise of (somewhat) equal opportunities played a fundamental role in explaining the failure of the Federation of Rhodesia and Nyasaland. Out of Southern Rhodesia, in particular, came a continuous string of reports of ongoing discrimination, including towards middle class blacks whom the system was supposedly trying to co-opt. Although the 'pin-pricks' of everyday segregation were fewer by 1959, the *Bulawayo Chronicle* said 'we provide our critics with sticks to beat us' because middle class blacks could still not go to a white cinema (quoted in King 2001, 269). Because of residential segregation, a black university lecturer and his white Dutch wife could not legally live anywhere in Salisbury where he was employed at the university. The *Central African Airways*, the official carrier of the Federation of Rhodesia and Nyasaland, had to revise its Blantyre–Salisbury flight so that black passengers connecting to London would not have to stay a night in Salisbury because the Jameson hotel, the only one with a multi-racial license, accepted only black guests who were normally resident outside the federation. The *African Daily News* (Salisbury) opined that 'something positive and progressive must be done quickly to encourage racial co-operation on the part of the African people and demonstrate to them in practical terms that this road holds out a better promise' (King 2001, 268). In the meantime Northern Rhodesia began to legislate against the color bar in 1960, going against the Southern Rhodesian instinct of allowing custom to dictate the speed of change.

However dated and patronizing the application of partnership was, the greatest achievement of the Federation of Rhodesia and Nyasaland in its short life was, paradoxically, to start lowering the color bar. This move was seen as the practical implementation of the policy of partnership, which was not necessarily out of step with developments elsewhere after World War II. In effect, and in contrast to South Africa, 'multiracial partnership' was an unfinished mechanism to establish the consent of the governed as opposed to simple (and often brutal) imposition of racial discrimination, and so built on traditional British colonial preference for consent and collaboration (Murphy 1995, 14).

Black discontent with the Federation of Rhodesia and Nyasaland was assured when despite the lofty rhetoric of partnership, a widening franchise and employment in the civil service, the continuing existence of the color bar reflected the failure to tackle the very essence of discontent among black Africans. In this setting, black support for federal arrangements (which was important for its legitimacy) virtually disappeared. The loss of the last vestiges of black support was acknowledged by the Monckton Commission that was set up by Britain to prepare for the 1960 Federal Review Conference on the future of the Federation of Rhodesia and Nyasaland. The Commission reported that dislike of the Federation was widespread among black Africnas in all three territories, and its recommendation that Northern Rhodesia and

Nyasaland be allowed to secede was accepted by Britain (Windrich 1975, 33), thus marking the end of the Federation which was finally wound up in 1963.

Conclusion

In examining the question of why the Federation of Rhodesia and Nyasaland failed, several interconnected issues should be kept in mind. The lack of meaningful progress towards democratic representation—as implied in the policy of partnership—with obvious repercussions in establishing the legitimacy of the Federation of Rhodesia and Nyasaland in the eyes of its inhabitants is obvious, and is tightly linked to the question of continuing discrimination against black Africans. This further reflected on the weakness and lack of imagination in federal institutions that could not manage the projected transition to more self-government, with a substantial black population, and stronger nationalist pressures from the northern territories against which the vague and incomplete promises of 'multiracial partnership' could not compete. The question of a lack of federal national identity, although important, was compounded by the failure to create the conditions for cohabitation between white settlers and black Africans. Finally, reluctance on the part of the British to support the white-dominated Federation of Rhodesia and Nyasaland against the pressures of African nationalism in all three territories at a time of accelerating decolonization meant that the imperial umbrella, beneath which the federation existed, was withdrawn. In the end, the Federation of Rhodesia and Nyasaland failed because the nature of its structures and assumptions could not accommodate the increasingly divergent political ambitions of its inhabitants.

The over-arching conclusion from the failure of the Federation of Rhodesia and Nyasaland that can be applied to other examples of defunct federalism is that a viable federal state depends on the establishment of credible mechanisms and institutions for the verification and continuous re-enactment of the consent of the governed. For this to happen, federal administrative structures should have the capacity to negotiate the conflicts between various communities (with their distinct and sometimes competing interests) that necessarily constitute a federation. These issues are not specific to federations, but are more prominent because by definition a federation recognizes and administers diversity in a way that a unitary state does not. As the case of the Federation of Rhodesia and Nyasaland indicates the lack of such mechanisms reflected its origins—i.e., it was a colonial creation which was a direct outcome of British rule. In this setting, the issues spurred by racial discrimination as well as the lack of common ground between the black and white communities reflected the intransigent 'one-size-fit-all' approach of the metropole that underwrote the inflexibility of the federal arrangements.

Chapter 5

The Games Elites Play:
Notes towards an Elite-Focused Understanding of the Failure of the Federal Republic of Cameroon (1961–1972)

Cyril Fcguc

To refer to Cameroon as 'Africa in miniature' the way its authorities tend to do with pride, is to imply that Cameroon is a reflection and presentation of Africa in terms of endowments (and only reluctantly in terms of pitfalls as well). While this may be true in many respects, it certainly stretches our credulity … Far from being Africa in miniature in this sense, the country has earned distinction as a burial ground for many a theory or generalization. As Cameroonians are wont to say: 'le Cameroun, c'est le Cameroun'. Meaning, Cameroon is a peculiar case, 'un paradis des paradoxes'… [Thus] the only thing that appears to unite Cameroonians is a common sense of ethnic ambition and difference, and the need to pursue these under the patronage of the godfather state. In this way mediocrity, corruption, exploitation, and a false sense of stability get perpetuated.

Francis B. Nyamnjoh (Nyamnjoh 1999, 101–102, 118)

Introduction

In a marked distinction from other defunct federalisms, the failure of the Federal Republic of Cameroon was not accompanied by the violent break-up of federal statehood and its 'balkanization' into separate sovereign entities. Instead, the federal arrangements came apart as a result of a popular referendum, which did not see a 'velvet divorce' between the federal provinces, but maintained the territorial integrity of the country within the arrangements of a unitary state. In its overview of these dynamics, the current chapter is premised on the assumption that Cameroon's federalism did not have a sudden ideological emergence, but that its origins reflect the protracted and problematic colonial experience that the country had faced.

From 1884 to 1916 Cameroon (or 'Kamerun') was part of the German colonial *Schutzgebiete* in Africa. In the wake of World War I, German colonial possessions were 'redistributed' among France and the United Kingdom. Consequently, Cameroon was partitioned into the French, Eastern Cameroons, and the British, Southern and Northern Cameroons. During the Anglo-French colonial era, these territories were recognized as Mandates of the League of Nations (LNM). After World War II they were converted into the United Nations Trusteeship Territories (UNTT) (Gill 1996). The project of federalism—understood primarily as the 'reunification' of the French and the British Cameroons—was, thereby, promoted as an arrangement that would facilitate (as well as manage) the decolonization process of these territories.

In this setting, the victory of the 'reunificationist' Kamerun National Democratic Party (KNDP) led by John Ngu Foncha in the 1957 general elections in the British Southern Cameroons and the results from the UN-sponsored plebiscite of 11 February 1961 triggered a series of negotiations between the political leaders of both Cameroons. These negotiations led to the Foumban Constitutional Conference (FCC) of July 1961. The FCC's final covenant became the foundation of a new constitution that gave birth to the Federal Republic of Cameroon inaugurated in October 1961. Formally, it was a two-state federation with two prime ministers, a federal legislature and a single president (Fonchingong 2005; Ngoh 1999). The existence of the federation was ended on 20 May 1972 with a popular referendum when the population voted to adopt a new constitution setting up a unitary state to replace the federation—which was lauded as 'the Glorious Revolution of May Twentieth' (Stark 1976, 423). Thereafter, the federal era tend to be viewed by some commentators as an onerous 'confusion' in Cameroon's history (Fossungu 1999).

The objective of this chapter is to discuss the 'intelligibility' of the federal failure in Cameroon and relate it to the identity tensions in the federation. As the assertion in the epigraph suggests, Cameroon has been and still is perceived by many as 'Africa in miniature'. In this respect, the president of the Federal Republic of Cameroon—Ahmadou Ahidjo—interpreted the 'reunification' of the Francophone and the Anglophone parts of the country as the first step towards the fulfillment of the dream of 'African Unity'. Ahidjo proclaimed on 1 October 1964 that:

> As far as culture is concerned we must in fact refrain from any blind and narrow nationalism and avoid any complex when absorbing the learning of other countries. When we consider the English language and culture and the French language and culture we must regard them not as the property) of such and a race but as an acquirement of the universal civilization to which we belong. This is in fact why we have followed the path of bilingualism since we consider not only that it is in our interests to develop these two world-wide languages in our country but that furthermore it offers us the means to develop this *new culture* which I have just mentioned and which could transform our country into the catalyst of *African Unity*. (quoted in Stark 1976, 434, emphasis added)

The emphasis on identity leads this chapter to adopt an interpretative examination of the stakes, the expectations, the situational opportunities, and the strategic moves made by relevant political actors. As the idea of reunification was promoted by various political elites in Cameroon, the trajectories of the federal experiment remained tied to their interests. In this setting, the projects of 'reunification' and 'federalism' were construed and perceived as synonymous by popular imagination. Cameroon's federal failure, therefore, demonstrates the complexity of understanding the phenomenon of defunct federalism 'in a manner which is neither abstract nor casuistic, neither programmatic nor purely speculative' (Bonhoeffer 1971, 89); yet manages to account for the political opportunism of party elites, the autocratic Gaullist tendencies of political leaders, and the impact of various international actors—mainly the UN, the United Kingdom, and France. The discussion of these issues informs the analysis of the failed experiment of the Federal Republic of Cameroon; the critical engagement underwriting this inquiry traces 'the birth, life, and death of a federation that was more shadow than reality' (Stark 1976, 423).

The Constitutive Social-Political Elements of Federalism

The federal momentum and its institutional maturation during 1961 in Cameroon were aided by an eclectic (and mutually-reinforcing) set of factors, which can be grouped into three categories: (i) nostalgic-emotional (ii) economic, and (iii) ideological-programmatic.

Nostalgic-emotional factors

Some commentators have stressed the centrality of the *Kamerun Idea* to the project of reunification (Ardener 1967, 293; Welch 1966, 155–159; Johnson 1970). The *Kamerun Idea* is a nostalgic, and (from the end of 1940s throughout the early 1960s) a romanticized and popularized concept that inspired large-scale mobilization usually labeled as the *Pan-Kamerun Movement* (Chem-Langhee and Njeuma 1980, 25–64). The adherents and sympathizers of that movement called for the re-institution of a Cameroonian national sovereignty premised on the territorial boundaries of the German colonial project. Thus, the *Kamerun Idea* reflected a form of nationalism, which seemed to reject sub-national identities—i.e., 'tribal' allegiance—to espouse a consciousness derived from the shared legacy of a German colony. The *Kamerun Idea*, however, did not manage to prompt a robust 'sentiment of cohesion' (Johnson 1970, 69; Kofele-Kale 1980, 3–23). The legacy of bifurcation had created real and imagined difference. At the same time, the fact that the Cameroons were formally designated as Trusteeship Territories also had noteworthy effects on the colonial powers: thus, that rather than following its centralizing tendencies, France was obliged to 'decentralize its relationship with Cameroon, while the British, noted for their decentralizing tendencies integrated their part of Cameroon into a region of Nigeria' (Stark 1976, 424; Westfall 1992). Nevertheless, despite the differences that these distinct experiences produced, the *Kamerun Idea* remained a powerful rhetorical symbol for popular mobilization. In this context, Awasom (2000, 94) concludes that although the brevity of the German colonization of Cameroon 'might have been too brief to create a profound and meaningful [feeling] of nationhood strong enough to evoke a strong sense of nationalism in its aftermath ... it left an indelible legacy of a common name—Kamerun—and a common German past'.

Economic factors

The second category reflects the distinct economic contexts in the French and the British Cameroons. These disparities meant that the idea of reunification in the British Cameroons was introduced and dominated by Francophone émigrés, who were living in the large Southern Cameroonian cities like Buea, Tiko, Victoria and Kumba (Ngoh 2000). They had migrated to the British Cameroons in an attempt to avoid the hardships of the French colonial administration. They earned their living through trade-related or minor commercial activities, and a sizable number of them worked on plantations (Njeuma 1995, 30). However, the Francophone émigrés suffered discrimination as alien residents and experienced difficulties while crossing the borders in the pursuit of their trade activities. Under the leadership of the businessman Joseph Ngu the émigrés founded an interest group in late 1940s, named the French Cameroon Welfare Union (FCWU). Its purpose was to protect the business interests of the Francophone émigrés in the British Cameroons (Amazee 1994, 199–234). Subsequently, the émigrés were also lobbying for the reunification and the establishment of a customs union between the French and the British Cameroons.

Ideological-programmatic factors

The establishment of the Federal Republic of Cameroon was aided by political formations that promoted the idea of reunification—hence, from its inception the idea of federation was tied to party manifestos. In 1947 the young charismatic leader of the *Jeunesse Camerounaise Française* (JEUCAFRA), Soppo Priso, created the first political party in the French Cameroons: the *Rassemblement Camerounais* (RACAM) (Njeuma 1995, 28). Priso was primarily concerned with France's commitment to the self-government and (ultimately) the independence of Eastern Cameroons. Dissatisfied with RACAM's moderate stance on independence, the party's Marxist wing splintered in April 1948 into the *Union des Populations du Cameroun* (UPC) (Joseph 1997, 92). The UPC's program included demands for immediate independence. In Southern Cameroons, the UPC was able to achieve wide popular support for the idea of a united Cameroon (Ozughen 1997, 27). At the UN, it also requested the separation of the British Cameroons from Nigeria and its reunification with its French counterpart (Awasom 1998, 163–183). Consequently, once the main political formation in the Eastern Cameroons—the *Union Camerounaise* (UC)—embraced the idea of reunification, federation became possible.

Navigating Contra 'Liberal Democracy': The Gaullist Factor

The establishment of the Federal Republic of Cameroon had been preceded by political events that undermined the practices of liberal democracy. In this respect, Frank Stark (1976, 432) has argued that 'although the birth of federation was celebrated, as a political system it was doomed to perish in the cradle'. In October 1959, only few months before the independence of La Republique du Cameroun (LRC) on 1 January 1960, the premier of Eastern Cameroons, Ahmadou Ahidjo, requested the legislative assembly to grant him *pleins pouvoirs* ('emergency powers'). He claimed that these were required for the suppression of a rebellion by the UPC (LeVine 1986, 20–52). Ahidjo, however, used his *pleins pouvoirs* to monopolize the constitutional process of the nascent state. He undermined the importance of the existing legislative body by appointing a 42-member Constitutional Committee that was tasked to prepare the draft constitution, which was approved in a referendum that took place on 11 February 1960 (LeVine 1971, 81). The new constitution was thereby Gaullist in character as it strengthened the powers of the executive vis-à-vis the legislative and judiciary branches.

During this constitutional process, the balance of powers between the political representatives of the British Cameroons and Ahidjo was tipped in favor of the latter. In this setting, the representatives of the British Cameroons had little (if any) ability to influence the contours of the federal project. As a result, the institutional architecture of the new federation resembled that of the LRC: for instance, it replicated the highly centralized state apparatus subservient to a president, who was elected by universal suffrage and held powers ranging from the control over finances, foreign relations, defense, culture, education to the territorial administration. After 1966, when Ahidjo attempted to hem in all political formations in the *Union Nationale du Cameroun* (UNC), he arrogated to the presidential office the prerogative to appoint the prime minister of Southern Cameroons. One of the most spectacular instances of this prerogative was when Ahidjo divested Augustine Jua, the leader of the KNDP, of his position as the elected prime minister of the Anglophone province in order to substitute him with the more pliant Salomon T. Muna (Frank 1976, 440–442).

Ahidjo's Gaullist tendencies undermined the democratization of the Federal Republic of Cameroon. Instead of consensual politics, he established a 'bureaucratic dirigisme'—an 'administrative system which basically ignored the "federal" nature of the country' (Stark 1976, 432). In lieu of the cultivation of political pluralism within an inclusive and ongoing dialogue involving political representatives from all federal units, Ahidjo promoted an autocratic style of political management. As Fonchingong (2005, 364) points out, Ahidjos's Gaullism was characterized by the main features of *neopatrimonial* rule: 'presidentialism, clientilism, and the massive redistribution of state resources'. This governing regime was also accompanied by the formation of ethno-regional political system in the context of Ahidjo's regional balance policy (*politique d'équilibre régionale*), which simultaneously fabricated and co-opted a multi-ethnic ruling class into the political enterprise of the UNC, while silencing 'alternative' political projects (Eyinga 1978; Nkwi and Nyamnjoh 1997). Borrowing from and reforming the colonial legacy of 'decentralized despotism', Ahidjo transformed Cameroon into a country where 'policy is less about balancing [between different interest], than it is about diverting attention from real to imagined problems and causes' (Nyamnjoh 1999, 105–106). Thus, in confirmation of the first hypothesis from the theory of defunct federalism outlined in Chapter 1, Ahidjo's ultra-Gaullism—which undermined the establishment of liberal democracy—was an important factor contributing to the failure of the Federal Republic of Cameron.

Negotiating a Safe Haven: The Anglophone Identity and Federal Institutions

It is often claimed that the establishment of federal statehood in Cameroon intended both the cohabitation between the Francophone and the Anglophone identity communities and the protection of the specificity and the rights of the Anglophones

(Fossungu 1999, 117–119; Konings 2005; Ngoh 2000). For instance, Nicodemus Fru Awasom (2000, 91) reminds us that when the reunification question was heating up in the 1960s, Victor LeVine allegorically referred to the British Cameroons as the 'bride', while the French Cameroons was the 'groom'. Awasom concedes that the imagery of stronger and weaker partners reflects the disparities between the two territories—the French Cameroons was ten times the area of its British counterpart, had four times its population, and 'had immeasurably greater resources and a much higher level of social and economic development'. Nevertheless, as Monga (2001, 202) points out such focus seems to occlude that Cameroon is ethnically highly diverse encompassing 'a mosaic of populations with different social structures, economic bases, and systems of beliefs, and about 200 languages and even more dialects' (also see Kleis 1980). Federalism was therefore promoted and legitimized as a device recognizing the diverse colonial experiences of different groups, containing the dominance of the political representatives of the French Cameroons, and creating a niche for Anglophone autonomy within a reunified Cameroonian state.

However, the political practices of federation did not seem to tally with these objectives—not least because of the activities of the dominant political representatives of the French and the British Cameroons (both before and after reunification) were often animated by instrumental interests and concerns, and tended to reflect tactical decision-making rather than any substantial strategic vision of the country's future. As indicated, the head of the federation—Ahmadou Ahidjo—did not seem to subscribe to the federal principles of transparency and accountability. Instead, he initiated a Gaullist project of creating a quasi-autocratic rule by forging 'a new national consciousness among people with different colonial experiences, political memories, and convictions' (Fonchingong 2005, 364). Although espousing to 'the ideal of an honestly pluralistic identity', Ahidjo's homogenizing project intended to suppress all particularistic tendencies (Bayart 1973, 453). For instance, in his statements he increasingly emphasized the distinction between 'reunification' and 'federation' to his nationalizing agenda—the latter merely facilitated the achievement of the former. In a speech on 3 November 1966, Ahidjo declared that:

> after the people of West Cameroon massively voted in favor of reunification and not for federation, after reunification itself we freely estimated that it was necessary to create a federation between the two states, and to create federal institutions. But that does not permit us to say that there are two Cameroonian nations. (quoted in Stark 1976, 437)

The Cameroonian context, therefore, confirms the outlines of the intrication between identity and federalism suggested in Chapter 1. As Yvette Djachechi Monga (2001, 199) indicates, the politicization of community identities 'does not just happen. It is processed and developed in a context of identity negotiation by culture brokers acting as self-proclaimed representatives of their respective groups'. Thus, in contradiction to Ahidjo's Gaullist nationalism, the representative of the British Southern Cameroons, Augustin Ngom Jua insisted that:

> It must be emphasized that the Federal Republic of Cameroon is a federation of two states, cultures, and traditions; the present arrangement was envisaged as the most ideal solution to the [problem of] reunification. Any exercise, therefore, that is designed to alter

this arrangement ... will throw our present system of government into complete disarray. (quoted in Stark 1976, 436).

It is, therefore, necessary to uncover the roots of the idea of reunification and indicate its instrumental nature. As Stark (1976, 424) insists, 'the idea of the reunification of the two trusteeship territories seems to have originated in early 1948 in the Kumba and Tiko areas of the [British] Southern Cameroons among the [Francophone] Bamilike who had resettled there and wished to improve trade by making border crossing easier'. At the same time, Anglophone politicians employed the discourse of reunification 'as an escape route from Nigerian domination' (Awasom 2000, 99). In the end, this 'chronic lack of [strategic] vision' (Nyamnjoh 1999, 111) in the discursive employment of reunification disadvantaged the political representatives of the British Cameroons.

For instance, Endeley—the first prominent Southern Cameroonian politician who led the Cameroon Youth League (CYL) in 1949 and established the Kamerun National Congress (KNC) in 1953, formed an alliance with the FCWU to create the Cameroon National Federation (CNF). In spite of the CNF's uncompromising call for the reunification between the French and the British Cameroons (Mbiakop 1996, 19), Endeley's political goal was either the achievement of the status of autonomous 'region' within Nigeria or the granting of full independence for Southern Cameroons (Njeuma 1995, 3–31). Thus, when the 1950 general elections were approaching, Endeley objected vocally to the enfranchisement of over 17,000 Francophone Cameroonians living in the British Cameroons, whom he considered aliens. In this respect, the idea of reunification offered Endeley effective means to internationalize the issue and to pressure Britain to support the autonomy of Southern Cameroons (Awasom 1998, 175). Following the July 1953 London Constitutional Conference, Endeley's plan seemed to have worked—Southern Cameroons had been granted the status of a semi-autonomous region within the Nigerian federation, endowed with a legislative assembly and an executive council headed by Endeley. Consequently, Endeley's agenda veered towards pro-Nigerian politics (and away from Cameroonian federalism).

These developments urged Foncha to leave the KNC and to found the KNDP. Influenced by radical UPC members, he advocated the separation of Southern Cameroons from Nigeria and the establishment of a federation with Eastern Cameroons (Johnson 1970, 129–130). The KNDP won the 1959 legislative elections and Foncha became prime minister. Although his professed goals were the secession from Nigeria and the reunification with Eastern Cameroons, he nevertheless requested from the British colonial administration an intermediary period of independence for Southern Cameroons. After the UN plebiscite Foncha emerged as the leader of Southern Cameroons, and led the constitutional negotiations with the LRC. In the Federal Republic of Cameroon, he became the federal vice-president and retained his prime ministerial position. However, owing to the federal constitutional rules in 1963 Foncha was forced to choose either his position as vice-president or as Southern Cameroons' prime minister. Foncha chose to give up his prime ministerial responsibilities and maintained his vice-presidential position (Johnson 1970, 263–265). Pursuing the goal of neutralizing his political opposition, Ahidjo called for what he termed the 'Grand National Unified Party'. Foncha rushed to form alliance with Ahidjo's, *Union Camerounaise* (UC) in April of the same year (Johnson 1970, 263). He feared his party would be overshadowed by Endeley's new Cameroon People's National Convention (CPNC), which had already merged with the UC (Johnson 1970, 262; Takougang 1996, 11).

This setting provided the facilitating conditions for Muna's political opportunism. He left the KNDP to form the Cameroon United Congress (CUC), set up an alliance with the CPNC, and merged with the UC (Stark 1976). Muna's public pronouncements tended to reflect Ahidjo's political views and he explicitly endorsed the idea of a loose federation and the abolition of the multiparty system. This allegiance was rewarded by Ahidjo who in December 1967 appointed Muna as the prime minister of Southern Cameroons and in March 1970 promoted him as the vice-president of the Federal Republic of Cameroon. The formal conditions allowing Muna to occupy both posts at the same time were created by a special constitutional amendment (Takougang 2003). Subsequently Muna was instrumental to the dismantling of federalism. On 6 May 1972 Ahidjo requested the National Assembly to establish a unitary system. On 20 May 1972 a referendum was organized, in which Cameroonians were asked if they wanted to continue the federation or allow for its transformation into a unitary state system (Takougang 2003). The result was a resounding support for a unitary state system. Thus, on 2 June 1972 through a presidential decree Ahidjo dissolved the Federal Republic of Cameroon.

Such overview suggests that the Southern Cameroonian elites used the issue of Anglophone identity either as a tactical ploy, or as a vehicle for political opportunism, or both (Mbaku and Ihonvbere 1998, 367–397; Takougang 2003, 434). Regardless of whether such stance was the outcome of political inexperience, of distinct historical contexts, or of insufficient resources, it prevented the political representatives of the British Cameroons to engage meaningfully with the instruments and arrangements of federalism and to establish a coherent framework for the accommodation of Anglophone identity. Reunification, therefore, remained 'essentially a Francophone affair, from its inception until it was ultimately imposed on reluctant Anglophones' (Awasom 2000, 112). Following the demise of federal statehood, the government unleashed an aggressive 'Francophonization' campaign that led to the stigmatization of the Anglophone community as 'uncouth', 'backward', 'uncivilized', and 'inconsequential' (Eko 2003, 81–83). In this respect, Bayart (1973, 453) brings out that the Anglophone community, 'who had few means of effective protest' paid a high price for reunification.

The 'Invisible Hand' of Federalism in Cameroon: The Ambiguity of Federal Imposition

The reference to the 'invisible hand' of federalism here relates to the contest between different forces in the Cameroonian context arguing in its favor or opposing it outright (Fossungu 1999, 87). The query therefore is, was Cameroon's federalism the product of an imposition? In other words, was it an outcome of the opportunistic manipulation of political elites or did it spring from different 'inducements' and/or 'predisposing conditions' (Springer 1962)?

Some of the factors contributing to successful federal arrangements are 'a sense of military insecurity and of a consequent need for common defense; a desire to be independent of foreign powers, and a realization that only through union could independence be secured; a hope of economic advantage from the union, some political association of the communities concerned prior to the federal union, geographical neighborhood and similarity of political institutions' (Fossungu 1999, 90–99). The elements of geographical proximity and security—especially from the point of view of Southern Cameroons—may have contributed to the federal enactment.

However, the contention here is that Cameroonian federalism was both conceptualized and imposed by the 'invisible hand' of political elites. As already indicated, through the promise of reunification, federalism offered possibilities for manipulating diverse interests for particular instrumental ends. The scheming between different political representatives (as well as Ahidjo's policies and rhetoric) suppressed federalism's popular appeal and ensured that it remained 'primarily an "elite" symbol and concept' (Stark 1976, 442). Yet, such domestic imposition was not without its international externalities. For instance, starting with Priso's RACAM, the political elites of the two Cameroons 'hoped to locate the legal battlefield' of their decolonization outside the UNTTs (Njeuma 1995, 28). Thus, the former colonial powers—the United Kingdom and France—as well as the UN were instrumental to the federalizing process in Cameroon and its failure.

The UN was concerned by the prospective formation of post-colonial micro-states, whose economic viability and sovereignty might not be sustainable. During the preparations for the 1961 plebiscite, after negotiations with the political leaders of the Southern Cameroons the UN agreed to put forth three questions for the referendum: first, a greater degree of autonomy within the Nigerian federation; second, reunification with the independent French Cameroons; and third, outright independence for the Southern Cameroons (UN Review 1959; Chem-Langhee 1976, Ngoh 2000). Surprisingly, and in contradiction to the agreements with (and desires of) Anglophone politicians, when the UN General Assembly Resolution 1352XIV of October 1959 was passed, it included only the first two plebiscite questions. Many commentators refer to this outcome as the UN's '*diktat*' (Awasom 2000, 110). The UN's refusal to permit the inclusion of the independence option in the 1961 referendum contributed to the subsequent trajectory of Cameroonian federalism and 'casts doubt on whether a federation in the sense of a voluntary relationship between political units ever existed' (Stark 1976, 441). As Awasom (1980, 58) comments, the plebiscite in the Southern Cameroons represents 'one of the most bizarre cases in history where a territory had to gain its independence by attaching itself to an already independent state'.

The position of the United Kingdom was somewhat similar to that of the UN. On the one had, it favored an enhanced autonomy of the British Cameroons within Nigeria, since London was apprehensive whether Southern Cameroon would be sustainable as an independent state (LeVine 1964, 210–215). However, the controversial stance of the United Kingdom—for instance, its attempt (against the UNTT agreement) to integrate Southern Cameroon into the administrative region of East Nigeria (Johnson

1970)—undermined its influence over the Anglophone political elites. In this respect, the latter were 'forced' to look for alternative ways to achieve their objectives, which initiated the cohabitation with their Francophone counterparts.

France, on the other hand, played a much more complex (although equally controversial) role. To start with, the relations between France and the LRC were very close and were crucial to Ahidjo's espousal of Gaullist principles (Blondel 1985, 115–117). Some have termed the political representatives of the Francophone community as '*collaborateurs valables*' (Awasom 2002, 5–7) in order to indicate their cooptation by the French neo-colonial agenda. It is often claimed that Ahidjo's centralizing policies were carried out with France's active support (Vershave 1999). Also, Paris bankrolled Ahidjo's assimilationist Francophonization policies in the Southern Cameroons (Eko 2003; Westfall 1992).

In this setting, different external actors contributed to and participated in the domestic political machinations of Cameroonian elites. The rhetoric and arrangements of federalism seemed to offer the representatives of different political formations a tactical means for achieving their goals. Thus, the reunification idea became little more than 'a barren political instrument in the hands of irresponsible and ambitious people' (Chem-Langhee and Njeuma 1980, 33). As Fossungu (1999, 102) indicates 'when only personal interests are predominating, realities are always bent to fit certain forms rather than forms bending to fit reality'. The ambiguous conceptualization of federalism by Cameroonian politicians, therefore, suggests that federal statehood was 'ultimately, a contingent phenomenon' (Bayart 1973, 454). Once the discourse and practices of federalism were no longer deemed pliant to the maneuvering of Francophone and Anglophone elites, the very same actors that imposed the federal arrangement dismantled the Federal Republic of Cameroon.

Conclusion

This chapter has claimed that the opportunistic nature of the elite games that brought about Cameroonian federalism also offers an explanation for its failure. Thus, in its assessment of the relevance of the hypotheses from the theory of defunct federalism outlined in Chapter 1, the case study of the Federal Republic of Cameroon draws the following conclusions. Firstly, it seems to confirm the '*liberal democracy hypothesis*' since the practices of federalism in Cameroon were subverted by the lack of liberal-democratic discipline stifled by the autocratic Gaullism of the political system. Secondly, as regards the '*just-institutional-setting-for-identity-accommodation hypothesis*', it seems that the ubiquitous clientelist relations and the political opportunism of the political representatives of the British Cameroons prevented the establishment of meaningful institutional accommodation of the Anglophone community. This setting allowed the Francophone elites to impose both their version of federal arrangements and, consequently, their dissolution. Thirdly, the '*imposition-of-federalism hypothesis*' also seems to be confirmed by this case study, although the complexity of its relationship to the federal trajectories in Cameroon have not been as straightforward as it might be expected. It was the ambiguous context of complex interactions between different political elites as well as various international actors (especially, the UN, the United Kingdom, and France) that contributed both to the initiation and to the demise of federalism in Cameroon. Additionally, as Stark (1976, 441–442) presciently suggest, the dismantling of the Cameroonian federation was made possible by federal divisions reflecting the 'colonial cultures and values that had to be broken down into a new indigenous culture; a breakdown that all Cameroonians could agree with'. However, the claim here is that the deleterious association of federal statehood with the colonial past re-affirms the utilitarian engagement of Cameroonian elites with federalism.

Thus, the legacy of the political machinations that first introduced and then subverted federalism in Cameroon indicates the practices of totalitarian system, which 'serves people only to the extent necessary to ensure that people will serve it, with anyone not playing their predetermined role running the risk of indictment as enemy of the system'. Because the 'ideological pretences of the system seduce people at every level of society, the system has succeeded in permeating life thoroughly with hypocrisy and lies' (Nyamnjoh 1999, 107). These dynamics, according to Oben Mbuagbo (2002, 431) render Cameroon 'always on the margins of disintegration and fragmentation' arising from the 'subversion of democratic principles to satisfy [the] parochial and sectional ambitions' of state elites. Confirming such observation, Monga (2001, 200) points out that the resulting social divisiveness and ethnic tensions produced by such politics produce 'fierce competition for diminishing state resources'—which are central to understanding the current patterns of identity accommodation in Cameroon, 'played among and within ethnic groups by their respective elites'. In the present context, for instance, the 'difficulties of establishing a single Cameroonian identity' (Awasom 2000, 113) are indicated by the campaign of the Sawa community for either an independent Anglophone state or the reestablishment of federal statehood in Cameroon (Fisiyu and Geschiere 1996; Konings 2000; Konings and Nyamnjoh 1997; Monga 2001). Thus, returning to the claim in the epigraph of this chapter, the origins, experience, and legacy of Cameroonian federalism seem to confirm its status as '*un paradis des paradoxes*'.

Chapter 6

The Failed Experiment with Federalism in Pakistan (1947–1971)

Farhan Hanif Siddiqi

Introduction

The chapter engages in a conceptual exposition of the factors that contributed to the failure of federalism in Pakistan—i.e., *how* and *why* federalism failed to take roots in the country. Such analysis is contextualized with reference to one of its provincial units—East Pakistan—which seceded and became the separate state of Bangladesh in 1971. Two factors make Pakistan unique: Firstly, the fact that the two territorial units, West Pakistan and East Pakistan, were separated by about a 1000 miles of Indian soil made Pakistan a territorially incongruent unit. Considering that territorial contiguity is one of the central principles of nation states in the modern era, Pakistan certainly constituted a major exception from the norm. Secondly, East Pakistan's secession from West Pakistan is peculiar in that a majority group seceded from the state (rather than vice versa). While in territorial terms the western wing of the country (the modern day Pakistan) was six times larger than the eastern wing, the population of East Pakistan at the time of the 1961 census was 50.8 million versus 42.9 million in the West (Jackson 1975, 15).

In terms of its ethnic composition, Pakistan comprised six major ethnic groups at the time of the partition of British India. These were the Bengalis, Punjabis, Pathans, Sindhis, Mohajirs and Baloch. Except for the Bengalis, all the other ethnic communities lived in West Pakistan while East Pakistan was the exclusive abode of the Bengalis, where they exercised an absolute majority. In this respect, East Pakistan resembled a nationality-based unit where there was a territorial concentration of one major identity group (Kymlicka 1998, 128), while in Western Pakistan there were federal units for the Punjabis, Sindhis, Pathans and Baloch (which were not however exclusively monoethnic).

Importantly, the Bengali majority in Pakistan did not automatically translate into political power of that ethnic group. Rather, political power and authority were concentrated in the hands of the Punjabis and Mohajirs in West Pakistan. Moreover, the failure of democracy to take roots in the new nation state meant that political power was centralized and monopolized in the hands of the bureaucracy and military. Punjabis and Mohajirs who made the bulk of the bureaucratic-military oligarchy were thus privileged by the institutions of governance, while the numerically stronger Bengalis, were excluded from the process of decision-making.

According to Choudhury (1969, 68), a 'federation comes into existence to overcome differences; it therefore has to work out a compromise between the desire for union and the anxiety to safeguard the interests of the federating units'. However, it is not imperative that states opt for a federal arrangement to manage their multinationality. They might implement devolution (for instance, Great Britain), or impose further centralization over the constituent federal units in order to preempt perceived threats to the territorial integrity of the state. Pakistan offers a clear instance of the latter. The ethnically heterogeneous nature of the Pakistani nation was managed by gearing the administrative machinery of the state towards rigorous centralization. This undermined the federal model in Pakistan and, ultimately, led to its unraveling.

Initially, this chapter reviews the historical pattern of Pakistan's statehood and traces the process of mobilization of Bengali ethnonationalism. It then discusses the 'secession' of East Pakistan in the context of the hypotheses from the theory of defunct federalism. Thirdly, this analysis proposes some additional factors that provide a more detailed context of Pakistan's federal failure. It also has to be mentioned that throughout this chapter Pakistan's 'federal government' is referred to by the term the 'central government' or 'centre'. This appellation seems to render the hegemonic features of the governing structures of Pakistan state comparatively better than the notion of 'federal government', which implies a shared agreement on the division of power between a government and its federating units.

History of Pakistan's Federalism and the Strengthening of Bengali Ethnonationalism, 1947–1971

This section outlines the political and constitutional history of Pakistan in the period 1947–1971 and explains how and why the experiment with federalism was doomed to failure from its inauspicious beginning. Being a multi-ethnic state, Pakistan could not escape the 'ethnic' predicament when it came to the simultaneous tasks of building state institutions and constructing a shared national identity. At the societal level, the organizational framework of Pakistan's statehood had to co-opt different groups in a manner in which their ethnic identity would give precedence to a national, Pakistani identity. The ethnic dilemma at the state level mandated that the institutional and administrative structure (namely the state administration and the military) be ethnically inclusive rather than exclusive. Viable state structures could only be sustained with a balanced and proportional representation of the ethnic communities inhabiting the state. Any state structure lacking such a system of representation would be bound to evoke critical responses on the part of deprived ethnic communities.

The political dominance of the bureaucratic-military oligarchy was manifest since independence. This meant that democracy and democratic institutions such as the parliament, political parties and their respective growth suffered. Consequently, the limited access of Bengalis (and other communities) led to their increased political mobilization. It has to be acknowledged that perhaps paradoxically (although not surprisingly) the pattern that Pakistan's federalism took was not that dissimilar from the 'administrative paradigm' of Indian federal arrangements described by Vassuki Nesiah. According to this model, federalism emerges as 'conservative and statist, its mapping of the relationship between state and nation evocative of images of the state as Leviathan, all-encompassing and standing in for all' (Nesiah 2000, 62).

For federalism to work in any country and in any political environment there needs to be a shared belief in its utility as a means of maintaining national unity and ensuring governance by consent rather than *diktat*. If such a conviction in the functionality of federalism is not supported by the ruling elites, the federation is very likely to be challenged by centralizing forces and to result in the institutional and political disempowerment of the federal entities. This intangible factor is often referred to as a basis for the successful functioning of federalism. Kymlicka (1998, 142), for instance, argues that for federalism to work, 'an enormous degree of ingenuity and good will, and indeed good luck' is required. Thomas Franck also argues that a 'union of federations only *begins* when the leaders agree to federate and their subalterns sit down to work out what is too often called "the details"'. Thus, undertaking a comparative analysis of the federal failure in Malaysia, Africa and the West Indies, Franck states 'that for a federation to be able to resist failure, the leaders, and their followers, must "feel federal"—they must be able to think of themselves as one people, with one, common self-interest—capable, where necessary of over-riding most other considerations of small-group interest'. This, Franck believes is a more effective framework in ensuring the success of post-colonial federations than a common colonial heritage, a common language or economic advantages associated with federalism (evaluated as secondary factors) (1968, 169–173 emphasis in original). Similarly, Kohli (2004, 282) attributes the non-willingness of ruling groups to share power with other ethno-national groups as the prime reason for overt centralization in ethnically diverse social settings.

The ruling elites in Pakistan certainly did not have the willingness or desire for accommodating the varying national identities cohabiting on the territory of the state. Political leaders like Ghulam Mohammad, Iskandar Mirza, Chaudhari Mohammad Ali, and Muhammad Ayub Khan (the most prominent decision makers in the 1947–1971 period, all belonging either to the state bureaucracy or the military) had a general dislike towards both federal arrangement and democracy. Ghulam Mohammad, the third Governor General, in particular, had no respect for parliamentary procedures and traditions, and he scorned the idea of parliamentary government in Pakistan (Choudhury 1969, 32). Ayub Khan (1967b, 213), who engineered the 1962 Constitution, states in his autobiography:

> My own analysis has led me to the conclusion that Pakistan needed a strong government capable of taking decisions which might not be popular but which were necessary for the safety, integrity and, in particular, development of the country. We could not afford the luxury of a system which would make the existence of government subservient to the whims and operations of pressure groups. On this I was not prepared to make any compromise.

As far as the federal arrangement of the new nation-state was concerned, Pakistan from 1947 until 1956 was run under the Interim Constitution based on the Government of India Act 1935 (GIA). Through the GIA the British colonial administration introduced elements of a federal structure to South Asia, which aimed at the flexion of calls for self-government through the creation of a sub-national state system (Setalvad 1960, 170; Nesiah 2000, 60). Under Section 8 of the Indian Independence Act (1947), the GIA became the provisional constitution of Pakistan (Ali 1996, 40). The GIA enunciated three legislative lists: federal, provincial, and concurrent. Although the Act established for the first time a separate legal personality of the provinces, the central government maintained actual power. For example, in respect of the concurrent lists, where both the federal and provincial governments had legislative powers, the GIA provided that federal law was to prevail and the provincial law was void to the extent of repugnancy (Choudhury 1969, 26). The powers of the central government were buttressed further by the powers of the Governor General to proclaim emergency if the security or economic life of Pakistan was threatened by war or internal disturbances, or the movement of refugee population in and out of Pakistan (Choudhury 1969, 26). The Governor General was the highest ranking official of the country (akin to the US President). The post was bequeathed by the British colonial administrators with Mohammad Ali Jinnah as the first Governor General of the new state. The post was subsequently abolished by the 1956 Constitution which provided for a President.

According to the GIA, in situations of emergency, provincial autonomy would be curtailed and the federal government would have the power to constitute laws for the federal units. Moreover, the Governor General and his powers were given a further boost by way of an amendment to the GIA. The Governor General under Article 92A could dismiss a provincial government if an emergency situation occurred that could compromise state security and thus impose Governor's rule (Choudhury 1969, 28). The Governor General was granted the authority (i) to determine whether an emergency occurred and, in such case (ii) to suspend a provincial ministry. Such powers of the Governor General were used to undermine and suspend the provincial governments of Sindh, Punjab and East Pakistan. As will be seen later, the provincial government in East Pakistan was dismissed by the Governor General after a Bengali nationalist party, the United Front, defeated the incumbent Muslim League government in the 1954 elections. The fact that local riots in East Pakistan were used as a pretext to dismiss the United Front government offers ample proof of the Governor General's power to interpret what constituted an emergency situation. These powers of interpretation accorded to the Governor General were highly disproportionate with regards to other levels in the federal structure (Tummala 1996, 373–384).

Moreover, the ethnic exclusivity of the bureaucracy and military meant that the Bengali majority was devoid of both power and representation. As numerous events in Pakistan's post-independence history demonstrated, the ruling elites of the country, including Muhammad Ali Jinnah, rode roughshod over the political, economic and cultural aspirations of the Bengalis. Jinnah's 1948 declaration of Urdu as Pakistan's national language both denigrated the Bengali language and failed to recognize the linguistic plurality of the Pakistani state. The declaration was met by protests by Bengali (student and other) groups, which resulted in armed clashes with the police. These skirmishes led Jinnah to visit East Pakistan where he categorically reiterated his earlier commitment to Urdu as the official language of Pakistan. He also made it clear that he would not tolerate 'quislings' and 'fifth columnists' (Jalal 1990, 85).

The language controversy raged on after Jinnah's death on 11 September 1948. The Constituent Assembly Basic Principles Committee in 1950 suggested that Urdu should be recognized as the 'state language' in the new constitution. The Bengali opposition to the Committee's recommendation took the shape of a mass movement, which organized itself as the 'state language movement' and aimed at, securing the equality of status for both Bengali and Urdu (Wheeler 1970, 48). The continuing intransigent response by the central government led to the politicization and consequent mobilization of Bengali identity. On 27 January 1952, while addressing an audience in Dacca, Prime Minister Nazimuddin (a Bengali) declared that Urdu was to be the official state language of Pakistan (Wheeler 1970, 48). This enraged the Bengali intelligentsia and the students organized a procession on 21 February 1952 defying a ban on public meetings and processions. The police opened fire on the demonstrators, which resulted in the death of four students and injuries to many more (Jalal 1990, 159).

Consequently, it came as no surprise that the ruling party, the Pakistan Muslim League was defeated in the provincial elections in East Pakistan in March 1954. As a result of that election, the United Front (a coalition of various Bengali parties) won 223 of the 309 seats in the Assembly (the Muslim League won only 10) and formed the first non-Muslim League government in Pakistan (Park and Wheeler 1954, 129). The United Front ran its political programme on a 21 point agenda, which included that (i) Bengali should be declared as a state language; that (ii) February 21 should be declared as Shaheed (Martyrs) Day; and that (iii) East Bengal should obtain complete autonomy according to the Lahore Resolution of 1940 (quoted in Park 1954, 73). The Lahore Resolution of 1940 laid for the first time the demand for a Muslim homeland in the Indian subcontinent. The resolution called for the Muslim majority provinces in the North-West and North-East of India be 'grouped to constitute Independent States in which the constituent units … [would] be autonomous and sovereign' (quoted in Jalal 1990, 15). The phrase 'Independent States' was later reformulated in 1946 to assert a single Muslim state to be known as Pakistan.

The central government's apprehension regarding the United Front and its political agenda reached a boiling point after the visit of the Chief Minister of East Pakistan to Karachi where in conversation with a foreign correspondent he was reported to have quipped a demand for the complete autonomy for East Pakistan leaving to the central government only the portfolios of foreign affairs, defence and currency (Park and Wheeler 1954, 131). Displaying its centrist and unitary tendencies to the fullest, the central authorities in Karachi dismissed the provincial government of East Pakistan in May 1954, barely two months after its swearing in. The Governor General Ghulam Mohammad under Section 92A of the Interim constitution took the measure to dismiss the United Front government on the grounds that it had failed to maintain law and order in the province (Sayeed 1954, 140). A Governor's rule was imposed on East Pakistan, which lasted from May 1954 until April 1955. This experience destroyed the basis of a federal framework, that is, shared rule, and made clear once again that Pakistan was a unitary and centralized state bent on wresting control from the provinces. In order to forestall the rise of nationalist governments in the provinces opposed to the centre, the state managers contemplated the implementation of what in Pakistan's political history is known as the 'One Unit' scheme (Callard 1957, 186).

One Unit was an ingenious scheme promulgated by Pakistan's ruling elite, which proved that their thinking was far removed from *sharing* power with the provinces, and endeavored towards the centralization of state governance. In essence, the idea of One Unit was designed to achieve *parity* between East and West Pakistan. On 27 March 1955 the Governor General amended the Government of India Act 1935 through an ordinance that empowered him to create the province of West Pakistan, comprising Punjab, Sindh, the North West Frontier Province and Balochistan (Khan 2005a, 142). West Pakistan was to be treated as a single entity at *par* with the majority unit East Pakistan. Prime Minister Mohammad Ali contended that the unification of West Pakistan would achieve national unity and curb the evils of provincialism (Ali 1996, 79).

The intention of One Unit was to bring the demographic majority of East Pakistan in line with the political dominance of West Pakistan. With the resulting parity specifically in representation to the central legislature, the numerical majority of East Pakistan was conveniently side-stepped by the ruling elites. The Bengali opposition to the idea of One Unit, as propounded by Hussein Shaheed Suhrawardy, was that its origins lay in 'the fear of domination by East Pakistan over the western wing and to capture power at the centre' (quoted in Maluka 1995, 144). Moreover, ethnic minority communities in West Pakistan that found their provincial identities subjugated to, and amalgamated, in a larger yet artificial West Pakistani identity detested the new administrative setup. There was a general and deep-seated fear in all units that unification would mean control of West Pakistan by Punjab (Callard 1957, 186).

When the draft of the 1956 Constitution was presented before the East Pakistani assembly, it provoked a critical response. The Awami League (AL), which was formed in 1949 as a protest against the homogenizing policies of the central government of Pakistan and played an instrumental role in the movement for the recognition of Bengali as the official language, started a powerful campaign against the draft. The AL insisted that no constitutional scheme would be acceptable to it if it failed to incorporate the '21 points programme', which brought the United Front to power in East Pakistan during 1954 elections (Choudhury 1957, 313–314).

Thus, by the time the country's first constitution was promulgated in 1956, Pakistan's political history had been tainted by the authoritarian practices of the central government in both wings of the country. The 1956 Constitution proclaimed that Pakistan would be a Federal Republic consisting of two units: East Pakistan and West Pakistan. The Constitution contained a Preamble, 234 Articles, and was divided into 13 parts and 6 Schedules. It was one of the lengthiest written constitutions in the world based on 'parity' between the two wings of the country (Maluka 1995, 145). The Constitution, however, was not adopted unanimously. The opposition, led by the Awami League, did not consent to it and staged a walk out of the House at the time of its approval. As many as 670 amendments were proposed, mostly by the Awami League (Jalal 1990, 214). In line with the GIA, the Constitution enumerated federal, provincial and concurrent lists (containing 30, 94 and 19 subjects respectively).

Though the provincial list had more subjects than the federal one, the erosion of the power of the federal units was implicated precisely by the large number of subjects, which necessitated a strong central management. Moreover, in case of conflict between the federal law and the provincial law the former was to prevail (Ahmed 1990, 77).

The 1956 Constitution provided for a unicameral legislature based on parity of representation between the two wings of the country. The National Assembly was to consist of three hundred members, half elected by constituencies in East and half by constituencies in West Pakistan (Choudhury 1969, 125). The executive authority of the federation was invested in the President who had discretionary powers to appoint and dismiss Ministers as well as to appoint the Prime Minister from the members of the National Assembly. Thus, the 1956 Constitution was a hybrid executive-parliamentary system in which powers were tilted in favor of the President.

In the provinces, the provincial Governor, as a representative of the President, was vested with discretionary power over the chief minister and his cabinet. Article 193 of the Constitution empowered the centre to dismiss the provincial government and impose direct rule in the province (Maluka 1995, 146). The Bengalis called for the right of their provincial legislature to appoint the Governor of East Pakistan, however, the power of the centre to nominate and appoint provincial Governors in both wings of the country was maintained (Choudhury 1969, 111). The Bengalis were not satisfied with the provisions of the constitution that gave the central government unchecked power to influence provincial politics. The 1956 Constitution which was in force for two years was marred by the constant meddling in parliamentary affairs by the centre and the dismissal of Prime Ministers and their cabinets by President Iskandar Mirza. This merely confirmed that the ruling elites viewed with contempt political parties and parliamentary politics. Parliamentary politics thus gave way to a presidential system of governance after the 1956 Constitution was abrogated in October 1958 and martial law imposed throughout the country by Ayub Khan (Choudhury 1969, 133–134).

As Pakistan's president in the period 1958–1969, General Ayub Khan imposed a new constitution in 1962, which made reference to the notions of 'federal' organization only in its preamble. In a radio broadcast on 1 March 1962, he declared that the text of the new constitution embodied 'a blending of democracy with discipline—the two prerequisites to running a free society with stable government and sound administration' (Khan 1967b, 216). With particular emphasis on democracy and discipline, federalism unfortunately lost out in the new scheme. The 1962 Constitution altered the name of the country from a Federal Republic of Pakistan to the Republic of Pakistan (Ahmed 1990, 58).

The 1962 Constitution concentrated almost all powers in the hands of General Ayub, and thus established a Presidential system (Shah 1994, 58). The President had the powers of legislation to issue ordinances when the National Assembly was not in session and to issue a proclamation of emergency. He could summon, prorogue and dissolve the National Assembly. The national budget, once sanctioned, could not be altered by the Assembly without his permission and the President enjoyed unfettered authority to appoint federal ministers, governors of the provinces and judges of the Supreme Court and the two High Courts (Khan 1967b, 210; Maluka 1995, 186).

A strong presidential institution was a *sine-qua-non* for a strong central government to the detriment of provincial autonomy. The centre–province disequilibrium continued under the 1962 Constitution. Article 134 affirmed that central law should prevail if there was a conflict with provincial law (Shah 1994, 75). Moreover, in a radical departure from the 1956 Constitution, the 1962 Constitution did not provide for a concurrent list (Shah 1994, 75). The provincial Governor was to be appointed and subjected to the 'direction' of the President (Article 80) (Maluka 1995, 187). This made the provincial Governor an agent that was entirely dependant on the central government.

Both the 1956 and 1962 Constitutions have proven that political developments in East Pakistan were subject to the political, social and economic prerogatives of the central government and the prejudices of its ruling elites towards the Bengali majority. By the mid-1950s, the Bengalis were complaining vehemently about the way in which they were treated by the Punjabi dominated central government. One Bengali legislator had this to say in the Constituent Assembly of Pakistan in 1955:

> the attitude of the Muslim League coterie here was of contempt towards East Bengal, towards its culture, its language, its literature and everything concerning East Bengal … far from considering East Bengal as an equal partner, the leaders of the Muslim League thought that we were a subject race and they belonged to the race of conquerors (quoted in Callard 1957, 172–173).

During Ayub's era, the economic disparity between the two wings widened further with disastrous effects for the territorial integrity of Pakistan. Since his constitution did not embrace any overt or covert mechanism for a federal setup, Ayub's centralization of the Pakistani state completely alienated East Pakistan. In March 1966, Shaikh Mujib-ur-Rahman, leader of the Awami League in East Pakistan, advanced a six-point programme to resounding public response. This six-point demand, which became the political battle cry of the Awami League in the 1970 elections and constitutional negotiations in 1971, distilled the various Bengali claims and frustrations over East Pakistan's perceived mistreatment in economic and national affairs (Siddiqi 2000, 110). After Awami League's victory in the 1970 elections and the failure of constitutional negotiations, the central government resorted to military action in order to quell the Bengali resistance.

The ensuing civil war precipitated the secession of East Pakistan and the creation of Bangladesh in December 1971 (Choudhury 1972b, 242–249). It is necessary to qualify this point with Patrick Riley's prescient assessment of the relationship between the pursual of 'territorial integrity' by the central government of a federal system and the demands for regional autonomy. The intrication between federalism and the idea of national sovereignty predisposes the federal center to represent the insistence of federal units on their 'legal rights' as a 'rebellion'. Riley illustrates this point with the '1971 civil war in Pakistan', which just like 'the American civil war' provoked the central government to act in the defence of the 'federal union' (Riley 1973, 120). The larger point from this detailed historical process tracing of Pakistan's federal experience is to illustrate the 'inherently unstable character of federalism', which is further analyzed in the following section.

Pakistan and the Hypotheses on Defunct Federalism

The claim here is that federalism in Pakistan failed because of the policy attitudes of the ruling elites whose fixation with state building undermined the basis for democratic politics and federalism. The ruling elite of Pakistan was never interested in sharing power with the Bengalis, a fact which manifested itself in the rigorous centralization pursued since 1947. This centralization was not only evident in the realm of politics but also in the socio-cultural sphere whereby Urdu was imposed on the Bengali population. The same status quo existed with regards to identity groups in West Pakistan. Besides military action against the Bengalis in 1971, the Pakistan Army was also involved in military action against the Baloch in 1948, 1958 and 1963–1966. Thus, it can be said that Pakistan's failure to establish inclusive democracy and to empower representative institutions vis-à-vis the executive in its highly politicized multinational context meant that the use of force was the only means available to maintain the continuity of the nation-state.

Federalism and liberal democracy

The claim that there is a positive correlation between federalism and liberal democracy is underpinned by the assumption that since liberal democracy gives voice to disadvantaged and minority groups, it ensures the stability and unimpeded functioning of the political system. An inclusive multinational federation is democratic to the extent that it allows the representatives of its respective national communities to engage in dialogue and open bargaining about their interests, grievances and aspirations (McGarry and O'Leary 2007, 202). Therefore, a liberal democratic federal organisation seems to be highly suitable to the needs of multinational societies. Requejo (2004, 260) calls this phenomenon 'plural federalism', by which he means a federal organisation that differs from mononational federations in its sensitivity to and empowerment of national minority interests. This is achieved through its accommodation of the principles of (i) constitutional recognition of the federal status of the national minority/minorities; (ii) a series of asymmetrical and/or confederal arrangements that bring to fruition the minorities' territorial self-determination vis-à-vis the whole federation and in international politics; and (iii) asymmetrical regulation of other administrative issues (Requejo 1999, 255–286; see also Requejo 2001).

The argument of this chapter is that Pakistan failed in establishing such a liberal democratic regime, which would adhere to the principles of public liberty, equality and representation for underprivileged group, at the same time minority and majoritarian. In the period under consideration, 1947–1971, Pakistan remained under a military dictatorship for thirteen years. In the period 1947–1958, the leaders of the new nation-state belonged to a bureaucratic-military oligarchy. Ghulam Mohammad, Chaudhri Mohammad Ali and Iskandar Mirza had distaste for parliamentary politics and contributed to the process of weakening the democratic system and the representation of political parties. In this context it seems correct to conclude that principles of liberal democracy, self-government and rights for distinct identity groups had no relevance in the case of Pakistan. Consequently, this meant that federalism in Pakistan remained largely irrelevant as a means of keeping the country together by way of shared rule. As the East Pakistan case study demonstrates, force was utilized in order to suppress the Bengali ethno-nationalist movement.

Pakistan's experience as a nation-state seems to testify to the correctness of the claim that *if federalism does not conform to the rules of liberal democracy it fails*. If the virtue of liberal democracy had been realized by Pakistan's ruling elites, it would have gone a long way in assuaging the demands of the deprived Bengalis to some extent and would have provided them with a sense of participation in the political system. However, prominent Bengali Prime Ministers such as Khwaja Nazimuddin, Mohammad Ali Bogra and Hussein Shaheed Suhrawardy were dismissed from office. Such undemocratic acts were peremptory and in consonance with the centralizing imperatives of a state which scorned the ideal of federal, that is, shared rule.

Federalism and its institutional setting

Kymlicka argues (1998, 123) that federalism in itself is not a guarantor of accommodating national minorities. Rather it depends on how federal boundaries are drawn and how institutional powers are shared. There is a possibility that the federally dominant groups will use their control of the state structure to impair ethnonational groups and transform the federating units into mere pawns. In short, when analyzing whether given federalism 'works' (and, more specifically, when concluding that given federalism has become defunct) it is essential to fractionate the existing institutional setting into its constative unit to discern how political power is *de facto* shared and distributed.

It seems that in the context of the Pakistani defunct federalism, the theory of a asymmetrical federal power division offers a huge explanatory potential. Its claim is that asymmetrical institutional arrangements are instrumental for federal organizations as they provide for a better accommodation of diversity (both normatively and pragmatically speaking) than symmetrical arrangements (Requejo 2004, 268–269).

Tarlton (1965, 869) defines the asymmetrical model as follows:

> The ideal asymmetrical federal model would be one composed of political units corresponding to differences of interest, character, and makeup that exist within the whole society. The asymmetrical federal system would be one in which … the diversities in the larger society find political expression through local governments possessed of varying degrees of power and autonomy … In the model asymmetrical federal system each component unit would have about it a unique set of features which would separate in important ways, its interests from those of any other state or the system considered as a whole.

It seems, therefore, that asymmetrical federal systems are best suited for multinational contexts where ethnic heterogeneity is prevalent. In post-independence Pakistan, the federalism debate was framed by an imaginary of a symmetrical federal model. The assumption was that such symmetry of the federal solution would institute political parity between the East Pakistan and the West Pakistan. The proclamation of One Unit and its legitimation in the constitutions of 1956 and 1962 proved that the ruling elites of the country intended to institute a model of political governance that would effectively silence, the Bengali population, the majority part. With political power concentrated in the western wing of the country, the symmetrical model failed to include the Bengalis within the state structure. Considering the geographical distance between the two wings, an asymmetrical model would have gone a long way in inculcating a sense of political participation amongst the Bengalis. Though an asymmetrical federal arrangement might be difficult to negotiate and implement, as Kymlicka (1998, 130–136) suggests, its emphasis on diversity would have potentially accommodated different ethnic and linguistic groupings in Pakistan, and enabled their participation within the newly-forged democratic structures.

The discussion of apposite institutional arrangements in federal contexts relies on two further points. First, it seems that executive federal arrangements provide better accommodation of diversity than administrative ones. Second, it seems that that institutionalization of identity might potentially contribute to the failure of federalism. The executive federal arrangement, which emphasizes a balance between the executives of each level of government and the political empowerment of disadvantaged groups, was again absent in Pakistan. Pakistan approximated an administrative arrangement where policy directions only flowed from the centre to the provincial units. Moreover, federal identity in Pakistan and its ideological compass was dominated by the Punjabis and Mohajirs who made up the bulk of Pakistan's federal administrative machinery. The imposition of an *exclusive* federal identity as opposed to an *inclusive* national identity which in essence excluded the Bengalis, in particular, was a classic recipe for the eventual failure of the experiment with federalism.

The Bengali sense of alienation from the power structure developed soon after Pakistan received its independence from the British Empire. It is interesting to note that Bengali leaders such A.K. Fazlul Haq and Hussein Shaheed Suhrawardy rallied the Bengali Muslims to the cause of Pakistan in the 1940s. Though Fazlul Haq developed differences with the Muslim League leadership in the mid-1940s and formed his own Progressive Coalition Party, Suhrawardy was instrumental in tying the fate of East Bengal with that of Pakistan. He played an instrumental role in the 1946 elections, under the colonial administration, which culminated in a sweeping victory for the Muslim League in Bengal with an absolute majority in the legislature (Banerjee 1969, 38) However, the enthusiasm for Pakistan amongst the Bengali elite evaporated quickly after 1947.'It seems Sir', said one Bengali Muslim Leaguer in March 1948, 'that in the present scheme of things East Bengal is really very much neglected' (quoted in Callard 1957, 174). Moreover, the Chief Minister of East Bengal presented a list of demands which included amongst other things Eastern Pakistan's 'fair and proper share in the Armed Forces of Pakistan' (quoted in Callard 1957, 174). Liaquat Ali Khan, the Prime Minister, responded by delineating such demands as 'provincialism' and the need to kill it for all times (quoted in Callard 1957, 174).

As late as 1956 there was no Bengali above the rank of joint secretary in the central secretariat. Of the 741 top jobs in the federal government, 93 percent were held by West Pakistanis with the Punjabis and Urdu-speaking migrants claiming the plums (quoted in Jalal 1990, 223). It was not until 1969, i.e. two years before

East Pakistan's eventual secession, that for the first time a few Bengali officers were installed as secretaries to the central government, at the head of some minor ministries. The bastions of power, namely, the ministries of Defence, Finance and the Planning Commission and the Establishment Division were still retained in trusted West Pakistani hands (Siddiqi 2000, 113).

The Bengali alienation and discrimination from structures of power played a consequential role in the federal failure in Pakistan. Federalism as a philosophical enquiry acknowledges group identity alongside individual identity and constructs political systems in which 'a balance is maintained between different forms of identity, individual, local, regional, national and, increasingly, transnational' (Hueglin and Fenna 2006, 37). However, by denying representation to the majority half of the country, the so-called federal experience in Pakistan negated the Bengali identity without providing for its equal treatment with other communities. The minimal Bengali representation in the administrative setup was contrary to principles of federalism based on a combination of self-rule and shared rule (Elazar 1991, xv). The Bengalis were not only denied representation at the state level but self-rule was also denied to them by political machinations of the centre as is evident in the dismissal of the United Front ministry in 1954 and the imposition of One Unit.

Federalism and its imposition

This brings us to the third and last hypothesis from the theory of defunct federalisms, which is that the mode in which federal structures are installed can be decisive for the success (or failure) of federalism. In other words, the hypothesis is that when federalism is imposed by an external or domestic group in a top-down fashion, and does not reflect any democratic convictions, ideas and sentiments, the possibility of its failure increases. Pakistan's case history confirms this hypothesis as relevant. Federalism, as applied in Pakistan under the 1956 Constitution was 'federal' only in theory. The imposition of centralized rule, in the garb of federalism in the 1956 Constitution, clearly belied any pretence of shared rule between the centre and East Pakistan. The imposition was troublesome in another respect. The ethnically constituted state dominated by the Punjabis and Mohajirs was an anathema to the Bengalis who were suppressed and their political, social and economic demands remained unheeded. This ethnic exclusiveness coupled with the absence of democracy provided a powerful mixture of discontent in East Pakistan. Since 1956 when the country's first Constitution was proclaimed till 1970 when the first general elections were held, the fate of East Pakistan was inextricably linked to the ruling elites which were non-Bengali.

Overlooking calls from the Bengali political leaders for greater autonomy, the Pakistani state exercised use of force to tame the Bengali populace. The ruling elites' readiness to impose its will on the Bengalis continued even after the Awami League had won a resounding victory in the 1970 elections. The League swept both the national and provincial assembly elections winning 160 of the 162 seats in the national assembly and 288 of the 300 seats in the provincial assembly reserved for East Pakistan respectively (Baxter 1970, 211). Despite the resounding victory, the Bengalis were denied the right to form a government and subsequently were subjected to an army operation which began in 1971 and ended with the separation of East Pakistan. The Bengalis whose political demands under Shaikh Mujib called for autonomy within a restructured federal system were pushed to the precipice of independence after military force was employed against them.

Reflections on the Federal Failure in Pakistan: Additional Factors

A detailed analysis of the federal institutions and federal practice in Pakistan 1947–1971 puts forward two additional factors that might be of causal importance in explaining the Pakistani federal failure in addition to those set out in the Introduction by the editors to the volume. The two factors relate to (i) the role of elites in establishing a federal framework of governance and (ii) the role of economic factors in (not) sustaining federalism.

The role of elites in establishing a federal framework to govern the polity is an essential requirement of a successful federalism (Franck 1968; Kohli 2004; Kymlicka 1998). It is a truism that a viable federal polity cannot be sustained 'without commitment, on the part of the politicians and the citizens they represent, to both effective self-rule for the states and effective shared rule at the centre' (Pinder 2007, 14). As Pakistan's political history demonstrates, the commitment to shared rule and the accommodation of diversity in the political setup were absent. This informed the nature of subsequent developments (including centralization), which made Pakistan move towards a more unitary rather than a federal state model.

Secondly, the dominant hypotheses from the theory of defunct federalism seem to obviate the role of economic factors, which at least in the case of Pakistan were central in the failure of identity accommodation. Generally, the literature on federalism does not associate economic differences with failed or successful accommodation. Ethno-national movements calling for autonomy or even separation can develop in poor areas such as the Kurdish region of Turkey, Northern Ireland and southern Nigeria as well as economically well-off ones (for instance the Basque country in Spain, the northern regions of Italy, and Quebec in Canada). However, this does not mean that economic differences between regions do not matter for the success or failure of federal arrangements. The suggestion here is that a region that is exploited and devoid of its economic rights provides the incentives for ethnonational mobilization and can strengthen a people's sense of regional solidarity directed against external intervention (Bermeo 2004, 458).

East Pakistan was the poorer of the two units and historically its economy had been linked to that of West Bengal (Bengal's Hindu-dominated province, currently a state in eastern India). East Bengal (Bengal's Muslim-dominated province, and now Bangladesh) was the major exporter of raw jute to the industries in Calcutta, one of the major port cities in British India. The province had about 78 percent of the world's crop of jute the export of which brought nearly Rs. 109.6 (about 30 million dollars) in 1948 (Ahmad 1950, 183). However, the central government in Karachi took over the jute trade. It set up a jute board, fixed a floor price with the board under the supervision of Ghulam Farooq, the non-Bengali secretary of Industry, and included such business luminaries as M.A. Ispahani, the elder brother of Karachi's ambassador in Washington and the 'largest Pakistani jute dealer' (Jalal 1990, 105).

The export of jute goods played an important part in the overall export earnings of the Pakistani state. Up until 1966–1967 the total exports of Pakistan amounted to Rs. 2871.00 million of which jute and jute goods provided Rs. 1451.23 million, approximately 50.54 percent of the total earnings. Much of the surplus generated from the jute export was put to fostering industrialization in West Pakistan. Thus, West Pakistan's development was built on a transfer of resources from the eastern wing, which got very little in return, and the process was initiated as early as the late 1940s and early 1950s (Zaidi 1995, 90). Such policies were against the interests of the Bengali majority resulting in inter-regional disparity between the two wings. The level of disparity between the two wings widened from 46 percent in 1964–1965 to 60 percent in 1969–1970 (*Economic Survey of East Pakistan* 1970, 16). Owing to this disparity, Shaikh Mujib-ur-Rahman called for the establishment of a 'federal reserve system in which there will be regional federal reserve banks which shall devise measures to prevent the transfer of resources and flight of capital from one region to another' (quoted in Sisson and Rose 1990, 20). Thus, with respect to East Pakistan, it was not merely the absence of federalism or federal institutions, which spurred secession; rather the whole gamut of political, economic, social and cultural exploitation was responsible in alienating the Bengali majority.

Conclusion

The chapter has made the argument that for federalism to succeed an acceptance and appreciation of its principles needs to be present amongst the ruling elites of a country. If such an acceptance is absent then federalism is at best a chimera. The first constitution of the country adopted in 1956 espoused a federal ideal, which however was subverted by the centralizing powers of the executive. Centralization, which has been a *sine qua non* of Pakistan's political history, survives to-date. The 1973 Constitution carried forward the legacies of the earlier constitutions by assigning more powers to the central government over the provinces. The root cause of much ethnic conflict and discord in Pakistan (even today) emanates from the centralizing imperatives of the state which is construed as detrimental to the interests of the ethnic minorities. To this day, the state of Pakistan continues to rely on force rather than the implementation of federal principles, which is evident in the recent upsurge of ethnic violence in Balochistan and Sindh. It seems that no lessons have been learned from the experience of East Pakistan's secession.

Moreover, the centralizing imperatives of the state are felt most in the economic sphere, which needs to be included in a critical appraisal of federalism. Recent ethnic activism in Balochistan and Sindh relates to dissatisfaction with the state's policies which undermine provincial economic interests. The experience of East Pakistan evidences that if relations between diverse identities in a multiethnic state are not managed to the satisfaction of deprived ethnic groups, secession can come about. Only with a credible democratic system and institutions, which provide adequate representation to disadvantaged ethnonational groups, can multinational states survive in the modern era. Moreover, it is not the mere presence of ethnonational groups, which makes federalism weak. Elazar is at fault when he states that ethnic nationalism is one of the strongest forces arrayed against federalism (quoted in Watts 2007, 228). As the Pakistani case persuasively demonstrates, it is when the state elites at the political center fail to exercise power in an accountable and legitimate form, that identity becomes politicized and identity groups start their mobilization against the federal government. It is in this context that ethnonationalism can present a challenge to federal institutions.

Last but not least, the theory of defunct federalism outlined in Chapter 1 seems to make a distinction between the practices of federation and the ideology of federalism. The argument is that the dissolution of the federation is not necessarily synonymous with the failure of federalism (for instance, as the cases of Cameroon and Czechoslovakia are sometimes interpreted). However, this distinction (which is largely functional) misses a key point. It is not merely federalism, *per se*, rather its application which determines the success or otherwise of various federations. Unfortunately, in the case of Pakistan, federalism as *applied*, did not (and still does not seem to) guarantee the smooth functioning (nor the stability) of the federation. Thus, what is required instead is an appreciation of the interplay between the theory of federalism and its application to particular contexts, which can offer more nuanced understanding of how and why some federations fail, while others maintain their resilience.

Chapter 7

The Demonization of Federalism in Republican China

Steven Phillips

Introduction

The failure of federalism in Republican China (1911–1949) and afterwards must be understood within its rhetorical, political, and historical contexts. During the 38 years between the collapse of the Qing Dynasty and the establishment of the People's Republic in 1949, China's most stable and coherent government was the Republic of China led by the Nationalist Party. The Nationalists, under Sun Yat-sen, then Chiang Kai-shek, made their centralization efforts synonymous with the welfare of the Chinese nation. They were successful to the extent that, as historian Prasenjit Duara writes, 'the two N/nationalisms have been fused and moralized' (Duara 1995, 198). Allegiance to political units other than the nation, or those who claimed to represent the nation, was defined as divisive, feudal, parochial, and anti-Chinese. As Duara notes, 'in the end, the interplay of power politics and authoritative language enabled the hegemonic, centralizing nationalist narrative to destroy and ideologically bury the federalist alternative early in the history of modern China' (Duara 1995, 177–78). Advocates of shared sovereignty between province and nation stood accused of perpetuating traditional local loyalties and of lacking the national consciousness needed to save China from imperialism and internal revolts.

The demonization and delegitimatization of federalism had significant long-term consequences. First, the Nationalists' experience on the mainland set the stage for politics and policies on Taiwan after their retreat to the island. Second, the Communists, who would win the civil war and govern the mainland after 1949, built upon this centralizing impulse when consolidating their rule. Mao Zedong and other Communist leaders agreed with Chiang that provincial identities prevented national solidarity, and they rejected the federalist ideal that sovereignty could be split or shared. Third, historians have generally followed the lead of the 'winners' in this conflict, focusing upon the nation and its centralization efforts over provincial prerogatives. They have tended to accept the narrative promoted by the centralizers—that federalism or any type of local autonomy stood opposed to the interests of the Chinese nation. As historian of Republican China, R. Keith Schoppa writes: 'For most historians of modern China, as with most twentieth-century Chinese, nation-building has been the central interest; as a result, provincialism has been seen as subordinate in value to nationalism' (Schoppa 1977, 661).

What follows is a chronological account of the Chinese experience with federalism. The first section lays out the basic debates over federalism in Republican China. It also introduces the political agendas that supported contending positions on federalism and the rhetorical tactics used to define any form of provincial sovereignty. Next, an overview of the Nationalists' 1947 constitution offers an opportunity to see how Chiang and his supporters sought to enshrine their anti-federalist agenda into the legal principles of the state. The third section examines the Nationalists' actual implementation of a highly centralized political structure after their retreat to Taiwan in the late 1940s. The following part of the chapter will illustrate how the Chinese Communists achieved the centralization that the Nationalists could not on the mainland. Finally, the Chinese case study will be connected to the larger issues of defunct federalisms raised in this volume. The role of history, as interpreted by those opposed to provincial autonomy, links these sections.

The Delegitimization of Federalism in Republican China

In the first half of the twentieth century, federalism (*lianbang zhuyi*) became part of a nation-wide discussion over local self-government (*difang zizhi*) in China. To some Chinese, federalism was one type of local self-government, meaning that provincial autonomy vis-à-vis the central government could mirror the relationship between the province and its cities, counties, or districts. Each level of this hierarchy would have clearly specified powers and obligations. In other cases, however, federalism was defined solely in terms of relations between the province and the central government, and local self-government was defined as administration below the provincial level. Federalism was often translated at *liansheng*, literally meaning a federation or confederation of provinces, while *lianbang* was often used to describe the phenomenon of federalism in a global setting.

The Qing Dynasty, weakened by foreign pressure and peasant revolts, sparked debate over local autonomy in the late 1800s through its belated reform efforts. In his study of local councils during the late Qing, Roger Thompson (1995) suggests that Qing leaders envisioned local self-government as a system that would facilitate China's gradual transition to a constitutional monarchy by formalizing the role of traditional elites and linking them to a reformed state. Growing out of this failed attempt at state building and from increasing knowledge of political structures outside of China, four constituencies (each with varying motivations and levels of commitment) campaigned for their conception of local self-government or federalism in Republican China: traditional Confucian elites, warlords, non-communist reformers, and the Nationalists. In many cases, the centralizers' criticisms were entirely correct. Provincial autonomy or federalism often represented little more than an excuse for rural elites to maintain power and block central government initiatives (Kuhn 1975, 257). During the late Qing, the traditional gentry, inculcated with the ideals of Confucianism, sought to protect their influence. For centuries, elites at the town, district, or provincial level promoted their own interests, thus preserving their social status and economic power, while performing government services by organizing people in their communities for tasks such as maintaining law and order, repairing public works, and assisting the poor. They accepted the sovereignty of the imperial state, but did not want it present in their communities, nor did they seek to become permanent bureaucrats. Their influence waned steadily throughout the early Republican period.

Later supporters of federalism on the mainland and Taiwan would have great difficulty divorcing themselves from the perception that they served the interests of the pre-1911 Revolution elites. Even language conspired against federalists, or any advocates of shared sovereignty. The traditional Chinese term for a high level of local autonomy within the imperial system, *fengjian*, was translated as 'feudal', and came to mean less an alternative administrative system than a set of pre-modern values. Federalism was thus tied not to modernity but to traditional local loyalties that undermined national unity and left China vulnerable.

In the beginning of the Republican period, however, federalism briefly held a position of relative political respectability. As the Qing Dynasty collapsed, a shaky alliance of traditional rural elites and revolutionaries in urban areas declared their provinces' independence from the faltering imperial government. The drive to keep local infrastructure out of the hands of foreigners or the Qing, nationalist antipathy toward the Manchu regime, and the lack of effective central authority justified their actions. Dissatisfaction with the increasingly autocratic Yuan Shikai, the Qing general turned President of the new Beijing government, became another incentive to limit the influence of the central government. Supporters of provincial autonomy, who often discussed their agenda in terms of federalism, generally sought to use the province as a building block to a unified Chinese republic. After Yuan's death in 1916, the Beijing government ruled China in name only, as warlords came to dominate many provinces. Most influential during the 1916 to 1928 period, these military strongmen grasped at any idea—including federalism—that would rationalize their rejection of the authority of the government in Beijing (Waldron 1990).

Federalism also became part of heated debates over separation of powers, limited government, and democracy in China, and was often advocated by those influenced by political thought from Western Europe and the United States (Hu 1984, 375–390). Frustrated by the lack of progress toward China's unification and political modernization after 1911, urban intellectuals and liberals turned to the provincial level (or below) to implement reforms they could not do at the national level (Chesneaux 1969, 135–136). Federalism, here defined as a form of local self-government, brought a package of values designed to divide power at all levels of the administrative hierarchy. Advocates tied doctrines of autonomy to their goal of a multi-party democracy—often portraying themselves as a reformist alternative, or 'Third Force', between the Nationalists and the Communists. To them, federalism required a relatively loose relationship between provinces and the central government. Furthermore, federalism would extend below the provincial level, as the division of powers and responsibilities between the provinces and the central government would mirror the ties between each province and the districts or smaller political jurisdictions it contained. Generally unarmed in a militarized China, urbanites in a peasant nation, and often out of touch with the vast majority of their countrymen due to their education and wealth, politicians who supported expanded autonomy for provinces found themselves relegated to minor parties. They struggled against the belief that their agenda was parochial, and thus detrimental to the Chinese nation. At best, federalists could claim that their efforts were no less legitimate than provincial governments formed by warlords, or the central government under a series of warlords.

To the Nationalists, local self-government and federalism came to represent little more than short-term compromises—fallback positions when they were unable to make progress toward their long-term goal of a highly centralized, bureaucratic state (Chesneaux 1969, 96). When Sun Yat-sen and his followers were weak and controlled one province or less, they accepted federalism and expanded local self-government. When they became more powerful, their emphasis on centralization increased. As historian Philip Kuhn writes: 'It is clear that Sun viewed both democracy and local self-government not as independent values, but as essential prerequisites to the supreme goal of national integration and strength. Self-government was to inculcate national consciousness, not local separatism' (Kuhn 1975, 283). Sun and other revolutionaries had called for a federal system of provinces as early as 1895. After 1911, in the wake of Yuan Shikai's increasing power, Sun and other leaders promoted the federal model as a way to limit Beijing's influence. This was presented as an orderly way to reunite the provinces of China that had declared independence after the 1911 Wuchang Uprising. After 1916, the Nationalists found themselves dependent upon shaky alliances with warlords for survival. In this environment, federalism provided warlords with a rationalization for their relative autonomy even as it gave the Nationalists a long-term framework for national unification. As late as 1921, Sun wrote that 'if we want to solve the long-running dispute between the center and localities (*difang*), the only way is for each province's people to have complete self-government, with provincial constitutions and the election of provincial governors. If the center divides powers among each province, and each province divides power among the districts, then maybe the divided nation can be associated through self-governmentalism (*zizhi zhuyi*) and once again be united' (Xu 1974, 100).

The 1920s was a key transitional period. Early in the decade, the image of federalism suffered due to its connection to attacks against Sun and his regime. Provincial strongman Chen Jiongming, under the banner of federalism, stymied Sun's attempt to create a new government in southern China. Chen's son, and some historians, may evaluate Chen as a leader who 'never entertained the idea of provincial independence. He embraced the federalist cause because it permitted him to build the province as the basis of the nation' (Duara 1995, 195; Chen 1991). The Nationalists, however, placed him squarely within the context of warlords. The 1922 split between Chen and Sun marked the point when China's 'progressive forces' turned away from federalism (Duara 1995, 202). Sun's temporary flight from Guangdong province fired hostility toward any form of provincial autonomy, and made it even more difficult for other political activists to support this doctrine. Sun's statement that on 'no account can we again allow the misleading principle of federation to serve as a charm to protect the militarists in their seizures of territory', became a mantra to the Nationalists (Sun 1928, 257). They returned to Guangdong determined to build a strong central government backed by military power. Further, federalism and local self-government became increasingly separate, the former becoming an anti-n/National excuse to weaken the Chinese nation while the latter represented a process of state-building—an integral part of China's revolution.

The four-year alliance between the Nationalists and the Communists beginning in January 1923 marked another step toward undermining federalism and ensuring that local self-government and federalism were separated. The Chinese Communist Party was founded in 1921 and was organized by the Comintern (the Communist International, established in Moscow in order to spread class-based revolution around the world) along a Leninist model. The Nationalists, desperate for support in the early 1920s, eagerly accepted Soviet aid and advice, and reorganized themselves along Leninist lines. The parties joined in a marriage of convenience in order to fight warlords, unify China, and expand their influence. In terms of governance, the Nationalists and Communists were more alike than different. They competed over which of them would create and control China's central government, consigning the advocacy of federalism to small political parties which had no independent military power or financial base. Both major parties accepted the need for local self-government, but redefined it in their own interests. They agreed that it would not involve shared sovereignty but would serve the central government.

Even while cooperating with the Soviets in the 1920s, the Nationalists drew inspiration from others, particularly the Japanese. Since the turn of the century, Japan had been an Asian model of successful political modernization and industrialization to many Chinese. The Japanese tended to conceptualize local self-government (*chihō jichi* in Japanese) as a way to depoliticize local administration, transforming partisan local leaders into bureaucrats beholden to Tokyo. Prefectures, analogous to China's provinces, were a unit of local administration, and not autonomous in any way. The goal was to prevent party politics and local loyalties—both of which were seen as remnants of a feudal past that hampered the centralization necessary for national wealth and strength. Japanese politicians and intellectuals had a great deal of influence over the early Nationalist leaders, despite hatreds that grew out of Japanese imperialism and invasion that caused Chinese to obscure this contact later (Jansen 1954). At the same time, the failure of Wilsonianism to help China, the lack of American support for Sun, and Washington's continued recognition of the warlord-dominated Beijing government made it difficult for many Chinese to see anything positive about the United States and its federal system.

The Northern Expedition of 1926 to 1928 gave the heirs of Sun Yat-sen, who had died in 1925, an opportunity to realize their goal of centralization. The Nationalists' military, under the command of Chiang Kai-shek, moved north from its base in Guangdong Province. Through a combination of military victories, intimidation, and alliances with warlords, Chiang's regime vastly expanded the area under its control and became the most legitimate national government China had enjoyed since 1911. After establishing the capital of China in Nanjing and launching a purge of the Communists in 1927, the Nationalists attempted to eradicate federalism and to limit local self-government by relegating it to the county level (Lindebarger 1937, 227–331). To most of the nation, military force and a short-lived alliance between Nationalists and Communists appeared to have achieved unity for China. At best, federalism was portrayed as inadequate—a system unable to meet China's needs; at worst, it was presented as dangerous—a cover for warlord intransigence.

Later the Nationalist' history of the Expedition obscured the fact that many supporters of local or provincial autonomy (often articulated as federalism) were reformist intellectuals or remnants of traditional rural elites rather than warlords. Further, many warlords joined the Nationalist ranks and became ardent supporters of centralization—another fact Chiang was willing to overlook. The province of Zhejiang offers one case study of how a warlord helped crush hopes for provincial sovereignty. As Schoppa notes, 'provincial autonomy was sought as the means to provincial security and integrity, to prevent Chekiang from being sucked into warlord struggles—and important corollary—to prevent consequent social disturbances' (Schoppa, 1977 673–674). This province's experience is particularly pertinent because Taiwan's future Governor, Chen Yi, served as Governor in Zhejiang there during the Northern Expedition. Chen controlled Zhejiang as an underling of warlord Sun Chuanfang. The provincial elite urged Chen to accept a new constitution and prevent the Nationalist forces from entering the province. According to the provincial elite, when seen in the context of federalism, the province could be the basic building block for a strong Chinese nation. They did not seek independence; rather they hoped to blunt the drive for centralization championed by Chiang's regime. Prominent leaders called for a government that would permit only those from the province to govern its people, compel militarists to leave the province, require that provincial military forces remain in Zhejiang, and assure that local military units remain under the command of a provincial committee. Zhejiang's elite, however, lacked the military power or the ideological legitimacy needed to obtain the level of autonomy they sought. Chen concluded that the Zhejiang plan was hopeless as the Nationalists had already begun to invade the province. He threw his support behind Chiang, thus beginning his career with the Nationalists and ending one province's drive to secure its autonomy within a federalist framework.

Continued friction between the Nanjing government and the provinces proved the survival of alternative visions of the national polity. The demonization of federalism or provincial sovereignty was more complicated than the Nationalists would have wished. Some provincial military leaders found common cause with the pro-democracy 'Third Force' activists. They shared antipathy toward Chiang's centralization, taxation, and conscription efforts, as well as his authoritarian rule. As was the case in Zhejiang, leaders in Guangxi province tried to emphasize that provincial stability and prosperity would build a strong China. In the early 1930s General Bai Chongxi, an important figure in the 'Guangxi Clique', attempted to reconcile provincial and national loyalties by combining them (Levich 1993). He claimed that 'the reconstruction of Kwangsi [Guangxi] serves as the basis for the restoration of the Chinese people'. The attempt by provincial leaders such as Li Zongren and General Bai to make Guangxi into a 'model province' and to stress self-government as one of the province's 'Three Principles of Self Reliance' did not placate Nanjing (Levich 1993). The downfall of the Guangxi Clique in the mid-1930s represented a major victory for the Nanjing government. The Clique was absorbed into the Nationalists, which greatly weakened its provincial powerbase. Opposition to strong central control over provinces, however, continued. In 1945 another provincial-level rival to the Nationalists, Long Yun in Yunnan, was overcome. Yunnanese support of autonomy was built upon Long's lust for power (not so different from earlier warlords) as well as upon the support of liberals who flocked to the relatively open political climate of Kunming, a remote provincial capital beyond the reach of the increasingly rigid political orthodoxy demanded by Chiang. The final destruction of Long's power relied upon threats and a military invasion of the province by forces devoted to Chiang. By 1945, the Nationalists had successfully overpowered, absorbed, or intimidated a variety of provincial elites, many of whom expressed support for federalism (or some other form of provincial autonomy). Each victory served to legitimize further the centralization efforts of the Nationalists, and enabled them to further manipulate the narrative of China's political development.

A New Constitution to Promote Centralization

In the wake of the bloody War of Resistance against Japan, the Nationalists emphasized the need for unity, which they defined as a strong central government that could direct resources where necessary without interference from provincial governments. This approach would be transferred to the struggle against the Communists as the civil war restarted in early 1947. The 'Third Force', however, continued to cautiously seek greater regional or provincial autonomy, largely as part of an effort to bring a separation of powers, limited government, and a modicum of democracy to the Republic of China. The Communists were willing to support such proposals immediately after the war, not because they wanted federalism for China, but rather because it fit into a larger united front strategy of cooperating with any political entity at odds with the Nationalists. The Communists' continued cooperation with these democratic activists further justified Chiang's hostility toward the principles and institutional practices of shared sovereignty.

Even at war's end, Chiang's regime still had to contend with a series of provincial-level non-communist revolts against its authority. For example, in early 1944, the Nationalist put down a short-lived uprising in northern Sichuan after rioters in one district attacked the Smuggling Investigation Bureau and the local tax office. As reported by central government observers, some of the slogans used by Sichuanese included 'Implement Self-government for Sichuan Province'. During their resistance, local citizens formed the 'Sichuan Peoples Self-Government Corps' (Hou 1995). Citizens from Gansu revolted due to the Nationalists' attempt to draft soldiers and requisition grain. In late 1946, Xikang (formerly a province straddling today's Sichuan and Tibet) was wracked by an uprising that involved as many as 50,000 people. Then, throughout 1947, the Nationalist confronted a challenge in the far west, as ethnic minorities in Xinjiang fought Han Chinese. The Nationalists used a combination of negotiation and force to settle these incidents.

Taiwan, the eventual home of the Nationalists after their retreat from the mainland, revolted against Nationalist rule in early 1947. The so-called, 'February 28 Incident' represented the failures of decolonization and reintegration, when the legacy of fifty years of Japanese rule clashed with the centralizing efforts of Chiang Kai-shek's government. After the Nationalists took control in October 1945 Taiwanese concerns over misrule and corruption grew rapidly. Taiwanese, generally defined as Chinese immigrants who came to the island prior to 1945 or their descendents, had no direct experience with the Nationalist struggles for centralization, and were tainted by allegations of collaboration with the hated Japanese. Discontent exploded into uprising in late February of 1947 when Nationalist troops fired on demonstrators. Unemployed youth, workers, students, peddlers, and small businessmen reacted with fury, and briefly wrested control of Taiwan from the provincial administration. The island's elite suddenly found itself caught between the mainlander-dominated state and Taiwanese society. Rather, the elite moved to limit violence and to restore law and order, then to press for reforms under the broad rubric of local self-government or federalism. After a week of increasing tensions, mainland reinforcements arrived and massacred thousands of Taiwanese, both those involved in the uprising or subsequent negotiations, and others unfortunate enough to be on the streets. From the start, leaders in Nanjing had seen the takeover of the island by Taiwanese as a rebellion, and placed it in the context of thirty years of struggle against warlords. The fact that some of the elite had put forth demands similar to those of mainland democratic activists did not help their cause.

By portraying provincial self-government, federalism, and Taiwanese independence as identical, the Nationalists made district-level reform the only acceptable system. For example, in July 1947, the prominent Taiwanese, Gu Zhenfu, and four others were tried for their role in the short-lived independence effort immediately after Japan's surrender (Shen and Zhang 1993, 13–16). Their indictment for 'war crimes' used the terms independence (*duli*) and self-government (*zizhi*) interchangeably to describe their activities ('Yanchang' 1947; 'Taiji' 1947). Islanders would have to be on guard to avoid having their own aspirations for greater local autonomy evaluated in this way. The Nationalists pointed out that students allied with the Communists repeated slogans such as 'end the civil war, remove American troops, and implement democratic self-government' (Li 1972, 246; Pepper 1978, 182–183). Provincial powers became further 'tainted' when tied to Xie Xuehong, a communist leader who had led the short-lived armed resistance to the Nationalists in central Taiwan after the 'February 28 Incident'. After fleeing the island in May, she helped established the Taiwan Democratic Self-Government League in December 1947 in Hong Kong, and served as its chair. This organization did not indicate the Communists' ultimate views on the province's role in the nation, but rather represented the strategy of building a multi-party, multi-class united front against Chiang.

In light of these ongoing challenges to his authority, Chiang sought a constitution that would allow a strong chief executive and limit local self-government, in particular by blocking autonomy at the provincial level. Non-Communist moderates continued to advocate the province as the basic unit of self-government and even request that each province have its own constitution (Chang 1952, 188–222). The National Constitutional Assembly took over in November in 1946. The Nationalists, ignoring boycotts by the Chinese Communist Party and a collection of liberal organizations known as the Democratic League, quickly completed a draft of the constitution, which was announced on 1 January 1947 and went into effect on 25 December of that year. The Nationalists' constitution focused on extending the reach of the central government, not sharing powers. It mandated the creation of 'Principles for Provincial and District Self-Government' by the government, which would authorize these jurisdictions to pass their own self-government laws. The Principles were drafted by the Executive Yuan, then passed by the Legislative Yuan in 1948.

Li Zonghuang helped mold the Nationalists' version of local self-government both before and after the retreat to Taiwan. Li held a variety of central government posts in the late 1940s, and authored many books on local self-government and administration (Li 1951). His ideas were legitimized by none other than the 'Father of the Nation', Sun Yat-sen. Li wrote that in 1918 Sun instructed him to study Japan's system of government during his time there. This, according to Li, gave birth to what became his life's work. His experience highlights a key facet of Chinese conceptions of self-government, that is, the attempt to emulate Japan's highly centralized system (Li 1972, 302–303). Li shaped many of the constitution's provisions concerning the division of powers between the central government and provinces or lower levels of government. He worked to prevent the adoption of any form of federalism when the draft constitution was debated in the National Assembly. He made the Nationalists' view clear when he echoed the words of Sun Yat-sen: '*xian wei zizhi danwei*' (The district is the unit of self-government). Li also explicitly rejected the idea of provincial constitutions (Li 1972, 277–78). This marked an important step in redefining local self-government downwards, pushing the relationship between the province and central government out of political debate. Nationalist commentators wrote that the relationship between the central government and province would be of two types: cooperative (*hezuo*) and supervisory (*jiandu*). In a cooperative relationship, the center and province were like elder and younger brothers. In the supervisory relationship, they were like father and son. Further, the areas of cooperation did not involve questions of sovereignty or divided powers, but rather concerned the division of administrative responsibilities. The province was to be an administrative jurisdiction of the center, not a unit of self-government (Shi 1946, 1). The 1947 Constitution was only partially implemented on the mainland before the Nationalists began losing the civil war against the Communists.

The Death of Federalism in 'Free China'

The humiliating defeat on the mainland and a well-justified sense of crisis reinforced the centralizing tendencies of the Nationalists. They had re-established Chinese control over Taiwan in 1945, bringing to an end fifty years of Japanese colonial rule. By 1949, however, Chiang's regime was retreating to the island, which would become 'Free China'. The themes, organizations, and personalities of mainland politics came to dominate Taiwan. This occurred due to the influx of refugees who had little interest in or knowledge of the island, as well as government policies designed to legitimize Nationalist authority by tying Taiwan more tightly to China's destiny. With slogans such as '*kang Ri kao shan, kan luan kao hai*' (Rely on the mountains to resist the Japanese, rely on the sea to put down internal rebellion) the Nationalists cast the island's image in terms of a vital base for a great national crusade. Building upon images of Ming resistance to the Qing and the more recent struggle against the Japanese, conflict with the Communists was defined in nationalist terms. Chiang's regime portrayed itself as engaged in a fight against an alien ideology, communism, promoted by foreigners, the (federated) Soviets. On Taiwan, therefore, the Nationalists built the Chinese state that they could not create on the mainland. Implementing the 1947 Constitution formed a key part of that effort.

Taiwan's experience with local self-government represented an excellent example of the Nationalists' approach to political activity—an extension of long-term trends from the mainland. The Nationalists brought to bear a broad array of methods to control the discourse and policies concerning provinces, towns, and districts. They wrote a constitution, laws, and regulations to maintain a dominant central government, and to limit local, particularly provincial, autonomy. Mainlander refugees also built a police state after the 'February 28 Incident' that grew into the White Terror. In May of 1949 the island was placed under martial law. These measures made the Taiwanese elite more malleable to the Nationalists' interests. On Taiwan, the regime could concentrate its attention, as well as its police and military resources, much more effectively than it had ever been able to do across the Strait. By the time the Korean War began in June 1950, Chiang was President, Director General of the Nationalist Party, and Commander-in-Chief of the Armed Forces, giving him the top positions in the state, party, and military. The fact that his personal purview, the Republic of China, and Taiwan were one and the same shaped politics on the island for the next three decades.

Under Chiang's leadership, several official and quasi-private groups publicized the Nationalists' program, including Taiwan Provincial Local Self-Government Association, the Taiwan Province Local Self-Government Research Society, and the China Local Self-Government Study Society. Justifying Nationalist authority and implementing specific policies such as local self-government required that Taiwan fit into the history of political development in Republican China. This history excluded the possibility of federalism. Because the Nationalists wanted Taiwan to represent all of China, officials such as Li Zonghuang and Zhang Lisheng discussed local self-government as though it was being implemented throughout the nation, not simply in its smallest (and perhaps least typical) province.

For example, part of Li's justification for local self-government on the island grew from his mainland-based timeline. First, he wrote, was the dark period (*hei'an shiqi*), when an autocratic monarchy—the Qing—prevented the establishment of democracy. During this time the people's knowledge was undeveloped, politics were corrupt, and local strongmen powerful. This lasted until the 1920s, when Sun Yat-sen began to publish his writings on local self-government, most important of which was the *National Outline for National Reconstruction* (*Jianguo dagang*). This marked the germinal stage (*mengya shiqi*).Although the Nationalists had unified the country, due to internal revolts and external pressure they could not implement self-government. Finally came the period of maturity (*chengzhang shiqi*), which began in 1938 when the Provisional National Assembly raised plans for self-government at the district level in preparation for constitutional rule (Li 1972, 306).That the laws and rules of pre-war China had limited relevance to Taiwan was of no interest to Nationalist experts, who were determined to create a history of inevitable progress toward their program of local self-government. To Li, reform on Taiwan would mark the culmination of almost fifty years of struggle against imperialists, warlords, and communists.

Ironically, now that the Nationalists had only one province to work with, they appeared to accept tacitly (though they could never acknowledge publicly) one key aspect of the ideology of federalism—that China could be strengthened from the provincial level upward. Li portrayed building a prosperous Taiwan as a blueprint (*zhangben*) for building a new China (Li 1972, 1). Taiwan was to be a 'model province', a concept previously raised by 'Third Force' advocates of federalism. Under authoritarian rule, however, the Nationalists no longer had to confront publicly such contradictions. Nationalist propaganda trumpeted the island's political stability and material prosperity in order to undermine the 'Communist bandits'.

It was in exile that the Nationalists offered some of their most detailed explanation for their plan for local self-government. The new system would concern the district level and below, and would not modify the relationship between the province and the central government, much less suggest a division of powers along the lines of federalism. The Nationalist program posited that the province could supervise (*jiandu*) and direct (*zhidao*) the promotion of local self-government in each district (Zheng 1948; Li 1948). The press, now more tightly controlled by the authorities, stressed that reform could in no way weaken the island's links to the central government ('Zizhi' 1948). Officials involved in local self-government like Zhang Lisheng reflected a common belief of the Nationalists: provincial identities would spawn movements disloyal to the central government. He attacked the federal system, connecting it to plots to keep China weak and divided. Zhang stressed that making the district the unit of local self-government was the best way to prevent national order from breaking down as it did early in the Republican period (Jin 1950). Li Zonghuang wrote that local self-government should never be confused with local sovereignty or autonomy (*difang zizhu*). *Zizhu* was a form of separatism tied to warlords and federalism (Li 1954, 17–18).

Taiwanese came closest to articulating the real agenda behind the Nationalists' program of local self-government when some complained that officials delayed reform because they feared that islanders had not received enough training and might elect 'bad' people ('Duiyu' 1949). The system was designed to transform Taiwanese into loyal Chinese, not empower them. Local self-government and implementation of all aspects of the newly promulgated constitution of the Republic of China became part of a broader program of 'citizenship training'. Li summed up the Nationalists goals when he wrote that local self-government should 'manage, teach, cultivate, and protect (*guan, jiao, yang, wei*)' (Li 1951, 97–98). Islanders would be taught to be the kind of citizens the Nationalists had wanted to lead on the mainland. The Taiwanese would have to earn the state's version of local self-government by assimilating into the Nationalist Chinese political order.

The final implementation of the new system of local self-government was anti-climactic. A special session of the provincial assembly met in January 1950 to discuss the upcoming reform. Assembly members met with government officials, military leaders, as well as the chairman of county or city level assemblies on the island. On April 5, 1950, Governor Wu Guozhen, who was appointed by the central government, announced that elections for mayors and district magistrates would be held soon. Candidates, however, were subject to government approval. Openly anti-Nationalist politicians were either under arrest or knew not to run for office. In early July 1950, the implementation of local self-government began officially with the elections to the Hualian District Assembly. Over the next few months, elections were held in districts and cities throughout the island. In December 1951, the Taiwan Provincial Provisional Assembly was established (and transformed in 1960 in the Taiwan Provincial Assembly [*Taiwansheng yihui*]). Federalism, or shared sovereignty of any type, had disappeared completely from public discourse.

Scholars often offer another mirror image of the Nationalists on the mainland and on Taiwan by focusing on how the regime improved due to the lessons learned in defeat. Much of the understanding of Chiang's rule of Taiwan is based on the idea that the Nationalists changed after their retreat, as the regime became a close American ally in the Cold War. According to this narrative, Chiang's chastened followers became less corrupt and accepted advice and aid from the United States. In particular, such an approach is often connected to the Taiwan 'economic miracle'. While defeat may have spurred fundamental changes in Chiang's macro-economic policies, the case is less clear in the realm of politics (especially, in terms of the images of institutional state-building).Federalism and local administration suggest that many Nationalist policies on Taiwan were extensions of mainland experiences, not dramatic breaks from them.

Four decades after the imposition of Nationalist rule over the island, the political system began a fundamental shift. Democratization and the death of mainland-born leaders made the idea of Taiwan as a province of China less important. Political change in the 1980s and 1990s opened the door to administrative reforms that essentially abolished the provincial government as an efficiency and cost-saving measure. Now, the central government shares a few powers directly with counties, and the major political parties focus their competition on controlling that government. Thanks to the end of the Nationalists' monopoly on power, the issue of federalism has become irrelevant to governance on the island itself.

The Communists Build Upon the Nationalists' Approach

The failure of federalism in China complicates our understanding of other Cold War dichotomies. Perhaps the best way to understand the similarities between the Nationalists and the Communists is through what Paul Cohen deemed the 'consensual Chinese agenda', which he defines as 'not only a set of *goals* that most Chinese, regardless of political affiliation, would support … but also certain *means, methods* or *instrumental strategies*' (Cohen 2003, 31). As another scholar would later comment, 'Indeed, the distance between Sun and Mao was not great; both were nationalists who felt that only a strong Chinese nation-state could survive and modernize' (Bedeski 1977, 354). Both parties' perspectives were shaped by the chaos of China's warlords and the failed state building efforts of the Republican era. For example, in the early 1920s founder of the Chinese Communist Party, Chen Duxiu, portrayed federalism as little more than a justification for warlord power (Waldron 1990, 122).

In this setting, the Communists would build upon Nationalist assumptions and policies. For example, Mao and his followers were even more strongly biased against the *fengjian* tradition than the Nationalists. To the Communists, feudalism was a stage of development that included local elites and the imperial state; nothing from it could be salvaged or adapted for modern state building. Further, the Communists saw the primary cleavages in society as class-based. The geographical divisions between provinces were insignificant compared to the differences between landlord and peasant or capitalist and worker. As had been the case with the Nationalists, the Communists' willingness to entertain the possibility of a federal China had been 'tactical' (Schram 1985, 81–125).

After Mao declared the establishment of the People's Republic of China on 1 October 1949, the Communists began to suppress or simply ignore other anti-Nationalist groups, including those that had supported federalism. Despite their ideological affinity for and dependence upon Moscow, the new leaders in Beijing rejected a union of socialist republics along the Soviet model as a way to manage minorities within China. Article 16 of the Communists' 1949 'Common Program'—the blueprint for the China's political structure until the 1954 Constitution—made clear that provinces and other administrative units answered to the central government, then led by the People's Political Consultative Conference (Solinger 1977, 30). Beijing did not devolve any sovereignty to provinces, but instead created a system of six regions in order to supervise provinces (Tung 1964). These regional administrations were 'to act essentially as agents of the central government in directing the work of the provincial, municipal and *hsien* (county) governments' (Thomas 1955, 83). The central government, however, would often by-pass the regions completely in order to direct provincial governments.

Factional conflicts within the Communist ranks helped spur further centralization, and came to illustrate the danger of regional and provincial powers. Gao Gang, party chief in Manchuria (the three northeast provinces bordering the Soviet Union) from 1949 to 1953, was one of the strongest advocates of following the Soviet model of economic and political development. He lost a power struggle with Mao, who wished to move toward a uniquely Chinese model of socialism then communism, and was suspicious of Gao's ties to the Soviet Union (Teiwes 1993, 45–50). In February 1954, Gao was removed from the Party's Central Committee, allegedly for creating a 'separate kingdom' in Manchuria. He would commit suicide in August. Mao would attack the original regional system, stating that it became a base for 'anti-party' conspiracies of his rivals. The Gao Gang affair 'proved' that dangerous sub-national loyalties remained a threat to the Chinese Communists, even after their military victory. Such anxiety informed the practices of constitutionalization.

As Yu-nan Chang evaluated, the 1954 Constitution, it 'does not intend to limit the power of the government; rather it aims to guarantee the unrestricted rule of the government and to augment the arbitrary use of power for the benefit of the ruling party' (Chang 1956, 521). He noted that the Chinese state 'is a centralized one with no power left to the local governments at all' (Chang 1956, 540). The sole legislative body under (and since) the 1954 Constitution is the National People's Congress. Clause 65 stated that the people's councils at each level of the administrative hierarchy 'have the power to suspend the execution of inappropriate decisions by people's congresses at the next lower level; and to revise or annul inappropriate orders and directives issued by their subordinate departments, and inappropriate decisions and orders issues by people's councils at lower levels'. Each level had the right to appoint or remove personnel at the levels below it. Schram notes that the document represented a 'quite clear and forceful repudiation of federalism' (Schram 1985, 98). At most, the Communists paid lip service to the idea that designated minority peoples, such as Tibetans or Uighurs (a Turkic people in northwest China), would be governed within special autonomous areas. In reality, these areas had no autonomy, and provinces and major cities answered to Beijing. Divided power of any sort was anathema to this party, which remained faithfully Leninist in structure. The constitution itself enshrined democratic centralism, a doctrine that called for party and state officials to listen to the masses then make decisions that are implemented without question. Mao's briefest definition called it a system 'in which the minority is subordinate to the majority, the lower level to the higher level, the part to the whole and the entire membership to the Central Committee' (Mao 1942). Regardless of the state structure, real power lay with the Communist Party, which was rigidly centralized.

Mao's determination to depart from the Soviet model and his dream of a rapid transformation to socialism overwhelmed any discussion of shared sovereignty or acknowledgement of provincial identities. In 1956, on the eve of the Great Leap Forward, Mao wrote 'On the Ten Major Relationships', where he stated that 'to build a powerful socialist country it is imperative to have a strong and unified central leadership and unified planning and discipline throughout the country; disruption of this indispensable unity is impermissible'. He added that 'the relationship between different provinces and municipalities is also a kind of relationship between different local authorities, and it should be properly handled, too' (Mao 1956). Thus provinces and municipalities (a few of the largest cities, such as Beijing or Shanghai, were "independent' of any province) were deemed local, and could not enjoy autonomy. Despite Cold War hostilities, Mao and Chiang had very similar visions of the sort of state needed to save China. The 1954 Constitution was modified slightly in later decades, but the basic relationship between provinces and Beijing did not change.

Even three decades after Mao's death, promoting federalism in China remains difficult for two reasons. First, advocacy of federalism within the People's Republic of China is often connected to larger agendas of democratization and an end to the Communist Party's monopoly on power (Davis 1999; Lee 2004). For example, Yan Jiaqi, a dissident who fled China after participating in the 1989 Tiananmen Square democracy movement, makes a case for fundamental political reform to protect the rights individuals and to expand the role of provinces through federalism. To him, these two types of reform were mutually reinforcing (Yan 1992). Yan and those like him are throw-backs to the 'Third Force' activists of Republican China, although they cannot admit the connection. As Diana Lary points out in her article on the discourse of regional and central conflicts, 'history has a peculiar authority in China' (Lary 1997, 183–184). The experiences of the Republican era, when federalism was connected to a host of agendas designed to undermine China's national strength and sovereignty, form the justification for attacks on federalism or any type of provincial autonomy. Lary concludes that efforts on behalf on 'provincial interests' are still 'dangerous' (Lary 1997, 193). The Communists' rejection of these reforms today sounds little different from Nationalist propaganda of 60 years ago.

Second, various models of federalism have been suggested in order to reunite Taiwan with China. While the issue of Taiwan's potential independence from China is extremely controversial, some in the Nationalist ranks who favor eventual reunification promote federalism or a Chinese confederation to define the island's place in China. The mainland government has rejected such a structure for cross Strait relations because it might give Taipei greater status than is acceptable to the leaders in Beijing. Further, the Communists fear that, if federalism is acceptable in any part of China, then other provinces could demand the same privileges, thus fatally weakening the nation. These concerns are similar to earlier fears that democratization on Taiwan would inevitably spread to the mainland, something that has not come to pass. Nevertheless, the centrifugal forces resulting from the explosive economic growth that is still concentrated in a few coastal provinces have only strengthened these beliefs.

Epilogue: The China Case Study

The case study of China's defunct federalism raises important questions about the role of democracy, political parties, and foreign influence. The hypotheses from the theory on defunct federalisms outlined at the start of this volume suggest that there exists a close, and complex, relationship between federalism and liberal democracy. Certainly China's 'Third Force' political activists saw the two as mutual reinforcing—and equally necessary. At the same time, the Nationalists and the Communists rejected both—that is, the two political formations made a strong case that federalism (here expressed as provincial autonomy) would not serve the needs of China. The fact that federalism was often attached to democratic reform was simply another reason for these two parties to reject it. Without democracy, or at least a democratization process, the advocates of federalism, who were unarmed in a heavily militarized environment, had no hope of obtaining the political resources necessary to influence and shape the institutional framework of China's polity. The analytical propositions of Chapter 1 also intimate that federalism prompts a mode for the accommodation of contending identities within a single state. In China's case, however, the two dominant political parties saw the accommodation of sub-national identities as the cause of weakness—provincial or local identities were a problem, a remnant of pre-modern political culture that needed to be eradicated in order to 'save' China.

In China, federalists tended to focus on the state as the most important political institution. The Nationalists and the Communists, who actually held power, did not agree. Each perceived *their* party as the sole realistic and legitimate vehicle for serving the national interest. For example, even each side's army grew out of the party structure (not a central government) and the officers of each military establishment took an oath of loyalty to a party, not the central government. There proved to be no way to reconcile the highly-centralized political parties with a decentralized federal state. The state—from the capital to provinces to counties—was not meant to be a forum for political competition, debate, or shared sovereignty, but an instrument for carrying out the will of the particular ruling party. Complicating these debates is the fact that it proved impossible to disconnect cynical self-interest from sincere patriotism. Both parties followed policies that they portrayed as selfless attempts to free China from backwardness and foreign influence, but actually served to solidify their domination. In short, provincial autonomy would have required that the two dominant parties change their fundamental nature and weaken themselves.

Finally, the hypotheses on federal failure accurately note that federalism requires consensual politics and popular support. Neither China nor Taiwan had consensual politics, nor was there much popular support for local or provincial autonomy. There exists no evidence that the majority of the Chinese people—the hundreds of millions of peasants who would eventually come to support the Communists' vision of national and land reform in the late 1940s—had any knowledge of federalism. In this context, federalism raises questions about how foreign political concepts are adapted to or adopted in China. The two forces for centralization, the Nationalists and the Communists, tied federalism to *certain* Western values and political forms, but bolstered their own centralizing project to other outside ideas, such as Leninism or the Japanese political system. The rejection of federalism might best be seen as part of a larger process of questioning the applicability of *United States* political forms and ideas to China. While the reasons for Mao's attacks on America are obvious, it is important to remember that Chiang and the Nationalists never accepted United States style democracy or federalism. The World War II and Cold War alliances should not obscure Chiang's fundamentally authoritarian nature. Supporters of federalism, often wealthy Western-educated urbanites in a few coastal provinces, relied almost exclusively on proving that the United States and its system could be adapted by China. Ultimately, federalism, like democracy, failed in China because most of the elite were not convinced that it offered a solution to the nation's problems, advocates of shared sovereignty were unarmed, and the bulk of the population was concerned more with survival than with issues of political decentralization.

Chapter 8

The Strategic Roots of Arab Federalism and Its Failure: Transnational Sovereign Power Issues, Military Rule, and Arab Identity

Corri Zoli

Introduction

Few commentators look for the roots of some of the more serious challenges facing the modern Middle East—sluggish political and economic reform, militarism, domestic instability, Islamic insurgency—in the legacy of federalism, let alone its failure. This chapter focuses on the brief moment when pan-Arab federalism—often associated with Gamal Abd al-Nasser and Egypt— became a general political desire, exemplified by several short-lived unions: the United Arab Republic of Egypt and Syria (UAR) and the United Arab States (UAS)—a confederation of Egypt, Syria and North Yemen from 1958 to 1961, as well as the failed Federation of Arab Republics (1972–1977) promoted by the Libyan leader Muammar al-Gaddafi. At the same time, this exploration contends that the aspiration for political unity (although transformed) persists in unexpected ways into the present day—most notably, in extremist forms of Islamic fundamentalism and Arab nationalisms.

There are several theoretical elements to contend with when framing pan-Arab federalism: the complexity of federalism in states with intense subnational conflict (Bermeo 2002; Kymlicka and Norman 2000); the cultural-regional applicability of traditional social science models to the Middle East (Mitchell 2003, 156; Burke 1998); the non-public nature of many of the region's historical archives (Gee et al. 1988); and the Eurocentric tendency to 'other' this region in essentialist, relativist, or exceptionalist terms (Said 1978; Gran et al. 1998). This exploration, therefore, scrutinizes some of these framing issues in order to engage with the problems of multinational federalism (Requejo 2004, 260; Kymlicka 2001, 91; Simeon and Conway 2001, 3) in the context of the Middle East. The chapter both adopts and adapts, Timothy Colton's (1990, 6) concept of 'sovereign power issues'—the question of who rules, who decides who rules, and who runs the state—from civil-military relations to the class of political events that characterize the birth of modern nations in the Middle East. Instead of treating the notion and practices of national identity in a vacuum, the analysis zooms in on the travails of federal identity in the idea of pan-Arabism. Thus, by focusing on the case of Egypt, the chapter indicates that the desire for federalism emerged not so much from some normative political beliefs (such as multi-tiered and shared governance. institutional checks and balances, and attempts to include diverse identities within a workable political union), but from the twin institutional challenges of state-building and combating political extremism. In this setting, the dominant hypotheses from the theory of defunct federalism outlined in Chapter 1, fail to generate an understanding for the complex dynamics that initiated and then undermined Arab federalism.

Reframing Civil-Military Relations from the Nation State to Transnational Sovereign Power Issues: The Coup d'État

It may not be obvious as to why a concept adopted from the interdisciplinary subfield of civil-military relations is relevant to the analysis of post-World War II Egypt and its experimental federalisms. On the one hand, its bearing lays in Egypt's own modern birth after a political coup in a region where coups have been, in fact, ubiquitous. The revolutionary Free Officers Movement, under the leadership of Colonel Nasser established in the aftermath of the 1948 Arab-Israeli War, deposed the corrupt monarchial regime of King Farouk I and its British advisors. A statement broadcast on *Cairo Radio* noted that 'the Army revolt was not merely a movement against the ex-King, but it has also been, still is, and always will be a force directed against corruption in all its forms' (Khalil 2002).

On the other hand, reflecting the particular contingency of their emergence, the aspirations of pan-Arab nationalists for federal unity were promulgated by ranking military personnel. In fact, the increase of national consciousness in the Middle East is usually associated with the activities among 'the Arab officers corp in the 1908–1914 period' (Haddad 1994, 205). One early commentator has noted, that probably the most comprehensive outlines for a unified Arab state were articulated by General Nuri as-Said, who held several terms as prime minister of Iraq and was no stranger to military meddling in civilian governance. General Nuri's plan for 'Arab Independence and Unity' demanded that:

> (1) Syria, the Lebanon, Palestine, and Transjordan to be reunited into one state; (2) the people of that state to decide its form of government—monarchical or republican, unitary or federal; (3) an Arab League to be formed ... (4) the Arab League to have a Permanent Council nominated by member states and presided over by one of the rulers of the states, to be chosen by the states concerned; (5) the Council of the Arab League to be responsible for (a) defense (b) foreign affairs (c) currency (d) communications (e) customs, and (f) protection of minority rights; (6) Jews in Palestine to have semi-autonomy, their own rural and urban district administration, including schools, health, and police ... (7) Jerusalem to have a special commission of three theocratic religions to ensure free access and worship; and (8) if required, the Maronites in Lebanon to have a privileged regime such as they had under the Ottoman Empire. (quoted in Khadduri 1946, 94)

Yet, once the League of Arab States was established, 'it was as if [its] founding members set out deliberately to create an Arab system, which did not in any substantial way threaten the vested interests of the respective regimes' (Barnett

1995, 495). Thus, on analytical level, the military involvement in civilian affairs reflects 'the ultimate problem of civil-military relations' (Taylor 2003, 6) which, at the same time, points to the fragility of sovereignty. Coups represent a perforation of the boundaries between political realms—civilian politics, on the one hand, and the professional military, on the other—that should remain distinct (Huntington 1957, 19). Yet, while scholars have long debated their motivation, meaning, and purpose the 'sovereign power issues' represented by the military overthrow of civilian administrations is not entirely unusual (Colton 1990, 6). Apart from coups there are other similar instances of 'political institutional decay' (Huntington 1968, 1–3) such as insurrections, military revolts, uprisings, guerilla warfare, racial, communal, and tribal violence, which provide the global context for what advocates tout as the 'peace-preserving' qualities of federalism to manage intrastate conflict.

The Middle East, in particular, according to James Quinlivan, seems to have provided a 'fertile ground for coups', seeing 55 coup attempts (about half of those were successful) between 1949 and 1980. Usually, their occurrence is attributed to 'many reasons'—some expected (such as, power struggles among officer corps factions) and others not (such as 'dissatisfaction of foreign states with an existing regime') (Quinlivan 1999, 133). In this setting, a shortcoming of traditional civil-military relations theory with implications for the Middle East is the focus on Western models and political experience that does not take into account that the presumed separation between military and civilian authorities might be limiting to our ability to understand the complex interactions between emergent actors, as well as sovereign power contestations in the Arab world.

Curiously, Samuel Huntington's alternative structuralism which sees the structure of a society as the most important cause of military intervention in domestic politics is a complex ally in a more critical approach to this region. In particular, it suggests that it is not the 'type', but the 'degree' of government, the presence or lack of socially and politically mature institutions, that makes a nation 'coup prone'. Thus, the key causes of a military incursion on domestic politics are 'not military but political'—a view that reflects the importance, 'not [of] the social and organizational characteristics of the military establishment', but of 'the political and institutional structure of the society'. Indeed, 'military explanations do not explain military interventions', Huntington argues, because such interventions into domestic politics are 'only one manifestation of a broader phenomenon in underdeveloped societies: the general politicization of social forces and institutions'. His key concept of *praetorianism*—the politicization of all aspects of social life (including the military)—can, thus, account for developing societies, places where politics lacks autonomy, where social groups (as opposed to professional politicians) engage directly in politics, and where society as a whole (not just the military) 'is out of joint'—leaving soldiers 'susceptible' to 'social cleavages impacting the society at large' (Huntington 1968, 193–194). Recognizing that the problem of civil-military relations is predicated on a problem of statehood is crucial for (i) the explanation of the chronic institutional problems in Middle Eastern politics; and (ii) the understanding of how the politicization of military institutions is also often accompanied by an ideological overlay, which has important identity implications.

Apart from structuralism, the sociology of organizations and the military establishment itself (Janowitz 1960; Huntington 1968, 194) are, however, also key to understanding aspects of Egypt's 1952 coup and its impact on Arab federalism. Nordlinger (1977, 63), for instance, takes the soldier's perspective to theorize the coup as a deliberately 'executed act' to defend or to enhance 'the military's corporate interests'. He argues that interventionist motives are 'activated when civilian governors fail to provide adequate budgets, interfere with military autonomy, create or expand militia forces, threaten the dissolution of the regular army', or when government performance fails or loses legitimacy. Just as every public institution seeks to enhance its own interests (i.e., budgetary support, preservation against encroaching rival institutions), militaries—in that they are highly cohesive, hierarchal units with a motivational esprit de corps—pursue corporate interests in a determined fashion. In fact, for Nordlinger (1977, 78), the military's ability to identify with the nation—i.e., what is good for the military is also good for the nation—not only 'rationalizes away' separate civilian interests, but politicizes the personal interests of the officers and equates them with those of the state (Khalil 2002).

Thus, in contrast to the traditional dichotomy between military and civilian institutions (Huntington 1957; Janowitz 1960; Perlmutter 1969), Timothy Colton divides civil-military relations into three domains: (i) the armed forces' professional concerns—i.e., defense budget, military doctrine; (ii) the non-military political, economic and social issues—i.e., the macro-economic context or educational policy; and (iii) the exercise of state sovereignty—i.e., who rules, who decides who rules, and who runs the state. This emphasis is in line with two critical paradigm shifts, mirroring larger theoretical trends (Horowitz 1980) and instructive for political transformations in the Middle East: on the one hand, perspectives questioning the applicability of classical western models of civil-military relations to non-western experiences; and, on the other, broadening the framework of analysis from the state to other arenas of political activity, including non-state actors, transnational influences, and the interplay between external determinants and domestic politics.

At stake in transnational sovereign power issues in the Middle East, then, is our ability to shift analysis from civil-military dichotomies to deep and persistent contestations over government legitimacy in what Olivier Roy calls 'transversal' as opposed to 'diachronic' analysis—looking to interactive dynamics with other states and forces (including colonialism, westernization, and transnational actors) and not only to the internal history of a given state (Roy 2004, 6). This does not mean ignoring domestic trends, but requires both placing them in the broader contexts that shape them and adapting better, more open and flexible, concepts for understanding the complexity and diversity of political actors vying for political authority and legitimacy.

Furthermore, the Egyptian experience with military coups, as Michael Thornhill notes, suggests that the traditional 'historiography of Nasser's consolidation of power' neglects 'the relationship between Egypt's internal and external politics'—i.e., the inseparability between Nasser's 'struggle to consolidate his own domestic position' and 'his role as Egypt's chief negotiator in defense negotiations' were inseparable (Thornhill 2004, 893). In this respect, Nasser's coup transpires into a kind of political language which articulates the terms for the strategic regulation of the challenges posed by the fragility of sovereign power (whether internal legitimacy or external post-colonial issues). Said otherwise, the coup is a far more dynamic mechanism than many have allowed, with the military functioning as an institution that comes to address, not only politics, but wide-ranging social identity struggles. Indeed, as the case of Egypt explicates, countenancing the tasks of defining the identity constellations for a transforming state, organizing national and transnational political constituencies (i.e., the people of Egypt, the Arab people, etc.), building institutions of governance, brokering power struggles, and inspiring regional coups suggests that the functions of the military are far more variegated and de-territorialized than narratives of modern nation-building suggest (Bishai 2004, 88).

Therefore, the following section indicates Nasser's symbolic role, not only in inspiring revolutionary transitions and building a post-coup political regime, but in using the coup as a region-specific organizational language and political template for a diverse set of Middle Eastern actors confronted by post-colonial administrative dilemmas. Egypt's political-institutional idiom, therefore, grapples with a confluence of pressures common in post-colonial states in the Arab world: corrupt indigenous monarchies, the legacy of colonial rule in political and social institutions, comprador class elites and interests, competition over land and resources with neighboring states and governments, and a dizzying array of political and social movements clamoring for political representation. It is in this transnational context that federalism transpires as a narrative of political opportunity.

Post-Coup Rhetoric and Military Rule: The Suez Crisis

While on 18 June 1953 'The Egyptian Republic' was declared by the Revolutionary Command Council, within five years—in February 1958—it was transformed into the United Arab Republic (UAR) in union with Syria, which lasted until 1971. Although Nasser was skeptical of Arab federalism (Jankowski 1997, 164–165; 2001, 101; Hudson 1998, 1), Egypt nevertheless retained the appellation of United Arab Republic, even after Syria's own military coup(s) forced its secession from the union in 1961. Moreover, Egypt underwent several additional short-lived confederations with Syria and Yemen (United Arab States, 1958–1961), Iraq and Jordan (Arab Federation, 1958), and Libya and Syria (Federation of Arab Republics, 1972–1977), and retains the reference to a unifying Arab identity in the current name of the state—the Arab Republic of Egypt (according to its 1971 Constitution).

This brief historical overview highlights the revolutionary objectives of intertwining federal and identity narratives in the state-building projects of the Middle East—that is, the transformation of monarchical regimes into modern republics was bound to a new political idiom indelibly linked to Nasser (Ismael 1971). As some commentators have noted, the historicized legitimation of pan-Arab unification intimated that 'nationalist allegiance did not undermine the supranationalist'—that is, the individual Arab aspirations for independence were part of a larger project for unity; thus, 'unlike Balkan nationalism this [pan-Arab movement for] autonomism was not considered as a first step toward independence, but a federation' (Haddad 1994, 217; Khalidi 1991, 1368).

The relevant query, therefore, is: Why did (transnational) federalism became a desired strategy in the post-coup policy-making of Nasser? There are three possible responses in the literature: First, as Nordlinger (1977) has argued, the perceived threats to the military by politicized non-state actors associated with (i) the popular liberal constitutionalism of the Wafd party, which had a parliamentary majority during the 1920s and the 1930s, and was still influential into the 1940s (Ginat 2003, 5); (ii) the Marxist-inspired leftist labor movement; and (iii) the pan-Arab, non-secular Islamist populist movements. The desire to preempt these threats urged Nasser to embark on an ambitious economic reform plan for an 'Arab road to Socialism' (Ansari 1984, 127). Second, the task of bringing into line the diverse (and often violent) field of non-state political actors fell to the ideology of Arab nationalism and its federalist aspirations (Beattie 2000). Third, the escalation of the Arab-Israeli conflict prefigured the need for federalism as a matter of 'common defense' (Al-Sayyid 2004, 111). In particular, the 1948 Arab-Israeli War was a serious blow to Egyptian military prowess (Aburish 2004, 26) and a catalyst for distinct discourses of Arab nationalism. These, however, were inchoate and not uniform—for instance, the sense of *Nakhba* (disaster) in reference to the 1948 Arab defeat infused this burgeoning Arab identity with a kind of negative pan-nationalism and a rationale of regional *self-defense* (a posture that hinted at the subsequent defensive brittleness of future federalist arrangements).

All of these factors—threats to the military by diverse politicized actors, the historical-ideological power of ethnic over political identity (i.e., separate Arab nationalisms), the experience of war—came into play in the articulation of Arab federalism. But given the emphasis on exploring the links between federal failure and transnational political extremism, the legacy of the Arab-Israeli conflict, in particular, points to the strategic impetus of pan-Arab federations. Moreover, since the (symbolic) onus of responsibility for Arab federalism usually falls on Nasser, this analysis recognizes the unintended consequences of the political idiom that he crafted especially for the articulation of transnational identity by extremist Islamist groups. In this respect, the strategic rationale of Arab federations seems to have undermined the potential for multinational federalism in the region owing to the distortion of the terms of political inclusion and representation.

The most obvious example of the ill-fated confluence between strategic, rhetorical, and identity issues in the project of Arab federalism is Nasser's nationalization of the French Suez Canal Company (which operated and built the canal) in 1956. The claim here is that two kinds of decisions, attesting to a post-coup style of rule (Decalo 1998) underwrote both Egypt's involvement in the Suez Crisis and the subsequent Arab federations: (i) the attempt to use military-style political decision-making and influence to achieve (often economically-progressive) societal development; and (ii) the deployment of asymmetric foreign policy strategies to improve a country's relative political influence. In each case Nasser's decision-making confused civil and military arenas, albeit, for strategic purposes and, thus, in the aftermath made federalism a savvy—but fleeting—political solution in a highly-volatile transnational context.

It should be noted that Nasser did not approach domestic politics (i.e., building the Answan Dam) and international politics (i.e., establishing Egypt's regional influence) blindly, but used the strategic vernacular so long as it gave him leverage in the face of regional and geopolitical challenges. For instance, having secured American and British funding for the Answan Dam, he played the wildcard of Cold War geopolitics by accepting an arms deal with Czechoslovakia, thereby prompting the USA and the UK to rescind their financial promises. On 31 August 1955, Nasser then publicly declared that the arms were required in preparation for a war with Israel (thereby, violating the 1949 Armistice Agreement brokered by the UN) (Ereli 1956). Such militaristic discourse, however, reflected a 'military managerial' style of rule that attempts to shift 'the source of executive power from force (control of the means of coercion) to authority', with a view to maintaining power on a 'more permanent and stable basis' (Decalo 1998, 52). What was unique in Nasser's case was his willingness to hybridize Egyptian with Arab identity as a means to legitimize his authority.

Angered by the US withdrawal of funds, Nasser's move to nationalize the Suez Canal was, then, not only economic (designed to replace funds for the Answan Dam), but politically symbolic—he intended to convey (i) Egyptian independence to and of the international community; (ii) that Israel was a pesky relic of the bygone days of western interference in the region; and (iii) to the Arab world the arrival of a leader capable of mobilizing the energy of an emergent pan-Arab movement. It is noteworthy to remember that such stance enlisted the burgeoning Muslim Brotherhood and the Young Egypt (*Misr al Fatat*, Green Shirts) movements (founded in 1928 and 1933 respectively), which were rapidly replacing the liberal Wafd party as key vehicles of popular mobilization, albeit with a difference: these avidly paramilitary organizations (the Muslim Brotherhood performed well in the 1948 War) argued for non-secular governance and the revival of the Arab Caliphate (Coury 1982).

Nasser's grandstanding provoked France and Britain (in collusion with Israel) to initiate military action against Egypt. As Adeed Dawisha recounts, the initiation of hostilities 'resulted in Arab cities erupting in anti-Western demonstrations and riots'. The conclusion of the tripartite attack on Egypt without the achievement of its objectives and the subsequent installment of a United Nations Emergency Force (UNEF) to maintain peace, propelled Nasser to the status of an Arab leader-*extraordinaire*, he:

> filled the Middle Eastern horizon, becoming … a regional hero. To restless and frustrated Arab nationalists he indeed seemed a second Saladin, turning the tables on Western imperialism. In those days many Arabs were bewitched by the power of the idea and seduced by the charisma of Nasser, whom they readily accepted as the leader of Arab nationalism and the keeper of its conscience. As a result, these Arabs came to believe passionately in the inevitable triumph of their nationalism … [a] belief [that seemed] confirmed in early 1958 when the United Arab Republic was born. (Dawisha 2000, 86)

But the Suez Crisis also contextualizes Nasser's decision-making style in terms of domestic legitimacy strategies. Decalo (1998, 23–33) describes the discrepancy between the conventions of coup-making (stated, idealized goals and intentions) and actual capabilities, how in 'the rearray of power that accompanies the overthrow of civilian authority' military juntas 'rarely follow up on pledges to cleanse society of its ailments' or corruption, and how stated tasks are often neglected for two common reasons: (i) to do so would 'threaten potential allies in the civil service', often a serious component of the military's post-coup stability; and (ii) because coup-makers often have 'a serious contempt' for governance, which they perceive as mundane 'public administration', suitable for civilians, not visionary leaders. Indeed, this disdain for the practicalities of governing often encourages military leaders to seek out *symbols* of governance, democratization, and populism, among others, evident in the post-coup proliferation of constitutions, but also in placing inordinate amounts of social energy into cultural-nationalist discourses, or establishing nativist identities obsessed with a glorious past. This tactic, particularly evidenced by Nasser's discourse, tends to lionize a charismatic leader as a substitute for absent institutions. Such strategy—born of a particular style of post-coup rule in Egypt—paved the way for the idea of transnational Arab identity.

Not only did confidence in Nasser as an Arab leader became evident soon after the Suez Crisis, it was also expressed in military terms. On 25 October 1956 Egypt signed a tripartite agreement with Syria and Jordan to make Nasser the commander of the three states' armies. This agreement became the institutional precursor for the United Arab Republic (UAR). Indeed, in many respects Nasser's military vernacular became the foundational element of the pan-Arab federalist culture. Thus, the 1952 coup in Egypt shaped a template of political behavior toward core challenges in the region that came together in a mode of a pan-Arab identity and a leadership inseparable from that of Nasser's militarism. This legacy both invades and undercuts aspirations for genuine multinational federalism in the Middle East. Nasser's strategic discourses of governance were, thereby, ideological tools linking the domestic and the diplomatic realms, outlining alternate values, and offering new terms of identity accommodation in regional geopolitics, but not a viable means for state building required by Arab federalism.

Transnational Identity Contestations

This section considers the complex identity configurations that have emerged in the wake of the frustrated ambitions of pan-Arab federalism. In this setting, the intrication between defunct federalisms and identity constellations is indispensable for the ongoing confrontation with the effects of weak statehood. According to Edmund Burke (1998), accounting for the Islamist movements in the Middle East has thus far confounded all theories in part because of a fixation on nationalism in the region. It is now well established that theories of history—i.e., *how* we study the past—relays (i) as much information as that which we study, conferring cultural, social, and political authority (on certain groups, areas of the world, important questions, authors); and (ii) the method and practice of writing the Middle East (Said 1978; Keddie 1992). The very idea of the Middle East, that it can be studied as a coherent, if internally variegated, cultural-political entity is the 'methodological byproduct of a long-standing hegemonic discourse on the Middle East which considers the region culturally unique' and 'therefore not amenable to study via 'conventional' social science analytical tools and categories'. At its core, such exceptionalism rests on 'the shallow historical vision and comprehension of difference and complexity' (Gran et al. 1998, 10).

In this respect, the contention here is that the emergence of Islamist extremist movements in the Middle East is contiguous to the same landscape of factors that have framed the failed projects of Arab federalism: crises of government legitimacy, the legacy of military rule in institutions and identity, fragile sovereignty, etc. Indeed, the dynamics of both Arab federalism and pan-Arab identity outline the provenance of regional conflicts in terms of transnational sovereign power issues, which attest to the residual military influence on civilian institutions. In this setting, the discourses of national identity, themselves, fall within the ambit of the framing pressures of military state-strategizing. The complexity of the historical, ideational, and political dynamics of the dream for pan-Arab unity in a federal state has:

> had an effect on Middle East history as compelling as that of Marxism on modern Europe. While both ideologies had lost appeal by the 1990s, pan-Arab nationalism continued to exercise an intellectual hegemony far in excess of that parallel utopian philosophy in Europe. [In the Arab case] identity was believed destined to create a state rather than the state consolidating a new identity. This gap between reality and ideology was a major factor shaping the turmoil and seeming political perversity of the modern Middle East. (Rubin 1991, 535)

During the period of British influence (1882–1952), Egyptians did not seem to identify themselves as Arab. Owing to the peculiar status of the country under the Ottoman system it remained autonomous and, thereby, distinct from the other Arab provinces of the empire. Thus, in response to the initial expressions of Arab nationalism the 'Egyptian public opinion remained hostile or at best indifferent, hardly perceiving what the point of it was' (Gerber 2004, 265). In 1918, Saad Zaghlul, the first popularly-elected prime minister, argued that Egypt's struggles for statehood were 'an Egyptian problem and not an Arab one'. Such an exclusive explanation emphasized a distinct historical trajectory that saw Egypt as 'virtually autonomous from the Ottoman Empire since the early nineteenth century' and with 'established modern-looking state under Muhammad Ali' and 'a secularist concept of citizenship revolving in particular around the 1919 revolution and the popular Wafd party'; indeed, such a formulation suggested that 'Egypt had its own concept of nationalism in which the nation (*umma*) was Egyptian, not Arab' (Makropoulou 2007). In fact, the pre-Nasser period is 'most significant', for 'the absence of an Arab component in early Egyptian nationalism' (Ahmed 1999; Jankowski 1991, 244–245).

As already indicated, the Suez Crisis—especially Nasser's stance—changed al this. Nasser's strategic attachment to Arab nationalism developed into a critical language for anti-colonial struggle, constitutional reform, and the instrumental means for the promotion of a post-colonial order in the Middle East. In acknowledging the strategic impetus of Arab federalism, Jankowski (1997, 151–153) argues that it was Nasser's participation in the 1948 Arab-Israeli War that 'solidified his conviction of the integral political link between Egypt and Arab Asia', by making him aware that 'fighting in Palestine was not fighting on foreign territory', which was inspired not so much by 'sentiment', but by 'the duty of self-defense'. Such pan-Arab awareness, however, still maintained its national specificities. For instance, while Syrian legislators tended to favor 'Arab over non-Arab foreigners in various respects, including the investment of capital, as well as the acquisition of citizenship and political rights, while fewer, if any, advantages of this sort were granted in Egypt' (Kienle 1995, 53). Thus, the strategic-military undertones of Nasser's budding sense of pan-Arabism although not devoid of content were instrumental to the extent that they advocated the 'coexistence' of 'Egyptian and Arab loyalties', his use of the term 'Arab Egypt', his sense of Egypt as 'a member of the greater Arab entity' (Jankowski 2001, 27–28). In her description of the rapid transformation of Egyptian into Arab national identity, Leila Ahmad (1999) indicates the qualitative shift from a category that had comprised multiple ethnic and religious identities— including 'ethno-territorial Egyptian nationalism' (or Pharaonism), secular Arab nationalism, and Islamism—into a more homogenous designation.

In the post-Nasser period, Anwar Sadat's policies of demilitarization, economic and political reform seemed to revive a separate Egyptian national identity imbued with a desire for an *Egyptian* and *not an Arab* role in the Middle East evidenced by the 'profound downgrading of the military's political role' from the 'very outset of his presidency' (Springbord 1987, 5). In short, the different identity constellations and their meanings—Arab, Egyptian, and Arab-Egyptian—emerged, achieved ideational hegemony, and then disappeared in relation to specific historical contexts and challenges. For instance, the Six-Day War of June 1967—which ended with Israel's occupation of Syria's Golan Heights, the Gaza Strip and the West Bank in Palestine and, most painfully for Egypt, the Sinai peninsula—marked the end of Nasser's pan-Arabism. By the late 1970s, Arab nationalism was once again replaced by the 'local nationalisms' that predated it.

Thus, it is the context of the strategic discourses of Arab federalism that offer nuanced interpretation of the origins of contemporary forms of Middle Eastern extremism. The price paid for Middle East exceptionalism, as Kennedy (1991), Burke (1998), and Anderson (1999) indicate, is not only paradigmatic blindspots on the mental maps of the Middle East, but the inability to notice, let alone understand or explain, crucial contemporary developments—in this case, the rise of transnational Islamist movements and their roots in military rule and its impressive pan-Arab vernacular. As Barry Rubin (1991, 537) has argued 'Arab disunity' can be treated as inevitable outcome of pan-Arabism—'by providing a rationale for each state to interfere in others' affairs, it actually strengthened the individual regimes and weakened unity'. In this respect, it is somewhat ironic (yet, not surprising) that with Nasser's death in 1970, there has been 'no ideology to capture the imagination of the Arab world except Islamic fundamentalism', even while Nasser, himself, 'never wavered in his opposition to Islam as an instrument of governance' (Aburish 2004, 4). In fact, some commentators have pointed out the doctrine of Arab nationalism shares several points of contact with Islam (Heim 1955; Zubaida 2004). Thus, Islamist extremism has emerged as one of the most conspicuous contemporary instances of the (unintended) effects of military strategic discourse and policies for transnational state-building. At the same time, these effects underwrite the emergence and failure of Arab federalism.

Conclusion

This chapter has argued that the roots of one of the more serious global security challenges today —the rise of Islamist extremists in relation to attendant issues such as weak/failed statehood, politicized social and military institutions, political vacuums that allow groups to leverage violence as a substitute for formal processes and institutions of political participation—are part and parcel of the story defunct Arab federalism. Its experience suggests that the context provided by the strategic/military impetus of Arab federations and pan-Arab identity-articulations is central to the failure of unification in the Middle East. The complex dynamics that animated pan-Arabism indicate the necessity of framing the history of federalism in the region in terms of transnational sovereign power issues (such as contestations over government legitimacy and sovereignty which are often fomented transnationally).

Although unsuccessful in terms of the sustainability of the specific federal arrangements, the attempts at federalizing the Middle East have nevertheless fostered a regional order of relatively stable expectations and shared norms among Arab states (Barnett 1995, 481). As Richard Pfaff (1970 156) notes, 'paradoxically, this inability of Arab nationalism to realize itself in any concrete fashion is the very reason it is able to survive'. The experience of federal failure—both in the Middle East and in other geographical locales—suggests that what is at stake is not only dealing with weak statehood (as one of the more challenging global security issues), but also the pervasive political vacuum that offers fertile ground for extremists to leverage violence as a substitute for formal processes and institutions of political participation. In the Arab context, the erosion of politics underwriting the simmering crisis of statehood, indicates that western projects of democracy promotion will most likely fail to the degree that powerful stakeholders—a legacy of the pan-Arab defunct federalism—are left out of the bureaucratic security umbrella.

Chapter 9

The Failure of the Socialist Federal Republic of Yugoslavia (1945–1991): A Story of Contradictions, Weaknesses and Tensions

Matt McCullock and Silvia Susnjic

Back in 1991, as the war in Slovenia was drawing to a close, a high-ranking Serbian official remarked that the coming conflict in Croatia would make what had happened in Slovenia look like Disneyland. Of course, picking up the Disneyland motif, one might note that Krajina could, properly enough, be translated as Frontierland, while Kosovo has perhaps earned the sobriquet Adventureland, recaling that most 'adventures' have a desperate character in them. Macedonia might be Neverneverland, at least in the eyes of Greek nationalists who wanted nothing less than to expunge its name and history altogether. I think of Bosnia as Tomorrowland, indicating a sense of foreboding for the future and offering a warning of a possible 'future' to be avoided. Serbia under Milosevic figured— dare I say *clearly*?—as a kind of Fantasyland, where fantasies of national salvation raised Serbian spirits to dizzying heights, only to see their spirits dashed in the course of eight years of War and privation. And dominating Fantasyland is, of course, Sleeping Beauty's Castle, where the slumbering beauty lies in repose until a princely kiss will awaken her. Serbia's Sleeping Beauty's Castle is the so-called House of Flowers, where Tito lies buried. But Yugoslavia's sleeping beauty, unlike Disney's will sleep forever. The only fairy tales still circulating in this Fantsyland are the dangerous ones.

Sabrina Ramet (Ramet 2005, 27, emphasis in original)

Introduction

The Yugoslav dissolution marked the return of war to the European stage after the nearly half-a-century-long peace of the Cold War (Bunce 2004; Critchley 1993). Ramet's metaphor in the epigraph, the violence accompanying the federal breakup disturbed the eunomic *Disneyland* not only of post-communist Europe, but also the linear Westphalian narrative (Kavalski 2007). This incidence urged the realization that 'while the politics of class has been retreating in the wings [during the communist rule], the politics of ethnicity has been moving in the limelight' (Hechter 2000, 2; Young 1993). Thus, the dismembering of Yugoslav federal statehood became a symbol for the destructive potency of ethnic discontent and unsatisfied identity groups. At the same time, the conflict in former Yugoslavia soon after the symbolic fall of the Berlin Wall appeared to indicate the *fragmegrative* (Rosenau 2003) tendencies of the post-Cold War turbulence of global life—not only was the conflict caused by the fragmenting and internal breakup of a state, the international response to the violent dissolution of the federation was also characterized by a multiplicity (and often disarray) of actors (Krahman 2005, 531).

Prior to its violent breakup, the framework of Yugoslav federalism was expected to 'play the role American constitutional law and political theory played during the last quarter of the eighteenth century' (Djordjević 1975, 79). Yet, the unraveling of Yugoslavia during the 1990s urged commentators to start looking for the tell-tale signs of such collapse. These explorations have ranged from the 'mono-causal' statements of Susan Woodward (1995) to the 'multi-causal' claims of Dejan Jović (2003). Moreover, a number of them explored the outside/inside dichotomy and the re-conceptualization of post-Cold War international politics. Unlike such studies, however, this chapter probes the relationship between identity and federalism and its bearing on the dissolution of Yugoslavia.

The claim here is that Yugoslav federalism was characterized by an *aporetic duality* (Parfitt 2006). On the one hand, it was promoted as a state building project that had to ensure the stability and territorial integrity of the country. On the other hand, federalism was envisioned as a temporary arrangement that would facilitate the establishment of Marxist/socialist consciousness among the peoples of Yugoslavia and would supplant their distinct national identities. The promotion of a unifying federal identity, therefore, was not central to the Yugoslav federal experiment.

The exploration of this duality of Yugoslav federalism will proceed in several steps. First, this chapter briefly outlines the evolution of Yugoslav federalism and suggests that its tensions derive from the internal political environment in which it developed. Then, the analysis outlines the intrication of these contradictions with the narratives of 'Yugoslav' identity. Third, these developments are assessed in the context of the hypotheses from the theory of defunct federalism. Fourth, such exploration emphasizes the weaknesses of the fundamental principles of 'socialist self-management'—as institutionalized by the 1974 Constitution—and their contribution to the Yugoslav federal failure. Finally, the chapter concludes with several inferences drawn from the experience of the Yugoslav federalism.

The Evolution of Yugoslav Federalism

From its tentative inception in 1943 to the dissolution of the country in 1991, Yugoslavia had four constitutions (1946, 1953, 1963 and 1974), numerous constitutional amendments (1967, 1968, 1971, 1981 and 1988), as well as various statutes that were accredited with a quasi-constitutional status. These divided the former Socialist Federal Republic of Yugoslavia (SFRY) into six republics: Slovenia, Croatia, Bosnia and Herzegovina, Serbia (including its two autonomous provinces of Kosovo and Vojvodina), Montenegro, and Macedonia (Malesevic 2000, 150). Traditionally, the origins of federalism in Yugoslavia are traced to the nineteenth-century anti-Ottoman struggles of the Slavic populations of the Balkans. Informed by the ideas of Pan-Slavism—a theory and a movement intended to promote political or cultural unity among the Slavic people—Yugoslavism (the idea of the unity of the South Slavs) emerged as a 'Pan-Slavism in miniature' (Sekulic 1997, 169). Its discourses animated the establishment of the so-called First Yugoslavia— the Kingdom of the Serbs, Croats, and Slovenes that lasted from 1918 until 1941. The appeal of Yugoslavism, however, proved too vague to counteract the existing religious, linguistic, political and historical differences and, instead, federalism was promoted as a practical solution to the problem of accommodating diverse communities in a single state (Frankel 1955, 417). This did not mean, however, that the aspirations for political unification became uncomplicated. The inter-communal tensions that reflected the increasing centralization of First Yugoslavia underwrote the mass extermination campaigns that all communities seemed to unleash on each other during World War II (Crawford 1998, 208).

Therefore, most commentators have noted that owing to the history of inter-ethnic conflict and in particular the violence during World War II, the architects of post-war Yugoslavia focused on institutional reforms that would promote reconciliation among the constituent units. Initially, the Second Yugoslavia was envisioned as a part of a larger socialist federal state encompassing Bulgaria, Albania and parts of Greece (Mastny 1996, 34–37). Formally, however, the immediate origins of the Second Yugoslavia—the Socialist Federal Republic of Yugoslavia (SFRY)—are traced to the declaration of the Anti-Fascist Council of the People's Liberation of Yugoslavia (AVNOJ) on the 29 November 1943, which introduced federalism as a principle for postwar state formation. This proclamation reflected the arrangement of AVNOJ's struggle against German occupation and its quasi-federal operational division. Thus, in Slovenia, the partisan forces were led by Edvard Kardelj, in Croatia they were under the command of Andrija Hebrang, in Montenegro by Milovan Djilas, and in Bosnia and the Sandžak they were led by Josip Broz–Tito (Bennett 1995).

Whether intentional or accidental, the nascent federal arrangements implicit in AVNOJ's resistance bespoke postwar developments and reflected the ideological bent of the partisan movement. In this respect, Yugoslavia's first constitution of January 1946 was merely a carbon copy of the Soviet constitution of 1936 (Hasani 2003, 144). There were several differences, however, relating to the omission of the right of the Yugoslav republics to maintain their own military and to conduct independent foreign policy. Furthermore, Yugoslavia did not adopt the Soviet concept of 'titular nation' and system of internal passports, which were central to the institutionalization of ethno-national federal units in the Soviet Union (Malesevic 2000, 168). The 1946 Constitution divided the country into three layers—the federal, the republican, and the administrative units. Similar to the Soviet model, Yugoslav federalism provided a façade for the high level of state-centralization under the League of Communists of Yugoslavia (LCY). In this respect, it was obvious that the character of the federal system was strongly influenced by the long-standing conviction that centralization is critical to the dynamics of state building (Shoup 1968). At the same time, however, it sought to assuage some of the regional tensions that had undermined the prewar Kingdom of Yugoslavia.

After Yugoslavia's dismissal from the Cominform in 1948, the state was forced to redefine its identity in domestic and foreign affairs. As a result, Yugoslavia's political leadership began experimenting with a 'national communist' path of state development (Carleton 1949; Gripp 1960). The new post-1948 state building charted a unique combination of communism and federalism: communism provided the political and ideational underpinnings of the state and federalism—the basic principle of territorial organization. Thus, while in its external relations Yugoslavia subscribed to a policy of non-alignment, in its domestic affairs it espoused a program of socialist self-management.

The practice of self-management was introduced in 1950 with the 'Basic Law on the Management of State Economic Enterprises and Higher Economic Associations by Work Collectives'. This law could be interpreted as a precursor to the 1953 Constitution. The text of the latter suggested that the Yugoslav leadership had ceased to perceive the federation as a community of nationalities, but rather as a 'community of producers' (Vucković 1997, 113). As a result, the Council of Nationalities introduced under the 1946 Constitution, which included representatives of the Yugoslav federal entities, was substituted by a Chamber of Producers whose representatives were elected by workers and peasants employed in state-owned enterprises (McClellan 1969, 136). This aspect of Yugoslav federalism was reinforced by the 1963 Constitution. At the federal level, the notion of workers' representation was further consolidated with the introduction of four specialized Chambers of Work Communities—the Economic Chamber, the Chamber of Education and Culture, the Chamber of the Social Welfare and Work, and the Organizational-Political Chamber (Rusinow 1977, 151). The members of these chambers tended to be technocrats— i.e., experts in their respective fields and therefore seemed 'more prepared' to debate controversial issues (Lampe 1996, 280). At the same time, although retained in principle, the status of the Yugoslav republics as sovereign states was redefined into 'state socialist communities' (Malesevic 2000, 152).

In this respect, by the mid-1970s, self-management became the defining feature of Yugoslav federalism. The institutional framework of federalism became the conduit for the experiment with self-management. This relationship, however, was not unidirectional. The practices of self-management impacted the pattern of federalism. They assisted the devolution of power to the periphery. As one observer noted self-management prescribed '*a new mechanism for decision-making which transforms traditional representative political structures* and creates a new synthesis of individual and common interests, of autonomy and unit, of participatory and representative democracy' (Djordjević 1975, 78, emphasis in original).

Consequently, the 1974 Constitution indicated a culmination of the Yugoslav experiment with self-management. It codified the shift from federalism to confederalism and facilitated the permeation of all aspects of public life by the principles of self-management. For instance, the units of the former Yugoslav federation were rebranded as 'states based on the sovereignty of the people' (Malesevic 2000, 153). Moreover, the name of the country was altered from Socialist *Federal* Republic of Yugoslavia to Socialist *Federative* Republic of Yugoslavia (Gow and Michalski 2005, 145). In this respect, the 1974 Constitution reflected the conviction of the Yugoslav leadership that the experience of socialism had made the pattern of federalism redundant (Jović 2003, 177). Some have insisted that 'federalism [was] not a final ideal, but a necessary step in the process of the socialist development of a multiethnic state, in the process of its withering away" (Hamdija Pozderac quoted in Ramet 1984, 71). Thus, as Kardelj (1975, 45) argued, the Yugoslav federal state was 'no longer an autonomous force above society, nor is it identified with society, but it is increasingly becoming a function of the society organized along self-management lines'. The arrangement of the 1974 Constitution aimed at the consolidation of communist rule, but did so at the level of the federal units, not the federation, which ensconced a system of 'socialist feudalism' in the country (Pavlowitch 2002, 231; Gow and Michalski 2005, 144).

Such formulations seem to acknowledge that the post-1948 process of state building in Yugoslavia charted a unique combination of communism and federalism: communism provided the political and ideational underpinnings of the state and federalism became the principle of territorial organization. Yet, the emphasis on these idiosyncratic features should not obscure the instrumental nature of the Yugoslav experiment. Despite the alleged legalization of state building, the Yugoslav form of federalism, however, was not *constitutional* in character. Its regulations clearly prioritized the rule of the communist party above the inalienable rights of the individual and the constitutional rights of the federal units. This prevented federalism from developing its own integrative dynamics. Instead the main integrative factors became the LCY and the Yugoslav People's Army (YPA), both overshadowed by the political and symbolic ubiquity of Tito's leadership. Consequently, these contradictions came to dominate the identity narratives of former Yugoslavia.

Sketching the 'Yugoslav' Identity

Historically, the debates over the identity politics of former Yugoslavia tend to be positioned in the context of the ideology of *narodno jedinstvo* (national unity) of the interwar Kingdom of Yugoslavia. The dominant interpretations of *narodno jedinstvo* reflect the dichotomous framing of identity between primordialists, who argue that it is 'profoundly rooted in, and generative of collective experiences', and instrumentalists, who view identity as 'an *ad hoc* supplement to political strategies' (Eriksen 2001, 44). The insistence of the latter concerns the question of whether political communities are created more or less consciously, or whether they grow organically, as it were, out of preexisting cultural communities. Consequently, it could be argued that identity is invented in the process of the creative constructions of peoples' experiences. From this point of view, *narodno jedinstvo* is perceived as a definition of an 'objective entity or as one which had a life, political, symbolic, or iconic, outside the consciousness of individuals' (Cohen 2000, 146). Its politics of identity intend to bring individuals together under the auspices of unity and to engage them in a constant interpretation and reinterpretation of the meaning and implications of its content. Thus, the evocation of *narodno jedinstvo* aspires towards the forging of clear boundedness, homogeneity, and continuity within a state (Fernandez 2000).

In this respect, the post-World War II attempts to advance a shared supranational identity in Yugoslavia were characterized by an internal contradiction: on the one hand, they were intended as a clear break with the project of *narodno jedinstvo*; yet, on the other, they maintained some of its characteristic traits. In terms of the former, there was a conscious attempt to advance a (generic) socialist identity, which was not necessarily envisioned as part of a program for the establishment of a Yugoslav federal identity or *jugoslavenstvo*. Thus, the promotion of a homogenizing socialist identity was self-consciously distinct from a common Yugoslav identity, owing to *jugoslavenstvo*'s redolence of the repressive practices of the Kingdom of Yugoslavia. The internalization of such socialist identity was sustained through symbols and rituals. There are two stages in the promotion of a shared socialist identity in Yugoslavia.

The first one—from 1945 to 1963—was premised on the conflated politicization of identity both as a national category and a socialist call for solidarity, equality and fraternity (Jović 2003, 160). Symbolized by AVNOJ's slogan *'bratstvo i jedinstvo'* ('brotherhood and unity'), during this period the architects of Yugoslav statehood relied on patriotism to overcome the differences between different national groups and unify them against internal and external enemies (Wachtel 1998, 132). Premised on the notion of relatedness, the appeal to *bratstvo i jedinstvo* aimed at the convergence of the interests of the different national groups into a supranational socialist identity (Judah 2000). In this respect, federalism was conceived as a matter of 'inter-national relations' that depicted former Yugoslavia as a 'state among the South Slavs which works and satisfies most of the people most of the time' (Rusinow 1998, 2). The brotherhood-and-unity doctrine also engaged in a strategic revision of the pre-socialist history of Yugoslavia, especially the experience of inter-communal strife during the Second World War (Bennett 1995; Critchley 1993; Djokic 2003).

The second stage of this attempted socialist-identity-building—from 1963 to 1980—reflected the institutionalization of the notion of 'producers' with the evolution of Yugoslav constitutionalizing process. For leaders such as Kardelj, this identity reflected the legacy of 'Yugoslav socialist patriotism' by emphasizing 'the strengthening of socialist workers community [in Yugoslavia]' (Popovski 1995, 188). This socialist identity was founded on and identified with the system of self-management (Vucinich 1969, 274). As self-management took hold, it 'resulted in a kind of social integration, but not into a Yugoslav [federal] society' (Wachtel 1998, 134). In fact, by the mid-1970s Yugoslavia had become 'a highly decentralized federation in which the constituent republics dominated the central government' (Burg 1993, 357). Such trend was already aptly summarized in a 1969 editorial of the Belgrade journal *NIN*, which asked '*Jugosloven—ko je to?*' (The Yugoslav—who is that?) (quoted in Burg 1983, 210).

Parallel to this project of constructing a supranational socialist identity, Tito promoted a distinct conceptualization of federal identity in which national identities were embraced but never took precedence over the Yugoslav one. In this respect, he subscribed to an understanding of Yugoslavism, which had its roots in nineteenth-century ideas of the South Slavic unity. Tito, therefore, favored a notion of *organsko jugoslovenstvo* ('organic federalism'), which intended a 'harmonious symbiosis between national specificity and affective attachment to the Yugoslav community' (Ramet 2006, 287). Tito, himself, insisted that:

> I have received these days quite a few letters just in connection with this [question of nationality], and mostly from children. Children understand what I am talking about. One little girl from Macedonia, a student in the fourth or fifth grade, whose father is a Slovenian

and mother a Macedonian, has written to me saying that she is happy that she can now be called a Yugoslav. Look, Comrades, a little girl wrote that in her own hand. That shows better than anything how absurd it is to force someone to belong to a nationality, Serb, Croat [or] Slovene (quoted in Shoup 1968, 224).

In this respect, the endeavor to forge a sense of communitarian federalist identity among the different ethnonational groups underwrote Tito's conviction that the peoples of Yugoslavia can be 'taught through patriotic education and rituals that unity means freedom, pride, and prosperity as opposed to ethnic strife which brings all groups back into poverty and humiliation' (quoted in Perica 2002: 100). Thus, Tito's unique position within the federal system as well as his charisma and virtual embodiment of the Yugoslav statehood, allowed him to provide a powerful alternative to the institutional program of socialist-identity-building.

The Hypotheses of Defunct Federalism

Federalism and liberal democracy

Despite the liberalization implicit in the practices of self-management, liberal democratic principles were never aspired to by Yugoslav federalism. For instance, Enver Hasani demonstrates that the formal recognition of self-determination (including the right to secession) in the constitutional makeup of the state was merely a disguise intended to coerce the construction of a homogenizing Yugoslav identity. Thus, the process of 'defining who the "selves" entitled to self-determination' was highly centralized and authoritarian (Hasani 2003, 142). According to Djilas (1991), the rejection of the procedures of political pluralism was adumbrated by the twin rationality of (i) the Marxist conviction that political parties are remnants of the capitalist social and economic order, and (ii) the demand for a revolutionary transformation of society, which required the LCY to maintain its monopoly on power. The rejection of the norms and values of liberal democracy was informed by an idiosyncratic understanding of the role of the individual.

For instance, Kardelj (1980, 134) argued that the treatment of the individual within a system of self-management is distinct from the conceptualization of the individual in liberal democratic system. He claimed that in the latter, the individual is reduced to an 'abstract political citizen', who partakes in an alienating political system which allows for the misrepresentation of individual needs by elected officials. Instead, the Yugoslav federal experiment endeavored to enable individuals to pursue their interests as 'real persons' within the 'complex system of relationships' that defines the 'actual working class'.

Therefore, the aim of socialist self-management was to identify and solve the 'actual' problems of individuals—defined as 'producers'—rather than the 'abstract' issues of national belonging (Todorović 1974, 3). The promotion of such a uniform political environment allowed for the development and maintenance of a totalitarian system of control and coercion, particularly in regards to the rights of the federal units to secession and the rights of individuals to exercise their freedom of speech. The ideological rigidity of state building underwrote the inability of Yugoslav federalism to influence underlying emotions and attachments (Shoup 1988, 69). In fact, Stancovic (1988, 36) insists that the form of federal statehood constructed a framework that 'thwarted the democratic political evolution of the basis of citizens' political rights'. In this respect, Yugoslavia's rejection of the norms and values of liberal democracy seems to corroborate the claim that in their absence the establishment of federalism would fail.

Institutional setting

The suggestion here is that the Yugoslav federal arrangement was only partially intended to accommodate diverse national identities and did not envision the promotion of an overarching federal identity. As already hinted, the ideological underpinnings of the Yugoslav state building process perceived such forms of identification as an artifact of the capitalist/bourgeois system. In this respect, it was expected that the practices of socialism would overwhelm diverse forms of national identification. Federalism, therefore, was perceived as a formality that would be removed once the processes of socialization would have created a homogeneous socialist identity (Ramet 1984, 54).

In this respect, the system of self-management intended the promotion of an identity of 'producers' among peasants and workers. Yugoslavia, thereby, has been termed an instance of a 'communal federalism' because its experience is so distinct as to necessitate 'an adapted conceptual approach ... a reconceptualisation which reflects Yugoslavia's special status among nominally federal systems' (Dunn 1975, 130).

The paradox of the Yugoslav institutional setting, however, is that the promotion of a shared socialist identity was not the only (and, probably, not the dominant) attractor in the country's federal arrangement. As already indicated, the commanding role of Tito—which he provided through a combination of personality and political power—was instrumental to the processes of state building. Robert Dorff insists that Tito's unique position allowed him to enforce an overarching *Yugoslav* perspective on the republics—thus, whenever, the interests of different national identities transgressed those of the federal state, Tito was there to rein them in and exert control from the center (Dorff 1994, 107).

During the 1980s the aporetic tension between these two projects—the identity of socialist 'producers' and Tito's *jugoslavenstvo*—became a conspicuous symptom of the weaknesses of the Yugoslav federal experiment. In the absence of Tito, his notion of *organsko jugoslavenstvo* was emptied of its meaning, while the framework of the socialist identity proved too abstract. Thus, the leadership of different federal units began increasingly to resort to 'populist nationalism [in order to] force acceptance of its demands' (Denitch 1990, 78). In this respect, the case of Yugoslavia tends to agree with the suggestion that the failure to advance (if not outright rejection of) institutional patterns for diverse identity accommodation is likely to undermine the viability of the federal experiment.

Imposition of federalism

While federalism—both as a form of territorial organization as well as a system of ideas—was established in Yugoslavia in a strict top-down mode by the LCY, this should not necessarily be understood as a contributing factor to its failure. A more plausible argument is that although imposed, there was not one, but *two types* of federalism that were being imposed concurrently. As it has already been explained, the LCY endorsed two distinct types of federal arrangements—Tito's *organsko jugoslovenstvo* and Kardelj's socialist self-management. Thus, the tensions between their impositions played a central role in the dissolution of Yugoslavia. Despite the apparent clash of objectives and understandings between those contradictory ideas they were allowed to coexist (Boduszyński 2004, 516). This experience weakened both public and elite linkages with the federal idea and federal level institutions (Seroka 2002, 104).

Therefore, during the 1980s, in the vacuum created by the absence of their main proponents—Kardelj and Tito—the contesting versions of state organization proved unable to respond to the internal tensions generated by the centrifugal forces within the federal entities. In this respect, the increasing devolution of political power to the federal units of Yugoslavia (which began around 1967 and was formally institutionalized with the 1974 Constitution) triggered an almost 'cyclical crisis environment' between different national identities rather than coalitions of 'common interest and mutual trust' (Ramet 1984, 18). As Katherine Verdery (1993, 182) notes the fact that the principle of national difference was constitutionally enshrined made possible the nationalization of the political discourse of the federal units. Thus, she insists that it was leaders

> of nationalities [that] held power as such in their republics. More important, this was so in a social environment that the party-state had worked assiduously to cleanse of *other* organizational forms that might compete with its own initiatives. When a system of this sort begins to decentralize and to encourage more initiative from the lower-level units, the only units having the organizational history and experience to respond are nationalities.

In this respect, the case of Yugoslavia seems to suggest that it is both the imposition of federalism compounded by the failure to devise a single conceptualization for the ideational framework of the state that contributed to the eventual collapse of the federal project.

The Contradictions, Weaknesses and Tensions of Yugoslav Federalism

The discussion of the dominant themes in the theory of defunct federalism elicited that the experience of Yugoslav federalism was underwritten by a number of contradictions, weaknesses and tensions. These inconsistencies in federal arrangement, therefore, provide for understanding the idiosyncratic features of the Yugoslav federal failure.

Federalism fails if it lacks coherence

The contradicting objectives of centralized statism and decentralized self-management underwriting Tito's and Kardelj's versions of Yugoslav federalism prevented its establishment both as a coherent political practice and form of state organization (McCullock 2006). Instead, the attempt to conflate the two led to a complicated and confusing process of constitutionalization. Thus, the 1974 Constitution contained over 400 articles, which together with the attendant laws explaining the content of a number of the constitutional clauses ensured a federal system, whose consistence was difficult to discern. Consequently, the 1974 Constitution created a 'confused, contradictory, self-paralyzed, and even self-destructive mixture of federation and confederation' (Stojanović 2000, 55). The increasing levels of complexity of the Yugoslav federal system made it difficult for the majority of the population to identify with it, not least because of the difficulty to grasp its content.

Federalism fails if does not address dominant social issues

The central weakness of Yugoslav federalism appears to have been its preoccupation with abstract issues such as alternative conceptualizations of the individual and their adaptation to Marxist dogma. Thus, the constitutional evolution of Yugoslavia is a reflection of such utopian undercurrent. An instance of such trend is the attempt to substitute the problems of national identity through the gradual assertion of a unifying socialist identity under the notion of 'producers'. Institutionally, therefore, since federal structures were designed to express support for the party program they never developed mechanisms for conflict resolution (Seroka 2002, 112). At the same time, despite its reliance on multiple local centers of power, Yugoslav federalism remained a 'top-down' construct—'an artificial construction frozen in its self-management ideology, and increasingly estranged from the masses and their emotional needs' (Shoup 1988, 70). In this context, on the occasions that the nationalities problems became too difficult to ignore, a solution was offered not through the constitutional framework of Yugoslav federalism, but through extra-constitutional means—i.e., reliance on Tito's charisma (as in Serbia in 1968 and Croatia in 1971) or the YPA (as in Kosovo in 1981). In this respect, the fixation on 'blazing new paths' (Kardelj 1977) failed to ensure a long-term vision for a sustainable federal arrangement.

Federalism fails if it is insulated from political reality

The Yugoslav federal experiment seemed to have develop in a vacuum. The contention is that the conceptualizations and practices of socialist self-management that characterized the post-1948 development in the country were made possible by the political and symbolic shield provided by Tito (Dimitrijević 1994, 31; Gow 1997, 35; Woodward 1995, 21). It was his charisma and authority that afforded Kardelj the cover to indulge in his federal experiments (Jović 2003, 172). This feature of Yugoslav federalism suggests its insulation from the political reality of the state. In this respect, the political vacuum created by Tito reinforced the increasing idealism of the project of self-management (Sirc 1979, 237). Thus, the 1974 Constitution seems to reflect such attempt for the creation of an ideal political order rather than address the Yugoslav political realities (Seroka 1993, 73). The failure of Yugoslav federalism, therefore, reflects its detachment from the political reality of the country.

These contradictions, weaknesses and tensions of the Yugoslav federal development reflect the absence of a strategic long-term vision for state building (Kavalski and McCullock 2005). Instead, they point to tactical decision-making aimed at the maximization of power. Thus, rather than solving existing problems, the implementation of the 1974 Constitution and its reform of the federation only accelerated the proliferation of conflicts between the republics and the federation (Malesevic 2000, 154). The underlying inconsistencies of Yugoslav federalism were reflected in the shift during the 1980s from the constitutional principles of socialist self-management to the notion of *organsko jugoslovenstvo* (Stanković 1981, 31). After the passing away of Kardelj and Tito, the Yugoslav leadership favored the latter's insistence on the practices of centralizing statism. This tendency was reflected in the proclamation 'After Tito—Tito' (Pavlowitch 1992, 88–89), which prompted a development from 'macro-decentralization to micro-centralization' (Malesevic 2000, 154). In this respect, the move away from the principles of self-management reflected the focus on territorial integrity. The invocation of Tito was intended to plaster over the cracks of the federal system. It promoted a Yugoslav patriotic mythology which pronounced Tito 'the creator and the savior, a peacemaker who abolished the religious hatred and united all of the Yugoslavs and the defender of the truth whose power derived from the love of the people' (Perica 2002, 103). These discourses were institutionalized in rituals—such as Youth Day (the celebration of Tito's Birthday) or the induction of children into Tito's Pioneers (youth communist) movement—performed throughout the territory of former Yugoslavia. Aimed at the reverence of Tito's legacy, these rituals acknowledged him as the symbolic embodiment of Yugoslavism.

The spectacle provided by these celebrations offered examples of identity-calcifying symbolic ceremonies that served the purpose of reiterating the importance of the Yugoslav federal doctrine. The decentralizing practices of self-management, however, had already ensured the erosion of the federal center as a central economic and political player (Bunce 1999, 221). In this situation, the institutions of federal government were gradually losing their significance (Malesevic 2000, 157). In this respect, Belgrade no longer represented the seat of 'real power' (Crawford 1998, 232). Thus, the inherent contradictions, weaknesses and tensions of the Yugoslav federal arrangement made it impossible to reconcile the contending versions of federalism (Ramet 2006, 334).

Conclusion

The instance of Yugoslav federalism seems to conform to the dominant hypotheses from the theory on defunct federalism. At the same it also generates additional context-specific suggestions that inform the practices of state building. In this respect the experience of federal Yugoslavia appears to represent a catalogue of contradictions, weaknesses, and tensions. It constructed an unsustainable political system, whose structure failed to accommodate multiple identities. Thus, during the 1980s, the institutional flaws of Yugoslav federalism began to be exploited by self-interested elites for the activation of nationalist myths (Heinemann-Grüder 2002, 8). As Steven Burg (1993, 357) has declared 'regional leaderships carefully protected the interests of their territorial constituencies at the expense of other regions and the federation'. Likewise, Sinisa Malesevic emphasizes that despite large-scale unrest in Croatia in the late 1960s and early 1970s, 'relationships between ethnic groups in Yugoslavia, unlike these between the individual party leaderships, were reasonably good' (Malesevic 2000, 155). This tendency towards legitimating policy discourses in terms of national identity ran counter to the politics of compromise and accession associated with federal decision-making (Seroka 1994). The increasing *nationalization* of Yugoslav federal units undermined whatever incentives there might have been for the acceptance of federal arrangements and prompted nation building not only as an available, but also as a viable alternative (Heinemann-Grüder 2002, 159).

In this respect, Branko Milanovic (1994, 64) has argued that the communist ideology of Yugoslav federalism created 'the proto-state' structures, which eventually became the vehicles for the federal demise. When the power of the federal center began to weaken (as well as was consciously eroded) during the 1980s, the Yugoslav political system shifted not toward 'a decentralized politics of accommodation, but to a politics of cutthroat competition between the center and the periphery and among the units of the periphery' (Dorff 1994, 104). The resulting tensions were further exacerbated by the profound changes in the international environment. In the context of accelerating domestic and external turbulence, the Yugoslav federal system lacked the ideational and institutional wherewithal to maintain its claim to 'brotherhood and unity'.

The story of Yugoslav federalism came to an end a few decades later during the 1990s, in what Ramet (1992, 251) has termed, 'the orgy of an inter-ethnic war'. As Gearóid Ó Tuathail and Carl Dahlman explain, the drive of Slobodan Milosevic to accumulate 'enough power' to become the 'new Tito' of Yugoslavia, initiated a polarization which tore the federation apart. In this setting, state governmentality was re-visioned along the demarcating lines of different identity communities—reflected in proclamations such as 'all Serbs in one state' or 'Croatia for the Croatians', which replaced the Tito-era slogan of 'brotherhood and unity' (Ó Tuathail and Dahlman 2004, 136). It has to be acknowledged that despite the critical contribution by domestic factors, the dissolution of the former Yugoslavia was also impacted by the end of the Cold War confrontation. In the discussion of the effects of the international context on domestic processes, it often remains overlooked that the end of bipolarity came as a result of the internal collapse of the communist bloc (accompanied by the federal disintegration of its hegemon); in the vacuum of political delegitimation contending projects for extensive political and economic reconstruction began vying for positions of authority (Lake and Morgan 1997, 346). For instance, Susan Woodward (1995) asserts that the inter-ethnic tension were exacerbated by the country's changing role in international life—from a favored recipient of financial credits during the Cold War to a relatively insignificant Southeast European actor. At the same time, the reluctance of external actors to bear the cost of appeasement as well as the extended discussions on the legitimacy of such involvement facilitated local conflict dynamics (Kavalski 2008).

This complexity notwithstanding, the claim here is that regardless of its demise, the case of the former Yugoslavia also reveals an original experiment with federalism within a multi-national environment. Thus, despite the failure of the Yugoslav *federation*, the claim here is that for the attentive scholar the experience of the Yugoslav *federalism* offers (and will continue to offer) a repository of ideas for further investigations. Returning to Sabrina Ramet's metaphor in the epigraph to this chapter, the contention here is that the Fantasyland of Yugoslav federalism requires neither a knight in shining armor, nor is it the abode of a disregarded Sleeping Beauty; instead, the extant relics of this federal experiment demand careful investigation and research.

Chapter 10

From the Second Best Option to Dissolution: Instrumentality and Identity in Czechoslovak Federalism

Jan Ruzicka and Kamila Stullerova

Introduction

In a recent exchange of views on regional cooperation in Central Europe, the Czech president Václav Klaus accused one of the country's leading political commentators, Petr Uhl, of grounding his arguments in '[his] well-known Czechoslovakism that exactly in the 1990s suffered its final defeat' (Klaus 2006). This was one of the few occasions that a reference to Czechoslovakism or Czechoslovakness appeared in Czech public discourse since Czechoslovakia's split in 1992. The low frequency and the negative connotation it carries suggest the ease with which the Czechs—and, as we argue in this chapter, also the Slovaks—abandoned the idea that defined their public space for over seventy years. But was the idea of Czechoslovak federalism ever the principal force of Czechoslovak politics and political identity?

This chapter discusses Czechoslovakia as a case of defunct federalism. We make a case that the signs pointing to defunct federalism were already present at the moment of the Czechoslovak Republic's creation in 1918 and were addressed only sporadically and erratically throughout the state's seventy-four years of existence. There was a marked inability to engage in a public debate about the differences between various ideas of what Czechoslovakia meant to different groups inhabiting the land and how their multiple identities were to be or could have been accommodated in a Czechoslovak federalism. This ultimately led to Czechoslovakia's dissolution into two nation-states, as contemporary Czech Republic and Slovakia see themselves.

We argue that Czechoslovak federalism always had an instrumental character. In this setting, whenever federalism became part of the public discourse it was rarely understood as a means to accommodate multiple, layered identities. Rather federalism was the means to achieve other political goals. This is what we call instrumental use of federalism. We do not claim that the federal Czechoslovak project was destined to fail. Openings conducive to successful federalism always accompanied indicators of its failure. Gradual popular identification with a relatively successful state (especially in terms of socio-economic leveling of its main constitutive parts) had the potential to produce a public formulation of and support for the values of federalism. This is best observed in the realm of collective identities, where the decades-long existence and success of Czechoslovakia did create a number of Czechoslovak identities.

Nevertheless, an accommodative, political Czechoslovak identity existed only among people in/from mixed families, a portion of Slovaks dissatisfied with the instrumental construction of the dominant Slovak idea of Czechoslovakness and a tiny number of Czechs critical of the backward-looking view of Czech identity and its patronizing inclusion of the Slovaks. Moreover, no version of federal Czechoslovak identity was explicitly discursively developed and argued for in the public realm.

Therefore, we identify the moment of the country's split in 1992 as a consequence of several otherwise benign actions that could have had much less detrimental effect under different societal, political and, importantly, collective-psychological circumstances. These actions coincided with, and were enabled by, an extremely open public climate in the aftermath of the Velvet Revolution, which at once unveiled both the pressing public need to address the issue of federalism as well as a critical lack of discursive practices, institutions and traditions to do so. Consequently, the people of Czechoslovakia, who only a couple of months before the dissolution had claimed in public opinion polls support for the common Czechoslovak state (Wolchik 1995, 233), accepted the new reality of two separate states.

The case of the Czechoslovak federation shows the necessity of a non-instrumental espousal of federalism in both the elite and popular political discourse about its underlying values (such as openness to diversity, greater potential for political freedom, better accommodation of non-standard national and ethnic identities, cultural richness, extension of we-ness). This discourse has to account for the challenges federalism presents to the collective meanings of we-ness and justice provided by its main competitor, nationalism (such as unambiguous criteria of belonging, the idea of a home, and solidarity based on an extended idea of family).

The chapter is divided into three parts. The first one provides a historical overview of the Czechoslovak state, highlighting the main challenges and changes from the perspective of federalism. The second part analyzes reasons we consider to have led to its failure, placing our contribution within the context of existing explanations. Using parts of the framework developed in this volume, we focus on, first, particular moments in Czechoslovakia's history when federalism itself could have been publicly addressed but was repeatedly redirected into the service of what was understood to be a more pressing political need at a given time. Secondly, we analyze key collective identities among Czechoslovak citizens from the point of their foundational myths, identifying in them components detrimental to development and acceptance of a strong federal Czechoslovak identity. The third part relates the Czechoslovak case to the theoretical hypotheses on federal failure, emphasizing especially the need of non-instrumental approach to federalism and questioning the claim that liberal democracy as a political regime safeguards the success of federalism. The conclusion reflects on the implications of the Czechoslovak experience on federal projects in general.

Historical Background

Czechoslovakia emerged as one of the new states in Central Europe after the demise of the Austrian-Hungarian Empire in the First World War. Formally, Czechoslovakia was a federation for only about a third of its duration, starting with the constitutional reform in 1968/1969 until the country's split in 1992. However, a vague idea of a just and accommodative institutional arrangement for more than one collective identity was a precursor to the state-building process. Therefore, it makes sense to examine Czechoslovakia's history from the perspective of federalism already prior to 1968/1969.

The Pittsburgh Agreement of May 1918, concluded by the prominent émigré advocate of Czechoslovakia and the country's future president, Tomáš Garrigue Masaryk, together with the representatives of Czech and Slovak emigrant organizations in the United States, expressed the will to form a common state of Czechs and Slovaks. It also stipulated Slovakia's entitlement to its own administration, congress and courts (Pittsburská dohoda 1918). Although Masaryk tried to subsequently downplay the importance of the Pittsburgh Agreement (Innes 2001, 6), it provided an important point of reference for later (Slovak) contestations of the unitary nature of the Czechoslovak state.

Upon the actual establishment of Czechoslovakia in the fall of 1918, the country's leaders opted for a rather rigidly centralized (if democratic) instead of a multi-tiered state. The Slovak National Council, proclaiming itself the sole representative of the Slovaks, was dissolved by a special minister for Slovakia in January 1919 (Bartlová 1995, 171). The state adopted an ideology of Czechoslovakism, according to which the Czechs and Slovaks were two branches of one nation. At the same time, however, a symmetric set of institutions, for example a minister for the Czech part matching the one for Slovakia, was not under consideration.

An institutional change came only in 1938. After the Munich Agreement, which substantially altered Czechoslovakia's shape by forcing it to concede parts with substantial German, Hungarian and Polish population to Germany, Hungary and Poland respectively, Slovak political representatives were able to gain political autonomy. In March 1939 the cropped Slovak territory became a Catholic clergy-dominated state. Recognized by Germany and its allies, the state was a Nazi satellite pursuing fascist policies.

The 1944 Slovak anti-Nazi uprising, although unsuccessful, provided for an opportunity to reintegrate Slovakia into the common Czechoslovak state. It allowed for an alternative narrative about the Slovak role during the war and gave to the originally underground, anti-Nazi Slovak National Council the legitimacy to claim to represent Slovaks both during and after the Second World War. While it distanced itself from the wartime regime, the Council did aim to secure a federalized state with an extensive degree of autonomy for the Slovaks (Rychlík 1995, 189–190). At first, the Czechoslovak exile government in London reluctantly accepted this. Nevertheless, once the war was over, these demands were watered down. During the first three years of post-war rebuilding, Czechoslovakia became part of the Soviet-led Communist bloc. Czechoslovak interwar institutional asymmetry aligned well with the Soviet 'special needs' asymmetry (Bunce 1999, 221), which also did not institutionally distinguish between the Russian and the Soviet. Hence, in addition to the asymmetric existence of the Slovak National Council alongside the Czechoslovak Parliament there was also the Slovak Communist Party existing alongside the Czechoslovak Communist Party.

Amidst the general reform process and political thaw of the late 1960s the Slovak National Council called for federalization in March 1968. This was quickly endorsed by the new Action Program of the Czechoslovak Communist Party. The Program argued that it was 'essential to recognize the advantages of a socialist federation which allows two equal nations to live together in a common socialist state' (quoted in Steiner 1973, 172). In June 1968 a Constitutional Law on the Preparation of the Federation was passed and in October the Federation Law itself was adopted. Thus from January 1969 on, Czechoslovakia was to be formally a federation of two socialist republics, with two national parliaments (National Councils) and republican governments as well as a federal parliament (the two-chamber Assembly) and a federal government (on these institutions and their powers see Rychlík 1995, 196–197). But the most important political power in the state did not undergo any change and remained divided asymmetrically into the Czechoslovak Communist Party and the Slovak Communist Party. In this arrangement the former made the most important executive and legislative decisions.

The brief period between autumn 1989 and summer 1992 provided an opportunity for an open debate on the question of federalism and arguably the most favorable setting for the strengthening and extension of the Czechoslovak federal identity. For the first time in its history, the country was both democratic and formally federal. And unlike in the interwar democratic period, the understanding that Czechs and Slovaks were two separate nations was well entrenched. Moreover, the uniformity of the post-1968 period ensured that people's lifestyle and values were largely similar regardless of national identity. The socializing effects of compulsory military service, enhanced student mobility as well as some mobility of labor and other forms of interaction brought about face-to-face contacts among Czechoslovakia's inhabitants resulting in numerous inter-ethnic marriages and friendships. As Erika Harris points out, in 1990 in Slovakia '57 per cent of the population had Czech friends and 31 per cent had Czech relatives', while among the Czechs 23 per cent claimed to have Slovak friends and 45 per cent had Slovak relatives (Harris 2002, 91).

Despite these rather positive conditions the last three years of the federation were marked by petty disputes that eventually led to its fast and surprising dissolution. The election results of 1992 empowered what came to be two incompatible visions of the future state. On the Czech side the economic reform-minded Civic Democratic Party led by Václav Klaus carried the day, gaining nearly half of the seats in both chambers of the federal parliament (48 out of 99 in the House of the People and 37 out of 75 in the House of the Nations). It got slightly fewer seats in the Czech National Council (76 out of 200). In Slovakia, instrumentally nationalist Vladimír Mečiar's Movement for Democratic Slovakia received a similar proportion of the vote, gaining 24 out of 51 seats in the federal House of the People, 33 out of 75 in the House of the Nations and 74 out 150 seats in the Slovak National Council.

The point of no return for the dissolution of the country was reached during the third meeting of the two parties empowered to form the federal government, eleven days after the elections (Rychlík 2000, 60). The main difference between the two came down to the question whether the federation is formed from bottom up (with its constitutive parts delegating some of their powers to the federation) or top down (with the federation delegating some of its authority onto the republics). Mečiar challenged the latter but Klaus took his demands for 'sovereignty' within a 'common state' as an unacceptable hybrid and decided to stop discussing federalism and start discussing the division of the country (Rychlík 2000, 60–61, Macek 2000, 244–245). As a result, on 1 January 1993 Czechoslovak federation ceased to exist.

Explaining the Failure

This chapter argues that the Czechoslovak federation dissolved because at various critical moments of its existence domestic political actors used federalism to serve other political objectives. From its beginnings the multinational state did not attempt to accommodate multiple identities. Instead, the institutional setup of the state reinforced, and in the Slovak case also promoted, the idea of two separate national identities, preventing the development of a federal identity that would be compatible with the respective national identities. Once federalism's instrumental function was exhausted, there was little left to hold the federation together as Czechoslovak federal identity was too weak to stop the decision to break the country into two. This explains both the pace and peacefulness of Czechoslovakia's dissolution.

Such contention diverges from some of the dominant explanations in the literature on the Czechoslovak breakup. This literature falls into two broad categories. The first one stresses the one-time failure of the post-1989 elites to keep the state together at the expense of more long-term causes and effects (Innes 2001; Macek 2000; Rychlík 2000; Kusý 2004). These explanations also stress that the population was against the split but the decision-makers ignored this. The elitist explanations capture three important issues. First, the narrow and closed environment, within which decisions regarding the country's fate were taken. Second, the interaction between two strong-willed leaders that made mutual accommodation difficult, if not impossible. Third, the speed and ease with which the country was split up. However, in this analysis they fail to account for the fact that the elite's acts simultaneously reflected the dissonant meanings Czechoslovak citizens ascribed to the federation. Although mostly taken by surprise, the population did not consider the split as principally undemocratic. This chapter builds on the elitist explanations but also goes beyond them, aiming to acknowledge underlying ideas about the federation that enabled the elites to act as they did in a democratic setting.

The second type of explanations argues that the federal failure was caused by the constraints imposed by the Czechoslovak Communist constitution, deemed not to be suitable in matters of federal power-division and the legitimacy requirements for a democratic regime (Cox and Frankland 1995; Kraus and Stanger 2000b; Kroupa 2000; Stanger 2000). The institutional explanations are in line with the instrumental approach to federalism that we see as the main cause behind the failure of the Czechoslovak federation. However, they fail to see the communist period as only one instance of instrumentality and careless institutional design. Moreover, they also omit the interplay of various identities and their impact on political processes.

Federalism's instrumental use

In the history of Czechoslovak federalism there were six moments in which some ideas pertaining to multinational federalism were publicly addressed. These key moments are: (i) Czechoslovakia's establishment as a homeland for the Czechs and Slovaks; (ii) Slovak Catholic challenges to unitary Czechoslovakism; (iii) post-war reconstruction and Communist takeover; (iv) the 'Prague Spring' era of public openness; (v) post-invasion Communist power-consolidation; and (vi) post-Communist transformation after 1989. The recurrence of these critical situations suggests that federalism as a normative concept was indeed perceived as important and its realization in the Czechoslovak context as inadequate. But using federalism instrumentally only led to half-hearted political measures. Issues of multilayered identity accommodation were politically addressed and thus temporarily settled, but the tensions and perceptions of actual federal deficiencies remained intact. As it will be explained, in all six instances dominant political actors used federalism and its alleged enhancement as an instrument to other political gains and purposes.

(i) Czechoslovakia's establishment as a homeland for the Czechs and Slovaks   While there were several reasons for ignoring views of Czechoslovakia as a multinational state at the country's establishment in 1918, one stands out. The new state was carved out of the former multinational Habsburg Empire and so, besides the Czechs and the Slovaks, sizable German and Hungarian (as well as other) minorities also lived there. According to the 1921 census, there were over 3.2 million Germans and 650 000 Hungarians out of Czechoslovakia's total population of 13 million (Kučera and Pavlík 1995, 15). The Czechs were a majority within the state by only a tiny margin. The unitary construction of a titular Czechoslovak nation, for which the new country should be the nation-state homeland, served a dual purpose. Domestically, it supported Czech and to a lesser extent Slovak positions vis-à-vis the Germans and Hungarians, formerly the two titular nations in the Austro-Hungarian Empire. Internationally, this created the impression of a quasi-nation state, boosting the claim for independence in an era when a self-determining nation was believed to be the best guardian of peace (Pomerance 1976).

(ii) Slovak Catholic challenges to unitary Czechoslovakism   The awkward construction in which the Czechoslovak nation was presented in ethno-national terms came under challenge already in the first years of the new republic. Some Slovak political leaders expressed disapproval with the unitary view of Czechoslovak nationhood. This is often interpreted in exclusively national terms, as a quest for Slovak emancipation and as Slovak's more insightful view of Czechoslovakness. But the clash is better understood as primarily involving social issues. It was religion, or more precisely religiosity as a mode of social integration and control, that was at stake in these challenges.

While the Czechlands were rich and industrially developed, rural Slovakia lagged behind economically. In the country's effort to reach socio-economic leveling, Czech professionals migrated *en masse* to Slovakia. Guardians of Slovak Catholic religiosity (and, of course, the Church's sphere of influence and power) viewed Czech influx to and intellectual influence on Slovakia as a danger to their dominance. The leading critic of Czech impact on Slovakia, Andrej Hlinka, was both a Catholic priest and a party leader. While nominally also Catholics, the Czechs had a wholly different approach to religion compared to the pious, relatively backward, and mostly rural Slovaks. The worldly Czechs living and working in Slovakia presented a dire contrast to the bigoted values of the Slovak countryside and small town. Hlinka's party was the only one expressing demands for Slovak autonomy (Leff, 1988, 78–81). The 1939–1945 Slovak state was a puppet of Hitler in all respects but religion, which was permitted to operate when all other civic associations or organizations were banned (Kamenec 1992, 31).

(iii) Post-war reconstruction and Communist takeover   After World War II there was an opportunity, and demand on the Slovak side, to institutionalize federalism. Since the German and Hungarian minorities had been expelled in the post-war retribution, the unitary construction of a titular Czechoslovak nation was no longer needed. Yet, once again federalism was not to be addressed as a primary issue. In the post-Yalta situation it was the 'internal enemies' of the communist power-grab that became the main threat and the primary political goal to deal with. The communists' position was much weaker in Slovakia than among the Czechs. Depriving the anti-communists of a relatively autonomous power-base by firmly incorporating Slovakia into a reinstalled, unitary Czechoslovakia eased the communist takeover. Slovak nationally-minded communists, many of them politically mobilized during the 1944 uprising, went along, somewhat naively believing that once the Communist Party asserted itself firmly they could reopen the idea of federalism (Steiner 1973, 77). This did not happen. Instead, most of them were sentenced during the 1950s show-trials as 'bourgeois nationalists' (Lipták 1999, 130–133).

(iv) The 'Prague Spring' era of public openness   In the 1960s, as the communist regime slightly eased its grip on the society and 'bourgeois nationalists' were released from prisons and allowed back into public life, the demand for formal federalization began to reappear in the public discourse. In spite of signs of change in Slovak political identity, dating back at least to the uprising, the Czechs were not fully cognizant of the shift in the Slovak expectations concerning the common state. Thus, one of the first and great clashes within the Czechoslovak reform process, which came to be known as the Prague Spring, was over federalization. In October 1967 Alexander Dubček, a Slovak and the soon-to-be First Secretary of the Czechoslovak Communist Party, criticized the government's fiscal policy towards Slovakia (Pithart 1990, 83–85). The Party was divided between those, mainly Czechs, who emphasized democratization as a precondition of federalization and those, chiefly Slovaks, who lobbied for federalization as a precursor to democratization (Enský 1978, 97–99). Communist hardliners rejected the idea of federalization altogether, worrying that it could provide a common ground for the reformists and at the same time erode the authority of the unified Communist party (Kaplan 1989, 343). Once again, federalism was used as an instrument to advance other political goals; the blueprint for institutional federalization was made primarily with the communist hardliners in mind.

(v) Post-invasion Communist power-consolidation   After the Soviet military invasion of August 1968 institutional federalization did take place. The quest for federalization played a crucial role in the actions of communist collaborators with the Soviets. Just one day after the invasion, the Communist Party of Czechoslovakia hurriedly held an extraordinary congress that expressed support for the reformist leadership. Given the circumstances, some Slovak deputies were not able to come. In accordance with the Soviet interests in the country the hardliners argued that the congress was invalid, because it 'was called to session without a consultation with the Central Committee of the Communist Party of Slovakia and therefore that the Slovaks were marginalized at [it]' (Pithart 1990, 87).

Two dynamics indicate the instrumental appropriation of federalism by the new communist leadership headed by the 1950's 'bourgeois nationalist' prisoner Gustáv Husák. First, the Communist Party remained asymmetrical—i.e., there were only two organizations, one for Czechoslovakia and another one for Slovakia, but without a Czech counterpart (Steiner 1973, 200). Only governments and parliaments (largely meaningless under the communist rule) were established symmetrically. Second, despite federal institutional setup, Husák's leadership emphasized the centralization of state-power. The 1970 amendment to the Federation Law turned federalism into a mere rhetorical device rather than a practical means for decision-making (Žák 1995, 246).

(vi) Post-Communist transformation after 1989   After the fall of communism, calls to improve principles of federal power-sharing were used by political actors who were otherwise unable, or unwilling, to express their reservations against what they perceived as harsh and overly rapid socio-economic reforms. These calls were interspersed with symbolic concerns related to the transformation process. Disputes over the official name of the common state started shortly after November 1989. Some— like Václav Havel and the majority of Czech politicians—called for reinstating the country's inter-war appellation Czechoslovak Republic (Československá republika), or Czechoslovakia (Československo). Others, predominantly Slovak representatives demanded a new name Czecho-Slovakia (Česko-Slovensko) in order to increase the visibility of the federal principle. A provisional compromise was reached in April 1990 when the country switched to the name Czech and Slovak Federative Republic. The issue was left settled permanently after the coming elections.

The attempts to amend the federal constitution, however, led to no conclusion. The legislative period 1990–1992 brought about initiatives to reconstitute federal principles but led to no real reform (for instance, Innes [2001, 115–146] provides a detailed account of numerous failed initiatives). Instead, the result was widespread disenchantment with federalism. Eager to move on with 'the real' (i.e. economic) reforms, many Czech politicians framed these debates as pointless, whereas many Slovak politicians were anxious about the impact of the fast-paced laissez faire economic reforms that were already starting to take place. Because of the industrial structure of the country, these reforms were almost certain to disproportionately affect the Slovaks (Příhoda 1995, 136). By 1991, unemployment in the Czech Republic rose from the full employment during communism to 4.4 per cent, while in Slovakia it was nearly three times as much at 11.8 per cent (Leff 1996, 183). In a situation when criticizing economic reforms bore the risk of being accused of supporting the fallen communist regime, discussing the symbolical and organizational aspects of the federation was a much safer route. Symbolic politics of federalism enabled the critics to express claims for differentiation without having to openly present a request for the reconsideration of the unitary policy of the economic reform. This informed the 1992 electoral campaign, which ex post can be clearly seen as critical for the fate of Czechoslovak federation and federalism. The quick deal between Klaus and Mečiar that split the country suggests that once again federalism was not addressed directly and the issue of national accommodation within the state became a smokescreen for competing ideas about and control of economic transformation.

Federal identity and its competitors

Czechoslovak federalism was repeatedly used instrumentally—both prior to, during and after the communist period—as a means to reach political goals other than self-determination of multiple selves, because of the weak conceptualization of the Czechoslovak political identity and the nature of collective identities competing with it. The six critical moments in Czechoslovak history uncovered the public need to address the issues pertaining to Czechoslovak multilayered identities directly and comprehensively but the country's foundational myths did not allow for federalist self-image, thus making such discussion extremely difficult.

Daniel Weinstock argues that foundational myths are critically important for federalism and distinguishes two ideal-typical situations of federation-building and two types of collective myths. Federations can be divided into integrative, formed in the fusion of formerly self-governing units, and restructuring, arising in an act of power-devolution (Weinstock 2001, 76). Foundational myths can be either nostalgic, 'mark[ing] the point at which a group awakens to its status as a collective subject … and becomes a nation *für sich*,' or aspirational, republican in character and 'future-oriented,' if they 'highlight an idealized historical event' this event 'is not represented as having given rise to the nation as such' (Weinstock 2005, 214). The most problematic configuration arises when a federation is formed out of formerly self-governing units that base their respective identities on nostalgic foundational myths (213). The constituent communities continue seeing their own groups as the primary object of solidarity and have difficulties in accepting overarching, federal sets of myths voluntaristically imposed by political elites dedicated to federalism as a normative concept (225). Moreover, nostalgic myths 'are often built around narratives' that cast their neighboring communities, which are most probably to be their federative partners, 'in a negative light' (213).

From the perspective of Wienstock's typology, the Czechoslovak case is approximating the most problematic constellation. Yet, it is not an ideal-type and its divergence from such a type shows possibilities to overcome the problems. First, neither the Czechlands nor Slovakia were self-governing units prior to 1918 as both were parts of the Habsburg Empire. Second, there were no mutual animosities in the Czech and Slovak foundational myths. Ordinary language discloses this. While having derogatory phrases involving all other nations from the former Empire, the two languages lack derogatory phrases referring to Slovaks and Czechs respectively.

Third, as both nations were formed during the incorporation into the Empire, Slovak and Czech foundational myths were partly also aspirational, aimed at future self-rule, though in the Slovak case expressed as only a cultural autonomy rather than full-fledged political independence. Fourth, Slovak collective identity around 1918 was still being created and thus was open to creative intervention that could attune it positively towards federalism.

At the same time, however, the two group's foundational myths presented serious hindrances to successful federalism. The Czechs centered their myths on the idea of past statehood that was lost to the Habsburgs and that should be regained (Suda 1995, 116). According to Ute Raßloff, the emblematic building block of the Czech myth was 'the existence of the Czech nation/rulers/culture' as 'a positive value' (1999, 257) which allowed for the 'non-Czech' to be easily equaled with 'barbarism' and a lack of value (1999, 255). Hence, the Czech foundational myth was, first, strongly nostalgic in Weinstock's terms and, second, potentially hostile to those who challenged its self-governing component.

The new Czechoslovak state provided an ambiguous fulfillment of the aspirational part of the Czech foundational myth. Indeed, in 1918, most Czechs considered the new Czechoslovak state as the fulfillment of their aspirations for self-determination. Yet, in keeping intact the myth of the Czech historical nation and at the same time acknowledging the reality of the Czechoslovak state, for Czechs the terms 'Czech' and 'Czechoslovak' became largely interchangeable (Pithart 2000, 229).

While Czechoslovakia as a country became part of the Czech national myth, the Slovaks as people did not. This 'led to a superior, or at best, patronizing attitude' towards the latter (Steiner 1973, 18). Over the whole existence of the common state the Slovaks remained the Czechs' 'younger brother', as if perpetually in a pubescent age (Pithart 2000, 231). 'The younger brother is always only of peripheral interest to us, even though we basically like him, because he bores us: we are going to dancing lessons ... and he is only beginning to smoke', writes Pithart. Yet, from the perspective of inherently adversary nature of the Czech myth, such infantilization should be viewed as an act of good will and as an attempt of inclusion: they have to remain minors, never reaching adulthood, as that would make them into 'non-Czechs'. In a prescient article published in an exile journal Jan Příbram (a pen-name) grasped the intertwining lines of Czech simultaneous inclusion and rejection of Slovaks:

> We take your burden onto ourselves, incorporating your poor land into our economy; we will develop your administration, school system; we will supply you with our experts. ... You will then set off the journey we already trod; you will appropriate our way of thinking and our view of the world; you will take up our understanding of history and values; you will develop your national community after our image, take up our customs, our sympathies and antipathies (and our inner conflicts) and will stand on our side in the political arena. ... We will help you get rid of everything that could prevent your from doing this, of your virtues and vices, anyway backward, of your memories and traditions, anyway clouded. ... You will, of course, speak Slovak; you will keep your eccentricity – we do like your folklore (Příbram 1976, 644).

The fact that the Czech foundational myth was capable of appropriating Czechoslovakia as the Czech homeland meant that it did not have to cope with the difference between Czechness and Czechoslovakness. The existence of Slovakness that could pose challenge to such an overlap was channeled through the idea of the young brother.

The unfinished formation of Slovak identity in 1918 paved the way to Czech fraternal infantilization. Yet, its different trajectory, developmental delay as well as certain nostalgic components proved to be incompatible with the Czech foundational myths and their incorporation of Slovakness and Czechoslovakness. Slovak nation-building was delayed vis-à-vis their referential neighbors, most importantly the Hungarians and the Czechs (Maxwell 2002; 2005). Indeed, the Slovak foundational myths were much less complex than the Czech ones, distinguishing only two moments of mythical past: a ninth-century Christian state of Great Moravia that was defeated by the ancient Hungarians and the nineteenth-century Slovak suffering from the consequences of the Hungarian national project that sought to 'Magyarize' non-Hungarian groups (Pynsent 1994, 159–170). Lacking a mythical idea of a Slovak medieval kingdom, Slovak political imagery was shaped by their life in the Empire. Their aspirational element was modeled after Hungary's successful quest for autonomy in Austria-Hungary, on which their idea of Czecho-Slovakia was modeled (Rychlík 2007, 15).

But nation-building is an evolving phenomenon that imports ideas from more mature nationalisms which it then indigenously adapts (Greenfeld 1992, 14). In this case, the Slovak political identity was subject to further development using the Czech identity as the primary point of reference. The war-time experience of self-rule, albeit severely limited and morally very problematic, as well as of a significant collective action in the form of the 1944 uprising, which was unprecedented in Slovak history, jointly added a political dimension to the Slovak concept of nationhood pushing the national self-image closer to developmental level of the Czechs. During the uprising the Slovak National Council captured this advancement well when it declared that: 'We [i.e. the Slovaks] stand for a Czechoslovak Republic as an independent and common state of Czechs, Slovaks and Carpathian Ukrainians [in the interwar period also belonging to Czechoslovakia] on the principle of equality' (quoted in Steiner 1973, 71). Yet, the fact that Slovak identity politically matured only within the context of Czechoslovakia provided for its inherent, if not sufficiently articulated or reflected, conceptual separation between Slovakness and Czechoslovakness, in which the latter is in instrumental service of the former, as opposed to the Czech unproblematic and thus egalitarian conflation of Czechness and Czechoslovakness.

While the Slovak foundational myths did not encompass any animosity towards the Czechs, their hostility towards the Hungarians eventually clashed with the Czech well-meant reception of Slovaks as young brothers. The mythical self-view portrayed the Slovaks as those who brought civilization to the backward Hungarians (Pynsent 1994, 154–155). The Czech transfer of human, civilizational and economic resources to Slovakia clashed with this component of the Slovak foundational myth, making the Slovaks resentful of both the Czech aid—leading some Slovak leaders to deny Slovak economic backwardness—and brotherly affection. This gradually made the Slovaks, in the subconscious myth-performing and myth-affirming realm, view their identity as being threatened by the Czechs.

Being at once the bearers of both Czech and Slovak predominantly nostalgic foundational myths and concurrently the founders of a new polity in an adversarial situation of post-war, post-Empire political reorganization, Czechoslovak leaders of the interwar era were unable to articulate (or understand) the value of Czechoslovakness as a federal identity in Weinstock's aspirational terms. Equally, federal identity was not formulated as inclusive of or compatible with both the Czech and the Slovak expectations formed by their respective foundational myths. Neither was Czechoslovakia publicly justified on pragmatic grounds. The understanding of Czechoslovakness in terms of greater cultural richness, exchange, broader scope of reference as well as of greater political justice and stability evolved within only a small segment of Czechoslovak citizens, mostly those with firsthand experience of mixed family or territorial mobility.

For difficult federal mythical constellations like the Czechoslovak one, Weinstock suggests that the articulation of the value of federation to each group does not need to be identical, allowing thus for certain incompatibility of mythical ties with the federation (Weinstock 2005, 226). This was indirectly attempted in the last public debate on the value of Czechoslovak federation, in 1990–1992, centered around and mockingly called after the meaning of the hyphen in the word Czecho-Slovakia as the 'Hyphen War' (Rychlík 2000, 52–52). The Czech claim that the hyphen was a sign of unacceptable and unnecessary divisions disclosed their leaning towards Czechoslovakia as a single political community that devolved chiefly on grounds of administrative convenience and efficiency (Weinstock 2001, 78). The Slovak claim that the hyphen joined the two equal components disclosed a tendency to see the federation as an integrative project fusing two previously self-governing groups. Obviously, both views were partially (in)correct, which explains the instinctive rejection of each respective party to the opposite conception. Memoirs of those present at the post-election negotiations in summer 1992 disclose the very moment when this realization of difference happened (Macek 2000, 242).

Czechoslovakia and the Hypotheses on Federal Failure

The Czechoslovak case directly relates to three hypotheses on defunct federalism. First, it invites a dialogue with the suggestion that federalism fails if a political community does not adhere to liberal democratic rules and principles. Second, it questions the validity of the claim that asymmetrical institutional arrangements are more conducive to successful federalism. Third, the Czechoslovak case gives support to the suggested correlation between instrumental use of federalism and its failure.

The Czechoslovak case suggests the possibility that federalism might 'succeed' within the framework of a non-liberal regime and, more importantly, in turn, also be vulnerable to the practices of liberal democracy. Rather than the actual institutions of liberal democracy, it might be the degree of openness to question all aspects of political nationhood as well as particular discursive properties of public discussion on the issue of federalism that provide for federalism's success/failure in liberal democracies.

Admittedly, the fact that practices of liberal democracy had been established only shortly before the federation's break-up makes this case less than ideal for examining the link between liberal democracy and successful federalism. One should ask whether the differences could have been reconciled had liberal democracy been more firmly entrenched. What undermined the federation was sudden openness of a previously restricted public sphere, in which even challenging the boundaries of the political community ceased to be taboo, meeting with a history of discursive inability and reluctance to address the tensions and differences between various existing expectations about the federal state. Federal legislative mechanisms inherited from the Communist period were, paradoxically, also exceptionally open to minority challenges on crucial questions of the state's existence (Stanger 2000, 143), as their Communist authors did not (have to) take institutional precautions against dissent. The popular feeling that the split came by surprise and too quickly does not suggest lack of liberalism or democracy but a lack of institutional and discursive mechanisms that would facilitate, deepen and most probably develop and lengthen the public discussion on the issue of federalism that might have brought Czechoslovakia close to, for example, the Canadian depth and length of the federal debate. The Czechoslovak case and the speed of its split in an exceptionally open setting signals a certain conservative tendency towards state boundaries in established liberal democracies, which, if federal, keep their comprehensive debates on the value of federalism to a less open and taboo-breaking period. Indeed, it might be this very tendency that contributes to the survival of multinational federations as liberal democracies, rather than an intrinsic link between federalism and liberal democratic regime.

The case of Czechoslovakia also challenges the second hypothesis, specifically its suggestion that asymmetrical institutional designs are advantageous. If there was one single institutional feature that had long-term detrimental effect on the success of the Czechoslovak federation, it was the lack of symmetry in state institutions, and in the communist period, also of the Communist Party apparatus. This institutional asymmetry reiterated and fostered asymmetry in the layered identities among Czechoslovakia's citizens. Those who understood Czech and Czechoslovak identities as interchangeable could not easily understand the relationship between Slovak and Czechoslovak as that of two different layers. In turn, the latter considered the unproblematic equation of Czechness and Czechoslovakness as exclusionary towards their own identity. Equally, those satisfied with Czechoslovakia as a unitary state considered federalism a wasteful institutional superstructure. To those demanding the institutional mirroring of multilayered collective identities, the asymmetrical federation did not go far enough. The compromise that was reached over the country's name during the disputes in the early 1990—Czechoslovakia for the Czechs, Czecho-Slovakia for the Slovaks—is only a bizarre illustration of the perils of asymmetry. Institutional asymmetries were attacked from two opposite directions: as signs of privilege rather than a principle of accommodation and as manifestations of lacking equal treatment.

The history of Czechoslovak federalism gives full support to the third hypothesis on defunct federalism, which links the failure of federalism to its imposition. More subtly, the hypothesis distinguishes between federalism as a means and federalism as an end. The instrumental function of Czechoslovak federalism, as identified in this chapter, is precisely a case of federalism that was, time and again, used as the means towards other political ends. It was never understood as a good in its own right. Equally, within economies of collective identities existing among Czechoslovak citizens, the two most dominant ideas of selfhood, Czechness and Slovakness, did not allow for the Czechoslovak identity as anything but an instrument for their own betterment and survival, rather than an identity that allows for a greater field of moral, cultural and political values pertaining to one's identity.

Conclusion

Thanks to its peaceful, swift, and smooth character, the dissolution of Czechoslovakia came to be known as the 'velvet divorce'. If they talk about the break-up of the common state at all, both Czechs and Slovaks tend to stress the orderly manner in which it took place, taking satisfaction and pride in showing how they managed the split, especially in comparison to Yugoslavia. The nearly idyllic view of the past gets support by references to intensive and friendly relationship between the two countries since 1993. Nevertheless, this rosy picture also reflects an aversion to deeper consideration of what went wrong with and in the common state. The remark of president Klaus at the start of this chapter typifies this attitude.

The fundamental question repeatedly asked by the students of the Czechoslovak case is whether the federation's dissolution was the culmination of a longer trajectory of discord or an accidental cluster of events that led to an unintended outcome? In his authoritative book on Europe's post-World War II history, Tony Judt leans to the latter conclusion, claiming that the division of Czechoslovakia was 'a product of chance and circumstances … with other people in control—with different outcomes at the elections of 1990 and 1992—the story would not have been the same' (Judt 2005, 664). Carol Skalnik Leff, who is one of few scholars working with the idea of Czechoslovak federal crisis and possible break-up still before the fall of its communist regime, gives support to the long-term view (Leff 1988). This chapter tries to show that both Judt and Leff can be right once federalism as a normative concept becomes the main focus of inquiry. As this chapter explains, the instrumental use and construction of Czechoslovak federalism could fill the gap of the absent Czechoslovak federal identity only temporarily and under certain internal and/or external conditions.

Such conclusion suggests that the success of federalism depends on the clear articulation of its values, of the contribution it makes towards political freedom, justice, and democratic accountability, to economic and ideational competitiveness as well as cultural richness. Federalism should not be construed as a second-best option—for instance to provide external security or achieve the suppression of domestic opponents. As any public articulation of values involves public discussion that is inherently open to disagreement, tension and contestation, successful federalism requires institutional and discursive mechanisms that keep discussion alive over a longer period of time, facilitating an environment in which the possibilities of the 'life and death' of a particular federation can be openly discussed while protecting the singular stages of the discussion, especially the initial ones, from being killed by the severity of the issue. Finally, the link between multinational federalism and self-determination places a greater burden on the articulation of the content of the multiple 'selves'. This process requires constructive work with communities' foundational myths that would lend support to the need for resolute dedication to the values of federalism.

Chapter 11

The Soviet People: The Rise and Fall of an Ideological Federalism

Ivan Gololobov

Introduction

The phenomenon of Soviet federalism—its emergence, development, and demise—have been preoccupying scholarly and policy imagination for a number of years. In this respect, the disintegration of the Soviet Union presents one of the more interesting examples of federal failure not only because of the size and geopolitical influence of the collapsed empire but also because of the particular historical contingencies of this event. Despite their variations, the dominant hypotheses of the theory of defunct federalism seem to share a conviction that the inconsistencies of particular federal arrangements emanate from a problematic relationship between the federal center and the substate units.

The claim here is that the Soviet case does not conform to this conceptual framework. The theory of defunct federalism assumes that the distinct identities of federal units exist *prior* the relations of federalization and the ideology of federalism. The experience of the Soviet Union contradicts such claims. There, federalism *preceded* not only the formation of state institutions, but also the *consolidation* of the identities of the 'Soviet peoples and nations'. In this respect, it is difficult to gauge the failure of Soviet federalism from the perspective of the theory of defunct federalism that seems to dominate the literature. Instead, the modalities of Soviet federalism need to be accounted for from the standpoint of the ideology that animated its processes and structures.

In this respect, prior to its discussion of the Soviet failed federal experience and the federal versus national identity of the 'Soviet people', this chapter briefly engages the dominant perceptions of the meaning and uses of 'ideology' in order to arrive at a useful understanding of its contextualization to the experience of Soviet federalism. On this background, the articulation of a Soviet federal identity is positioned within the discursive uses of communist ideology. The contention is that despite its analytical opacity, the narrative analysis of Soviet federalism illuminates the constructs that animated its dynamics (Seliktar 2004, 6). The dislocations apparent in the discursive articulations of federalism underwrite the explanation and understanding of the failures of Soviet statehood and its accommodation of diverse identities. The chapter concludes with a discussion of the inadequacies of the Soviet-promoted ideological federalism.

Ideology

The focus on the ideological dimension of Soviet federalism requires a clarification of its meaning. Clifford Geertz has long acknowledged that 'it is one of the minor ironies of modern intellectual history that the term "ideology" has itself become thoroughly ideologized' (Geertz 1993, 193). Similar doubts were expressed by Robert Putnam, who suggested that 'diving into the cold and dark water of the literature on "ideology" is a shocking and disappointing experience for any promising supporter of social science' (Putnam 1971, 651). Despite the seeming definitional confusion, the 'dark waters' of the concept of ideology indicate a clear infusion with the notion of identity. In a federal context, ideology is sometimes conceived as the idiomatic articulation of a vision of imaginative unity: in a sense, therefore, ideology is a combination of a mediating role between the utterances of social knowledge whose function is to organize different representations of identity with the mystification (in the sense of flexible exploration) of cultural and subjective phenomena (Kavalski 2005, 29; van der Linden 2008). Said otherwise, ideology and identity evince a symbiotic interconnection, which cannot be feasibly disentangled. Thus, whether it is through a reference to the Marxist 'false consciousness', which subverted the 'true class identity' (Marx and Engels 1970), a mention of a tool or an instrument used by elites in their political games (Putnam 1971), or a post-Marxist allusion to creating particular social groups (Althusser 1971), the issue of identity has been at the centre of understanding and explaining ideology.

Contemporary social theory considers identity as a fluid process (rather than a fixed state), whereby in the context of multiple interactions particular social arrangements obtain their objectivity (Laclau 1985; Laclau 1990; Howarth 2000; van der Linden 2008). In this respect, identity is seen more as a project aimed at obtaining impossible fullness of social agency that requires a particular method of its analysis focused on temporal, rather than spatial dimensions concentrating on the processes rather than static 'relations'. The remainder of this chapter, therefore, accounts for the failure of Soviet federalism by exploring the alterations in Soviet Marxism—the overarching ideological doctrine of the Soviet state—and the transformations in the identity-perceptions of the 'Soviet person' or the 'Soviet people' during the last decades of the Soviet history.

The Soviet People

> Twenty-six attempts preceded the present genesis, all of which were destined to fail. The world of man has arisen out of the chaotic heart of the preceding debris; he too is exposed to the risk of failure, and the return to nothing. 'Let's hope it works'… exclaimed God as he created the World, and this hope, which has accompanied all the subsequent history of the world and mankind, has emphasized right from the outset that this history is branded with the mark of radical uncertainty (Prigogine et al. 1985, 313).

It did not. And the 'twenty seventh attempt' to create the world was not the last one. The entire subsequent history of humanity consists of eternal struggles between the organizing reason seeking to bring a particular order in the world of humans and chaos dissolving this order into a stream of spontaneous, unpredictable and irreversible events. This research is devoted to one example, where a formerly stable social order falls into pieces, one more time proving the truth of the Creator's concern. It is the dissolution of the Union of Soviet Socialist Republics (USSR), the first socialist state, which, like all other 'attempts', was thought to be the last response to the challenges of the chaos and the final organisation of the eternal world.

Among the many reasons for the disintegration of the Soviet Union some of the more oft-quoted are economic problems related to the mismanagement of the plan-economy and the bureaucratization of the party-state (Boettke 1993; Dowlah et al. 1997; Xenaxis 2002). Yet, this event can also be explained from a different perspective—namely, the Soviet Union collapsed as a result of the profound ideological crisis of its society. The devaluation and impoverishment of the communist ideology underwrote the crisis of the common Soviet identity and set the stage for the divorce in the federal 'family of peoples'.

The Soviet *people*, the Soviet *family of peoples*, the *people* and the *peoples* (plural) of the Soviet Union: all these terms used interchangeably in the texts of the Soviet epoch may confuse any unprepared reader. Indeed the Soviet identity was a complicated discursive construction based on the interplay of ethno-national differences, the modalities of class and ideological equivalences whose particular combination resulted in the fixture of a particular articulation of the 'Soviet people'.

The October Revolution of 1917 was mythologized as a revolution of the working people. Following Marx, the idea of the class dominated the debates on political embodiment of the new society. The leaders of the Revolution appealed to the 'working people', or the 'workers and the peasants' as the dominant identities recognized (recognizable) by the emerging order of the 'liberated world' (Kowalski 1997). The other divisions, including the national ones, were not regarded as remnants of an anachronistic past. With regard to the possible federalization of the new state on the basis of national principle, Lenin said:

> Marxists are, of course, opposed to federation and decentralization, for the simple reason that capitalism requires for its development the largest and most centralized possible states. Other conditions being equal, the class-conscious proletariat will always stand for the larger state. It will always fight against medieval particularism, and will always welcome the closest possible economic amalgamation of large territories in which the proletariat's struggle against the bourgeoisie can develop on a broad basis. Capitalism's broad and rapid development of the productive forces calls for large, politically compact and united territories, since only here can the bourgeois class—together with its inevitable antipode, the proletarian class—unite and sweep away all the old, medieval, caste, parochial, petty-national, religious and other barriers (Lenin 1964, 45).

Yet, straight after the success of the October Revolution the views of the Bolsheviks shifted radically. In 1918, the Russian Civil War broke out and the revolutionary government found itself besieged by a number of aggressive enemies. Although all of these posed an existential threat to the 'Red' Soviet government, the 'White' counter-revolutionary armies were billeted for particular securitization (Lincoln 1999; Wade 2005). In order to confront them, the Bolsheviks had to galvanize popular support for their cause and, therefore, found themselves appropriating the modalities of nationalism. Thus, while the Whites relied on their 'Great Russia' chauvinism, the fledgling Soviet authorities recognized the existence of different 'peoples' and 'nations' on the territory of the Soviet state and acknowledged their right for some degree of autonomy (Lenin 1964, 423). As some commentators have noted, Lenin made a U-turn from his previous statements by arguing that 'self-determination was a useful revolutionary slogan' which would lose its force once the revolutionary class had seized power and multinational states merged into a unitary socialist order—i.e., a 'socialist (communist) federation' (Hasani 2003, 71).

This ideological intervention certainly had the great tactical value of bringing non-Russian national movements under the banner of the Soviet government. However, it also had significant longer-term consequences. The national dimension entered the project of socialist revolution. The existence of different national groups was not only formally recognized, but it was also enshrined in the legal framework of Soviet statehood. Federalism, thereby, became an ideological tool for the Soviet regime. It created federal units on the assumption that they would satisfy the aspirations of different national identities. Branko Milanovic (1994, 63–64) remarks that in this way the ideological federalism of the Soviet Union 'helped others who lacked strong national feelings ... and [who] most likely would have been absorbed, had Czarist Russia continued to develop along capitalist lines ... to "discover themselves" and also created state structures for them'. In this respect, Philip Roeder (1991, 197–199) observes that:

> [T]he architects of the Soviet regime came to understand that federal institutions could expand their control over the politicization of ethnicity. Within each homeland, the regime created a cadre of party and state officials drawn from the indigenous ethnic group but dependent upon Moscow for its members' positions. As the cadre was assigned monopoly over the mobilizational resources within the ethnic community, it determined when the ethnic group would be mobilized to action. It was a strategy that achieved interethnic peace not so much by removing the root causes of ethnic grievances as by eliminating mobilizational opportunities for independent ethnic protest.

Such instrumental use of federalism—i.e., the subjugation of federalist structures to the objectives of ideology—allowed the Soviet regime to manipulate and suppress the expression of national identities; however, as the Soviet Union industrialized, the 'indigenous cadres "became instruments of the new ethnic assertiveness"' (Dorff 1994, 103). These developments towards the politicization of national identity prompted the task of articulating a novel discursive legitimation for the narrative, functional and political coexistence of the unity of the working class (the driving force of the socialist revolution) with the recognition of ethno-national differences (and their federally-constituted political entrepreneurs). A new discourse was about to emerge—the discourse of Soviet Marxism.

Discourse

The notion of discourse is apprehended here as a sphere '[that] includes all the practices and meanings shaping a particular community of social actors. In these perspectives, discourses constitute symbolic systems and social orders, and the task of discourse analysis is to examine their historical and political construction and functioning' (Howarth 2000, 5). The fact that all identities are assumed to be the objects of discourse, however, does not refer to the debates on the primacy of thought over matter or the other way around (Wodak and Chilton 2005).

Laclau and Mouffe, for instance, argue that the focus on the discursive emergence of identities does not mean that there is no world external to thought. What is questioned is that the reality external to thought has its meaning independent from the discursive condition of its emergence.

> The fact that every object is constituted as an object of discourse has *nothing to do* [emphasis original] with whether there is a world external to thought, or with the realism/ idealism opposition. An earthquake or the falling of a brick is an event that certainly exists, in the sense that it occurs, here and now, independently on my will. But whether their specificity as objects is constructed in terms of 'natural phenomena' or 'expressions of the wrath of God', depends upon the structuring of a discursive field. What is denied is not that such objects exist externally to thought, but the rather different assertion that they could constitute themselves as objects outside any discursive condition of emergence (Laclau et al. 1985, 108).

In this respect, the main focus of discourse analysis appears to be defined by the question of why the materiality of surrounding realities becomes interpreted in this way, rather than another. Why, for example, does the forest standing on the path of a proposed motorway become an 'obstacle' to be passed through, the 'nation's heritage' to be saved or the 'object of naturalists' interest' (Howarth 2000, 101–102)? These differences are assumed to be constructed discursively through the production of a certain knowledge, which constitutes the object of the 'forest'. It is this process which entails the construction and dissolution of things, events, and social identities as 'objects' from the surrounding realities.

In order to see how particular identities are constructed, how they change and how they dissolve we need to look at the discursive conditions of their articulation. In this respect, it is necessary to analyze the production of certain concepts—for instance, the fixing of the meaning of class, nation, or any other form of identity— and, then, to investigate their translation into the fabric of actual social relations. The discursive construction of reality, however, is not a linear process. Referring to this unevenness, Laclau distinguishes between two types of social situations: the 'period of stability' and the 'crisis' (Laclau 1979, 102). In general terms the periods of stability are characterized by the capacity of active knowledge to 'neutralize' the contradictions invoked by certain social events, and also the ability of discourse to retain its ideological unity. In other words, 'stability' is understood as the time when the totality of happening events is more or less explainable within a given system of knowledge. The crisis, on the contrary, is the situation when actual reality and the structures of knowledge appear to be split. This makes events meaningless and meanings unable to be discerned in real practices and relations. In the situation of crisis, existing social formations loose their stability and become a complex narrative terrain where processes are unpredictable and contingent.

Discursive Construction of the Soviet People

The construction of the Soviet people is a result of a number of discursive articulations aiming at the fixing of a particular system of meaningfulness to the Soviet society. Its narration was triggered by the immense discursive rupture of the October Revolution. The old system of social organization was destroyed but the new one was still to come. Several steps were undertaken before the new identity was fixed in the ideology and the institutional organization of the Soviet state. As already mentioned, the classical form of Marxism was confronted with the need to recognize the tactical importance of national demands and ethno-cultural heterogeneity. What might have been at first recognized as a disturbing presence of national sentiments was strategically inscribed within the logic of Soviet Marxism (Kemp 2001; Martin 2001; van der Linden 2008). It outlined the narrative of the *socialist state,* which supplanted the imaginary of a *socialist world revolution.* The project of building a socialist state became a ground which attempted to achieve the reconciliation of particularistic national interests and identities on the one hand and the universalizing demand of the liberation of the working class on the other.

Although a Soviet statehood had officially been proclaimed, the *socialist state* was still very much a 'work in progress'—that is, the formal institutional content of the state still had to be established (Kenez 2006; van der Linden 2008). In fact, there was little clarity as regards the outlines of territorial borders; the economy was collapsing; there were no identifiable state symbols, no constitution, nor any other stable corpus of state-legislation. The USSR was, thereby, an 'empty signifier'— or, rather, *a signifier of absence.* Thus, on an analytical level its political reality bore resemblance to the Hobbesian 'order'. In other words, in a situation of total chaos it meant literally anything but the absence of disorder; nevertheless, *being* (and, at the same time, *becoming*) a nodal point fixing the sense of other notions such as sovereignty, authority, etc.

The emptiness of the model of Soviet statehood was a powerful discursive instrument that permitted multiple sectors of the society to identify their hopes and interests with this concept (i.e., *fill in* its void). Its *dispositif* allowed Lenin's Bolsheviks to assume the symbolism of the Soviet state. They established a discursive hegemony, which postulated that the way in which different groups could fulfill their identities was not in opposition to each other but in equivalence to the common struggle *for* the Soviet state. In an environment characterized by the actual absence of such a state, this demand for equivalence was essentially fixed by the antagonism to the common enemies (Laclau et al. 1985, 122–127).

Antagonism should not be seen as a real opposition of two actors with autonomously constituted identities, as is advocated, for example, by the Kantian tradition. Neither does antagonism imply a logical contradiction. Discursive antagonism is viewed here as a situation where the actor *A* appears to be unable to reach his or her identity because of the presence of the actor *B*. Illustrating this situation Howarth points that 'peasants expelled from their land by capitalist farmers and forced to become workers in the city, are literally prevented from "being peasants" and thus experience a "blockage" or "failure" of identity' (Howarth 2000, 105).

Clarifying the importance of antagonism in constituting a discursive formation, Laclau argues that an identification of the 'other' draws a frontier between the 'inside' and the 'outside' of a discourse, which reveals the limits of intelligible social organisation and makes possible achieving one's own identity (Laclau 1990, 17–18). In the Soviet discursive articulations the world of capital was identified as this antagonist blocking any possible realization of the national identities, while the prospects of building the socialist state were seen as this discursive space where such identities could be finally achieved.

Such a narrative construction turned out to be quite valuable in the process of legitimation of the Bolshevik ideology. The discursive power of its expressions was enhanced by numerous re-articulations of the actual threats to the system and the ever-growing list of 'enemies', which assisted the identification through relations of equivalence: (i) during the 1920s these were the new bourgeoisie and the New Economic Policy-promoters, 'selling' the revolutionary passion; (ii) during the 1930s these were the 'enemies of the people' betraying their 'Soviet Motherland' and sabotaging the 'constructing sites of communism'; and (iii) during the 1940s the threat to the socialist state was even more existential as it became an object of military aggression, etc. (Schapiro 1960). In the wake of the World War II, the inception of the Cold War provided the USSR with an omnipresent ideological, political, diplomatic, economic and military 'other'. The constant articulation of the threat posed by the antagonist in the post-war period ensured the stabilization of the discursive structure of the Soviet society (Daniels 1993). The Soviet propaganda vilified the allegedly oppressive nature of Western capitalism and accused it of threading heavily on the right to national self-determination. For instance, individuals such as Nelson Mandela, Angela Davis, leaders of indigenous movements, and other political activists against the 'capitalist oppressors' were *sacralized* by the Soviet propaganda—not merely as freedom-fighters, but as advocates of socialist statehood. In this respect, both the legitimation and the realization of individual identity through the discursive frames of the socialist state remained valid.

Yet, the suggested stabilization of the Soviet federal narratives had another important implication. The pre-communist array of social distinctions and differences was increasingly diminished, and under the project of 'building a Soviet state' appeared to be getting more and more homogenized. The ethno-national differences between various groups of the Soviet society lost their value in the struggle with the 'capitalist bloc'. In both scholarly and policy discussion, the 'peoples' of the Soviet Socialist Republics were gradually substituted by 'nationalities' and 'ethnic groups'. The title of 'people' in its turn started to be applied to the new social formation—the Soviet people (Baghoorn 1956). The concept of the 'Soviet people' was enshrined in the Soviet Constitution (Kukushkin et al. 1987, 315–317) and endorsed by innumerable academic reflections in the Soviet social sciences (Kim 1972). A peculiar instance of the discursive reality of the Soviet identity was the October 1972 conference on 'The Soviet People—A New Historical Unity of the People'

(Kenez 2006). In this respect, the empty signifier of the common identity (which made it a politically pliable tool permitting the inclusion of a wide range of diverse demands) appeared to be finally fixed by the rhetorical enunciation of homogeneous supra-national Soviet people.

Ideological Ambivalence of Soviet Marxism and Multiple Dislocations in the Soviet Discourse

Much ink has been squandered in attempting to understand and to explain the historical failure of the alleged unity of the Soviet identity and its institutional embodiment—the USSR (Kempton et al. 2002; Walker 2003). The suggestion here is that the disintegration of the Soviet federal experiment (and the federal identity with which it was intertwined) is linked to the internal inconsistencies of the Soviet brand of Marxist ideology rather than predetermined by any particular historical abnormality or contradictions of institutional organization (Hickey et al. 1996; Kux 1990; McAuley 1991; van der Linden 2008).

In this respect, Rachel Walker (1989) points out that the Soviet theory of Marxism-Leninism evinces a profound structural inconsistency. It is fostered by the conflicting rhetorical demands creating (and upholding the conceptual integrity of) the Soviet people as 'builders of communism'. On the one hand, there was the insistence on maintaining the revolutionary fervor and creativity; and, on the other, the call for almost religious admiration and unquestionable respect for the grand ideologues of the Soviet communist trinity—Marx, Engels and Lenin. The latter demand—with its assertions of the necessity of 'loyalty to Marxist-Leninist teachings'—hindered (if not made unfeasible) the very possibility for constructive debates.

Such contradiction of Soviet Marxism generated a discursive tension within the identity-doctrine of federalism, which reflected the dislocating potential implicit in its ideology. The notion of dislocation is understood as a disruption of the symbolic organization invoked by occurrences which cannot or can be hardly symbolized within a given discursive order (Howarth et al. 2000, 13–14). The dissolution of ideological unity leads towards the inability to apprehend the ongoing performances of the surrounding reality. It is a situation in which meanings (and meaningfulness) appear to fall out of the field of intelligibility.

There have been a number of serious dislocations in the genealogy of the Soviet people. For instance, the institutionalization of forced labour during Stalin's regime was a marked departure from the notion of 'liberated labour' (Lenin 1965, 126), which underpinned the Bolshevik Revolution. The fissures opened by this contradiction were further compounded by Khrushchev's liberalization, which caused a massive dislocation among Stalin's admirers and apologists. At the same time, the analytical unpacking of the 'untouchable' ideas of Marx and Lenin undermined the conviction in the Soviet doctrine as the 'only correct social theory' (McLean et al. 1961; Tokes 1975; Amalrik 1970). As a result of this critical challenge, during the 1970s there emerged a dislocation in the ideological unity of Soviet Marxism (Baghoorn 1975). Having grown in a post-Stalinist atmosphere of social, artistic and political liberalization, the 'generation of the 1960s' (*shestidesyatniki*) appeared unable to reconcile the post-Khrushchev restrictions on public debates.

This concatenation of dislocating experiences precipitated the crisis of Soviet identity. The occurrences of the dislocating discourse made individuals incapable of representing the ideal frame of their 'self' in a material fabric of social relations (Laclau 1979, 103). Taken literally, this means that in the moment of dislocation the social agents are unable to be themselves. Being unable to reach their identity within an actual social order the dislocated actors face the impossibility of finding their place in society. It is possible to say that the dislocation does not just make one's identity impossible, but it also transforms the social subjects (whatever they might be) 'back' into mere (detached) individuals. The loss of 'subject' identity is not necessarily liberating. The exclusion of individuals from the structure of social organization transforms them into marginal figures. Exactly because of such profound dislocation in the post-Marxist theoretical tradition, the marginalized elements are regarded as *subaltern classes* (Gramsci 1971, 52–54).

As suggested, the historical experience of Soviet federalism distinguishes several such dislocations which led to the proliferation of subaltern identities. For instance, the conservatism of the 1970s impeded the liberal identity of many actors in the Soviet society (*Bol'shaya* 2002). Thus, the liberal intelligentsia was prevented from being itself because it could not perform its roles in the absence of open social debates (accompanied by the threats from prosecution for noncompliance). Such labeling of some forms of 'Soviet identity' as deviant from official doctrine triggered the process of *dissocializing* characterizing the development of Soviet society in the post-Khrushchev era.

Such dissocialization prompted forms of 'passive resistance' (Beddulph 1975; Feifer 1975) that aimed at minimizing an individual's relations with the society—such as emigration, for instance, whose scope during the 1970s and the 1980s articulated a 'third wave' of Russian emigration, following the 'White emigration' after the Civil War and the expulsion, removal and escape in the wake of World War II (Pilkington 1998; Raeff 1990). At the same time, the feeling of dislocation led to the 'internal displacement' of individuals towards the social (and geographic) periphery of the country. By the mid-1980s, this dissocializing among the Soviet people had become a dominant undercurrent of social and political reality. The dynamics of dislocation were further reinforced by the profound economic crisis that marked the end of Brezhnev's rule. During the 1960s, Khrushchev had proclaimed that the 'next generation of Soviet people will live in communism' (Frankland 1966; MacGregor-Hastie 1959; van der Linden 2008). The failure to implement the ambitious declaration to establish 'communism' was compounded by the verification of a quotidian regime of shortages (*deficit*) and disintegration of public services. In addition, the resulting impoverishment of the 'working Soviet people' was contrasted by the affluence of the 'Party aristocracy'. Commenting on this ideological disruption, Stayer (1998, 138) noted that by the mid-1980s 'even the workers [seemed] unable to find satisfaction or even expression in the workers' state'.

Such inability of the formal 'title' group of the Soviet state—the workers—to achieve a resilient (and comfortable) accommodation of its identity points to the massive dysfunction of the discursive system of ideological federalism. The consequent massive dislocation of the social order led to the expansion of marginal groups and a feign attempt at maintaining the ideological unity of Soviet discourse by designating them as different forms of 'deviations' ('criminals', 'dissidents', 'mad' or 'hooligans'). The pervasiveness of these 'de-subjectivated' elements prompted the profound distantiation of the Soviet federal narrative (Kozlova 1996, 59). This led to a legitimation crisis for the embodiment of its political architecture—the Union of Soviet Socialist Republics—and the profound discrediting of the communist ideology which had to glue millions of people in a common federal project.

Perestroika and the New Nationalisms

By the end of the 1980s the ideological unity of the Soviet people tied in a common state and guided by the mission of building communism, was rapidly loosing its ground. The society was struck by a crisis of identity and left without any organizing impulse. '*Quo vadim?*', 'Who are we?', 'What are we living for now?' were the vital questions for people formerly identified as Soviet. Thus, the reconciliation of the tension between national self-determination and ideology became increasingly untenable within the framework of 'Soviet Federalism' (Hasani 2003, 72–78).

Hechter argues that, 'while the politics of class has been retreating in the wings [during the communist rule], the politics of ethnicity has been moving in the limelight' (Hechter 2000, 2). The cognitive gap opened by the explanatory inconsistency of Soviet Marxism was gradually being filled with new nationalisms. Masked under the guise of political programs construed *for* and *on the behalf of* different social groupings diverse agendas representing the interest of particular 'constitutive nations' and/or 'peoples' gained popular and policy momentum in the second half of the 1980s. Thus, the ideas (as well as ideational potential) of national revival grew to dominate the political discourses across the Soviet federal entities. In this respect, Gorbachev's proposals for 'more democracy' through the grassroots of perestroika and popular glasnost offered an outlet for the demands (as well as urged the emergence) of various 'national' formations. Initially, these were started as cultural associations devoted to the 'revival', study, and promotion of national history, literature and (folk) traditions (Hosking 1991; Lapidus 1992). Yet, in the absence of formal limitations national imaginations envisioned not only cultural revival, but also engaged in the articulations of specific political demands. Pereistroika, thereby, dented the seemingly unchallengeable hegemony of communist ideology over the Soviet territory (Beissinger 2002). The strengthening of the national counter-narratives in the Soviet republics completed the disintegration of the Soviet discourse. Thus, although there was a proliferation of idiosyncratic and distinct 'national' formations, all of them seemed to share an aversion towards (what they perceived as a bankrupt) Soviet federal system. In one way or another, their agendas for the future involved the denial of all that was deemed *Soviet*, and its substitution with *national* paraphernalia.

In this respect, the process of perestroika, contributed to the further undermining of the ideological project of Soviet federalism (Birgerson 2002; Kagarlitsky 1996). The gradual rejection of communist ideology undermined 'the basis for the state' and legitimized the claim of different national identities to sovereign statehood (Huntington 1991/1992, 587). At the same time, the dynamics of 'cognitive liberation'—that is the process of progressive broadening of the scope of glasnost—served not only as a catalyst for the revival of political and cultural nationalisms, but also called into question the entire gamut of ideological assumptions, institutions, and values that had formed the core of Soviet federalism (Lapidus 1992, 47). Therefore, the founding project of Soviet statehood—the building of communism—became an enemy-image in itself and the focus of a shared antagonism towards *Soviet* paraphernalia. In the wake of perestroika, the tides of the democratic euphoria prompted strategies for the 'de-ideologizing the state' (Sakwa 1996, 397). Bound with the notion of 'Soviet', the concept of ideology itself became a prey to the onslaught of the 'democratizing' revolution. And thereby, when no ideology can be perceived as a 'good one', no ideas for new identities can be articulated and no possible universal identity can be thought.

Conclusion

The Soviet Union was a federal state whose unity was premised on the articulation of a common supranational identity transcending the differences of numerous national groups living on its territory. Not merely the sum of its parts, this overarching Soviet identity was a complex discursive construction based on a representation of particular national demands in the project of building the common socialist state. This project appeared to demonstrate high mobilizing potential framed by the actual impossibility for the full realization of its aspirations. The discursive power of the unity of the federal Soviet identity held together diverse populations through the shared framework of Marxist-Leninist ideology.

Ideology, thereby, was promoted as a mechanism, a set of ideas, and a locus of power for shaping social destiny by recruiting individuals into a certain imaginary unity. This recruitment is the process of creating social identities. In the Soviet state it set a specific form of social organization where various particular identities—regardless of whether they are defined by class or national belonging—seemed pliable to federalization through a common 'historical mission'. Administrative distribution of power, the balance between the center and the federal legal systems, economic and other dimensions of 'traditional' federalism came to be perceived as secondary (if not outright insignificant) in the framework of its ideological vocation became purely decorative elements of Soviet federalism.

In this respect, the suggestion here is that the entire history of Soviet federal statehood and its experiment with an ideologically-based federal identity should be seen in the context of the October Revolution. Thus, the Soviet federal project was promulgated as a form of *re-identification* in the face of the foundational uncertainties of the emerging state. For several decades such model of ideological federalism proved to be more than just functional. Yet, as any ideological system it was not free from internal discontinuities. The ambivalence towards the intellectual sources of the Soviet Marxism, the constant interplay between the sacralization of the 'founding fathers' of communism and the on-going demand for maintaining the revolutionary passion construed a dislocating modality, which in the second half of the 1980s evinced its destructive potential by undermining the Soviet federal discourse. Having lost its discursive consistency, Soviet federalism failed under the weight of its decrepit ideological precepts of federal re-identification.

The Soviet Union no longer exists, so does the 'new historical unity of the Soviet people' united various ethno-national groups into a common society. The history showed us that this model of ideological federalism failed. However, this does not undermine analytical value of such experience. At least we know what we have lost, and in the end—who knows—maybe in other circumstances, in other places, at other times, precisely this response will dominate the search for a new identity in a dis-identified society. Thus, reflecting the emergent dynamics of fragmegration (referred to in Chapter 1 of this volume), the experience of Soviet federalism attests to the unpredictable globalization of contingency:

> We know now that societies are immensely complex systems involving a potentially enormous number of bifurcations exemplified by the variety of cultures that have evolved in the relatively short span of human history. We know that such systems are highly sensitive to fluctuations. This leads both to a hope and a threat: hope, since even small fluctuations may grow and change the overall structure. As a result, individual activity is not doomed to insignificance. On the other hand, this is also a threat, since in our universe the security of stable, permanent rules seems gone forever. We are living in a dangerous and uncertain world that inspires no blind confidence, but perhaps only the same feeling of qualified hope that some Talmudic texts appear to have attributed to the God of Genesis (Prigogine and Stengers 1985, 313).

Chapter 12

Conclusions:
Whither Defunct Federalisms

Emilian Kavalski and Magdalena Zolkos

But readers want to have a sense that it all adds up. Many even want a conclusion that ends on an upbeat note that celebrates the realization of common themes! That's why so many reviews of edited books rue the absence of a concluding chapter that ties all the contributions into a coherent whole and that thus demonstrates the wisdom of collecting the essays between the same covers. [Therefore], to write an Epilogue is to strain for what may be a misleading sense of closure. It amounts to having the last word, just like superpowers do. They use all kinds of guises to impose their outlooks in such a way that they seem to be merely playing by the rules … No. Here my normative and analytical impulses converge. Normatively, an epilogue is the last word and, as such, it does impose. And analytically, I'm not so sure that I can highlight the diversity without implying an underlying coherence that readers may mistake for conclusions shared by all the contributors and their characters. I can't fake it!

James Rosenau (Rosenau et al. 1993, 127–128)

Introduction

Relying on the privilege of editorial 'superpower', this epilogue drafts a hesitant outline of some of the themes zigzagging across the analyses of the preceding chapters. The following remarks, therefore, are not *the* authoritative version of a 'concluding chapter that ties all the contributions into a coherent whole', but just one of many possible versions. Thus, rather than 'impose an outlook', this chapter illustrates *a* perspective on the discussions of defunct federalisms in this volume. The query guiding such interpretative reading is: What inferences can be gleaned from the discussion of the preceding cases of defunct federalisms and how do their highly speculative explorations interpret the juncture between federal demise and identity accommodation? The central value animating such inquiry is the potential for *uncovery* inherent in the comparative assessment of the experience of federal failure—that is, the intention is not only to *discover* new and previously untouched perspectives on the context of defunct federalisms, but it also implies the *uncovery* (i.e., the *excavation*) of viewpoints from underneath layers of ossified or never-problematized knowledge (Bially-Mattern 2005, 5).

The insistence is that such parallel examination of defunct federalisms has a bearing on the interpretation of federal designs and trajectories. This claim echoes Thomas Baty's observation that while 'federalism has failed where it was not wanted is no reason why it should fail where it is. Federation has frequently seemed very desirable; has been tried and has failed. But the mistake has been made of applying a right principle in a wrong measure and in a wrong way' (Baty 2005, 315). Thus, despite the certainty of wanting federalism, very often there is great uncertainty about how to achieve it.

Therefore, it should not be surprising that the 'immediate'—observable—corollary seems to be that the failure of federalism (just like its emergence) is the product of design, rather than chance. The contingency attendant in the promotion of federal arrangements impacts the provisions and frameworks of their institutional and ideational makeup, whose abstruseness offers opportunities for the manipulation of federal principles and the radicalization (through extreme politicization) of distinct identities. The cases of defunct federalisms included in this volume indicate the ongoing requirement for the reconsideration of the treatment of identities in an increasingly fragmegrating world. Thus, while federalism offers a range of useful tools and perspectives for apprehending the complexity and fluidity of identities, the contexts of federal failure suggest that its diverse incarnations are often incapable of meeting the demands of institutional flexibility and the required 'overture to the "Other"' (Gaudreault-DesBiens and Gélinas 2005, 58).

In this respect, the investigations included in this volume intimate that the notion and practice of federalism involves much more than the manner of apportioning sovereignty. In fact, it seems that it is the very treatment of federalism as a mere technical arrangement for the formal distribution of power and resources, which tends to underwrite its proclivity to failure.

Before proceeding further, however, it is necessary to assess the relevance of the conceptual map provided by the theory of defunct federalism on this volume's journey through the ruins of federal failure. The next section examines the contextual relevance of its hypotheses and outlines the additional inferences teased out by the case-studies. The final section discusses the implications of these discussions for contemporary conceptualizations of federalism.

The Case Study of the Theory of Defunct Federalisms—The Failure-Identity (Missing) Link

The study of defunct federalisms cuts across the controversies surrounding alterations in the organizational forms, processes, and content of states under the pressures of globalization, emerging forms of regional governance, and the reanimation of the conflict propensity of the link between territory and national identity. Said otherwise, the experience of failed federal arrangements has important lessons both for state building and the prescription of federalism as a remedy in multiethnic settings. In spite of their different contexts, the preceding chapters confirm identity as a form of social capital, which can be drawn upon by political entrepreneurs both for challenging federal arrangements as well as for their dissolution. Hence, in intricating the conversations among the contributors to this volume with broader discussions on the ongoing transformations of global life, it seems that most (if not all of them) would concede that the instances of defunct federalism confirm the proposition that:

> there is little, and maybe nothing, that is global that does not have some sort of a local manifestation. And each local manifestation changes the global context. Place centeredness is the amalgam of global change and local identity. Every place reveals itself at a variety of scales. Local perceptions are shaped by global influences, the combinations of which process local actions. These in turn are fuelled by local aspirations, many of which are the product of global images and expectations. All these local activities accumulate to create chaotic but global outcomes (O'Riordan and Church 2001, 3).

The problematization of federalism through the discussion of the role(s) and impact of identity politics on the moment of its failure outlines (at least) three main advantages of this perspective: (i) prompts a set of restrictive conditions under which federalism matters in the 'political accommodation' of different communities; (ii) allows for overcoming the concept and practices of a monolithic Westphalian statehood in explaining federal arrangements; (iii) facilitates outlining the preferences of relevant actors (Solingen 1998). Therefore, this section begins by examining the performance of the hypotheses of the theory of defunct federalism in the preceding analyses. Consequently, it details the additional contextual conjectures gleaned from that experience.

The hypotheses of the theory of defunct federalism

The diverse experiences documented in this volume under the label of 'defunct federalism' recognize that such a term—as an analytical notion and the inferences gleaned with its assistance—is necessarily a generalization. As the preceding chapters indicate, not only do the contributors analyze cases characterized by very different geopolitical and temporal circumstances, but also these cases range from very tentative and short-lived experiments (such as the only four-year-long Federation of the West Indies) to the long-standing and, arguably well-developed state projects of Yugoslav and Soviet federations (48 and 69 years respectively). The contention here is that the 'failure' shared by all federalisms discussed in the preceding chapters does not connote any commonality of genus. In this respect, this section briefly accounts for the contextual engagement with the theory of defunct federalism in the cases analyzed in this volume.

The first hypothesis from the theory of defunct federalism is that the failure of federalism is closely related to its dissociation from liberal democratic processes and institutions. While it has not been the ambition of this volume to establish linear causality, the context provided by the case studies represents either instances of post-colonial transition to sovereign statehood or the democratizing of non-liberal ex-communist systems (or a mixture of the two). In the cases of pan-Arabism, the West Indies, Ethiopia, Indonesia, Pakistan, and Rhodesia and Nyasaland the complexities of the transitional situations did not seem to allow for the formulation of any straightforward conclusion about the relationship between federalism and liberal democracy. There seems to have been a coincidence (if not a correlation) between periods of increased authoritarian tendencies, on the one hand, and moments of federal unpopularity, on the other; a dynamic which seemed decisive for the eventual collapse of the federal arrangement. A fitting example here is Pakistan in the early 1960s when the increase in autocratic inclinations during general Ayub Khan's presidency, together with the discrimination of the Bengali population, and the reactive rise of the Bengali ethnonationalism coincided with the emerging consensus among Pakistan's political elites that the federal arrangement was neither desirable nor feasible as a solution to the internal identity tensions in the country.

At the same time (albeit to a different degree), the post-colonial experiments with federalism indicate that the political coincidence of un-democratic tendencies and the consequent federal failure was an outcome of a dissociation between democracy and federalism—which was not only institutional and political, but also discursive. Such a discursive dissociation opened up for the political possibility of uncoupling the federal idea from democratic procedures. In this permissive space, the collapse of federalism was accomplished without the sense that democracy was being undermined. As suggested, the case of Pakistan demonstrates that while democracy, national unanimity, and coherence were included among the desirable goals in the text of the 1962 Constitution, federalism itself was sidelined in political practice (while discursively it was construed largely through its potentially subversive impact on national security). Similarly, this seems to have been the case with the transitory federal experience in Indonesia. There the discourses on post-colonial self-determination and popular democracy became interlaced with nationalist ideas opposing federalism as an ideology prompted by the Dutch colonial administration and supported by the local conservative elites. In other words, while the post-colonial cases might not provide sufficient evidence to conclude that there was direct correlation between weak (liberal) democracy and weak federalism, they do suggest that the lack of discursive synergy between the federal practice and democratic empowerment constitutes a political trajectory that ultimately undermines the former (and possibly also the latter).

In the cases of former Yugoslavia, Czechoslovakia and the Soviet Union it seems that federalism had become so tightly connected to the practices of socialist statehood and communist ideology that federalism (almost) should have been expected to crumble during the early 1990s in the absence of its ideological underpinnings. More importantly, however, it appears that federalism as institutionalized in and practiced by those three former socialist states, became one of the constitutive elements of a polity that undermined individual liberty and civic empowerment vis-à-vis the state. Consequently, the chapters on the Yugoslav and the Soviet federalism suggest that the accommodation of federal arrangements within the socialist theory of the state (either by Tito, by Kardelj, or by Lenin) reveals 'inconsistencies' and 'internal contradictions' of that theory. To rephrase this assertion into a positive statement, one has to acknowledge that the concept of federalism constitutes a relatively 'rigid designator' (Kripke quoted in Margalit 2002, 24) to the extent that its content (although flexible) is not always malleable. At the same time, there is a strong conceptual nexus between the federal focus on the 'empowerment of the people' and 'self-determination' on the one hand, and the normative democratic perspective on the relationship between the individual and the state on the other.

In this respect, the findings of the case studies on the second hypothesis from the theory of defunct federalism—the association between the institutional setting of identity accommodation and federal failure—are even less conclusive than with the first hypothesis. The reason is that 'identity' connoted very different historical situations in the analyzed cases. For instance, the analysis of federalism in the West Indies did not permit for advancing any convincing inference on the 'sufficiency' of its accommodation of diverse (insular) identities. In this context, Amanda Sives argues that while diversity in the Federation of the West Indies was abundant and rather well represented in its institutional setting, it, nevertheless, failed to articulate an overlapping West Indian identity that could be projected through (and, thus assist in maintaining) the federation. The absence of a regional West Indian sense of 'community of destiny' became apparent in the aftermath of the 1961 Jamaican popular vote against the federation.

The analyses of both the Yugoslav and the Czechoslovak cases confirm the proposition that the construction of a federal identity remained a tenuous and elitist project that was dissociated from the identification with popular political practices. At the same time, the study of the Federation of Rhodesia and Nyasaland points out that in some instances there was very little (if any) formal attempts to construct a federal identity that would give meaning to the project of cohabitation between different communities. This lack of tangible symbols and discourses of shared federal attachment allowed for the politicization of racial identities.

In this respect, the case of the Ethiopian–Eritrean federation highlights the political importance of identity bifurcated along religious lines (Christian and Islamic), the instance of Pakistan's federalism is more concerned with the problematization of a shared religion (Islam) by ethnic/regional identities, while former Yugoslavia exemplifies the politicization of both ethnic and religious signifiers in the securitization of identity. While very different from each other, all three cases tend to indicate a correlation between an inadequate institutional setting of identity accommodation and the elevation of identity as a site of political resistance. Consequently, the rise of Bengali ethnonationalism, the formation of Eritrean national unity as a response to Ethiopian oppression, and the complexification of diverse Yugoslav identities contributed to the federal dissolutions in these three cases. Therefore, while there is some probability of a causal connection between the federal failure and identity mobilization, it seems that sketching linear and unidirectional causality is misleading and inaccurate. Likewise, it seems that both symmetrical and asymmetrical arrangements can be problematic. Thus, while some cases (Yugoslavia, the USSR) found federal symmetry insufficiently accommodative of identity complexities, others (Cameroon, Czechoslovakia) suggested that federal asymmetry was problematic to the extent that it translated into (perceived) inequality in the distribution of powers between different levels of government.

The third hypothesis from the theory of defunct federalism—that the imposition of federalism presages its failure—was indicated (to a varying degree, of course) by all contributors to have been of secondary importance in their explanation of the dynamics of federal failure. Rather, the issue of imposition (as an ultimately un-democratic occurrence) functioned as a modality of the broader considerations about the relationship between democracy and federalism. For instance, in the post-colonial cases, it seems that the designation of federalism as 'imposed' and its recognition as a neo-colonial project functioned as synonymous constructions. Again, the recognition of the historical particularities in the discursive embodiment of federalism has been central to these considerations. In the Yugoslav case, for instance, while federalism was practiced in a centralized manner and remained largely dissociated from societal concerns, it was ideologically represented as derived from the popular consensus in both its 'nationalistic' form of pan-Yugoslavism and in its 'civic' version of federal self-management. In addition, the purportedly nonviolent multiethnic coexistence within the framework of the Yugoslav federal arrangement was deeply accommodated within the discourses of the innovative version of socialism, which functioned as alternative to the Soviet model.

Connected to the discussion of the three hypotheses of federal failure (i.e., vis-à-vis the considerations of liberal democracy, identity accommodation, and institutional imposition) is the reflection that constituted a *leitmotif* in all of the preceding chapters—that federalism (in its variety of forms) was *not an end in itself* but rather *an instrument to achieve other political goals*. This is an interesting, if also somewhat equivocal thought, that seems to capture a variety of meanings that invite deeper examination. The point is that even in the case of the federal arrangements that might be considered *successful*, it can be argued that federalism is *instrumental* (in the sense of both being crucial and also of constituting a tool for) in the achievement of a variety of (higher) political goals. These include the political empowerment of individuals and collectives, the just distribution of goods, the peaceful coexistence of (ethnic and other) identity groups, etc.

Therefore, the suggestion is that the claim of instrumentality made in the context of defunct federalisms seems to capture, first of all, the thought that there occurs a strategic dissociation between the functioning of federalism on the one hand, and the achievement of political goals on the other, which are not its consequences *sensu stricto*. Thus, federalism is used as a tool that serves as a systemic concealment of the occurring power struggle in the political game of the day. It is important to spell out the specific meaning of instrumentality precisely because it could be argued that federalism is 'instrumental' by its very nature. That is, federalism constitutes ends for the achievement of socio-political and socio-economic goals that are immanent to the federal institutions and practices, *per se*—namely that of non-violent coexistence of diversity within different levels of government. In contrast, the argument about the instrumentality of federal arrangements in some of the contributions to this volume suggests that the failure of federalism in these historical instances has been connected (i) to the *missing recognition* of both its possibility and its desirability in providing the conditions for peaceful social life; and (ii) to its opportunistic employment by individuals and/or political formations.

Secondly (and probably more importantly), the assertion that defunct federalisms have not constituted an end in themselves captures the impression that their functioning was tentative and provisional. This seems to have been a commonality shared by all the analyzed cases, even the long-term and relatively stable ones, like the former Yugoslavia and the USSR. This quality of tentativeness and impermanence of the defunct federal structures in turn suggests the absence of structural stability and relative predictability for the political life (intrinsically unstable and unpredictable in itself) to unfold and play out within (and across) the federal structures. This is not to suggest that it is desirable or historically accurate to assert that the nature of federal arrangements is *apolitical*. However, this observation can be re-articulated into a constructive analytical claim that federalism will be considered successful if, among other criteria, it will facilitate, on the one hand, the stability and reliability of social agreements and social rule and, on the other hand, will open up for the radical unexpectedness and uncertainty of democratic politics.

Context-specific suggestions

Federalisms become defunct as a result of the interaction between multiple details and changing contingencies. The following discussion generalizes some of the supplementary inferences prompted in the case studies. As suggested in Chapter 1, the contributors to this volume have organized their investigations into the instances of defunct federalism around the hypothesis from the theory of federal failure. However, they have also pointed out additional factors, which enhance the understanding of specific occurrences. It is important to restate that these factors have contributed to federal failure not in isolation, but through their interaction with idiosyncratic sets of issues, contexts, and dynamics. It is the unique mixture of these complex ingredients that has prompted the failure of the federal experiment.

One of the additional inferences advanced by some of the contributions is that the contexts of defunct federalism indicate the problematic dictate of political geography on the parameters of federalism. The dynamic environment provided by the focus on identity accommodation draws attention to the observation that human interactions are rarely (if ever) governed by the territorial logic of federal organization (Gaudreault-DesBiens and Gélinas 2005, 68). In this respect, the imposition of political arrangements can alter the trajectories of such interactions, but cannot deny the identity politics informing their dynamics. Instead it is the politicization of identity that endows territoriality with meaning. Attachment to geography is 'a perception susceptible to change over time', whose implications however are dependent on the content of the relationships between different identity groups sharing (or claiming) this territory and the levels of government involved in their regulation (Toft 2003, 313). The intrinsic (strategic) importance of territory in federal organization is, thereby, determined by the significance of symbolic attachments rather than its measurable value (Hensel 1999, 117–119; Huth 1999, 68; Kahler 2006, 6). The instances of failed federations indicate the limits of thinking about federalism primarily as a principle for the distribution of power across territorial subdivisions. In these contexts, failure is indicated by the lack of consideration for the management of identities, which more often than not straddle territorial divides.

The analysis of defunct federalisms also attests that their failure to survive reflects an inability to *generate a new and complex identity* (Gaudreault-DesBiens and Gélinas 2005, 73). Such inability to network creatively the plurality of identities undermines the validity and the legitimacy of the administrative rationalization of the federal idea. Such failure of constructive identity accommodation offers sites for resentment and mobilization that tend to impact on (for instance) a cost-benefit assessment in the participation in (and the necessity of) federal structures. In particular, the instances of Ethiopia, Indonesia, Pakistan, and Yugoslavia stress the critical role played (or not) by state elites in this process. In these cases, it is especially pronounced that the federal leadership failed to engage in federalizing the imagination of the population. Owing to a mixture of personal, ideological, and economic motives theses state elites marginalized (and in some instances repressed) the diversity of identity groups in their political discourses and practices. The examples of defunct federalisms indicate the effect from overemphasizing homogeneous identities at the expense of complex and layered identities; in particular, such tendency overlooks that 'social life is the reign of contradictions whose outcomes escape all rational planning' (Kavalski 2005, 50–53).

The contexts of defunct federalism, therefore, reflect the inability to achieve a continuous reconciliation (and re-articulation) of the interaction between functionality, solidarity, and legitimacy in the dynamics of identity accommodation (Gaudreault-DesBiens and Gélinas 2005, 73). Thus, another addition to the theory of federal failure is the inference that federal arrangements need to maintain their *re-constitutive flexibility*. Such process comprises of both the conception of structures of governance as well as its substantive context—i.e., this involves the recognition that structural frameworks are intimately bound up with substantive patterns about 'the central or primary locations of human identity and belonging across a wide range of relational experience' (Macdonald 2005, 267). The proposition of *re-constitutive flexibility* appreciates that while 'federalist ideas might help contribute to the creation of a political union', such federations might 'subsequently fail precisely because it results from ideas rather than [continuing] calculations relating to the interests of the component states' (McKay 1999, 35).

In this respect, another inference from the parallel examination of the case studies is that federalisms tend to become defunct owing to a failure of *mythologizing their creation*. Weinstock (2005, 215) asserts that by picking out the historical moment of federation as central to 'a nostalgic mythic narrative', this event takes on 'normative force for the future' that contributes to the resilience of federalism. Thus, nostalgic memory is transformed into an aspirational force that ensures the vivacity of federal contexts. None of the defunct federalisms investigated in this volume attempted the discursive construction of such narratives of origin. Instead of their *founding*, they became involved in the mythologizing of either a *founding father* (Yugoslavia, Rhodesia and Nyasaland, pan-Arabism), or a *founding ideology* (the USSR, Yugoslavia, Czechoslovakia), or a *founding party* (the USSR, Yugoslavia, Czechoslovakia), or a *founding enemy* (Ethiopia, Indonesia, pan-Arabism, the USSR), or a combination of several of these aspects (while in the instance of Republican China, federalism was de-legitimized outright as a nightmare from the past rather than a dream for the future). Such narrative absence of nostalgic aspiration contributed to the failure of instituting a (homogenizing or layered) federal identity. Indeed, this argument fills a gap in the literature by proposing that the task of identity accommodation is not about the weakening of federal government as is so often assumed, but about increasing the capacity of government (Ziblatt 2004, 98). Federalism, thereby, is not about less government, but about more appropriate forms of government. In this respect, the instances of federal failure suggest that the inability to engage different identities in the dynamics of creative interaction underwrite the decreasing capacity (and legitimacy) of federal government—i.e., federalist structures become predisposed to unraveling when they are unsupported by 'effective accommodative processes' (Dorff 1994, 104).

Thus, in the vacuum effected by the lack of meaningful interaction between different identity groups, federalist structures become not only party to, but also tools for the suppression of identity difference. For instance, in the experience of communist federations, federalism became associated with the commanding and ideological structures of the ruling regime. Likewise, the failure of federal arrangements in post-colonial contexts seems underwritten by their association with the neo-imperial designs of external actors rather than aspirations of internal constituencies (Ziblatt 2004, 97).

The Theory of Defunct Federalism and the Study of Failed States

The contention of this volume is that the instances of federal failure are part and parcel of the larger continuum of state building and state collapse. Both as a unit of international organization as well as a mode of analytical inquiry, the 'state' (regardless of whether it is a federal or a nation state) has been (if not inaugurated then at least) consolidated as the dominant entity in the study of world affairs by the 1648 Peace of Westphalia. Most observers assert that sovereign statehood remains 'the fundamental way in which the world is politically organized' (Jackson and James 1993, 6) and that it is without any 'serious challengers as the organizing principle for the political life of humankind' (Buzan 1995, 392). At the same time, other commentators have remarked that the state, if not dead, has at least reached the age of retirement (Mann 1993, 115). Thus, despite its respectable age, the notion, form(s), and practices of statehood have increasingly become the subject of popular, policy, and scholarly contestation and assault.

In recent years, these challenges to traditional statehood have led to a proliferation of 'awkward', 'collapsed', 'contested', 'failed', 'fissile', 'fractured', 'uncertain', 'weak', 'quasi', etc. states (Kavalski 2006; Rotberg 2003). The abundance of such terminology acknowledges not only the methodological and pragmatic quandaries emanating from the transformations in the post-Cold War international environment, but also draws attention to the diverse (and diversifying) content and context of global statehood. To borrow from a different context, the state that identity communities encounter is not the 'rational-actor model' deployed in the study of political science, but a fragmented actor caught in a 'broad web of state-society relations'; therefore, rather than viewing the state as a 'neutral arbitrator of domestic society or a preference aggregator', the focus on identity communities and their experiences suggests that states are very much shaped and influenced by the societies with which they interact (O'Brien 2005, 221). In this setting, the pervasiveness of various types of states populating the globe tends to reflect the *topsyturvydom* of current world politics, where the domestic life of states is becoming increasingly anarchic, while their international relations are orderly. Such intra-state anarchy tends to pressure political actors to engage in 'self-help' strategies (more often than not these involve the use of violence and force to achieve political objectives), rather than strategies that emphasize accommodation, bargaining, institutional channeling (Adamson 2005, 44).

The metamorphoses implicit in the attempts of failing states to contain threats from within, however, mirror the modalities and the conceptualization of weak federal arrangements. As William Stewart has presciently argued, the instances of 'coerced', 'facade', 'imposed', or 'primitive' federalism intimate 'a universe of complex phenomena' indicative of federal shortcomings. According to him, the addition of adjectives for the description of federalism not only 'politicizes the term', but also offers an important way of knowing about the complexity of state forms (Stewart 1982, 5–10; Kavalski 2007). In this respect, the literature on federal theory has begun to question the dominant conviction of political science that states are functionally similar—i.e., that they are 'like units'—and differ only in regards to their capabilities. Such inquiries have focused not only on what types of statehood are more relevant for overcoming different sources of insecurity, but also whether the dominant interpretation of Westphalian statehood—both as a form and as a concept of political and territorial organization—is the desired (as well as appropriate) vessel for achieving such stability (Kavalski and McCullock 2005; McCullock 2006).

Following Thomas Hueglin and Alan Fenna, the origins of such inquiry can be traced to the philosophical underpinnings of federal theory which define federalism as a way of 'approaching politics that acknowledges group identity alongside individual identity'. It is the particular forms of the group identity (i.e., its spatial, locational, or territorial modalities) that spur different sets of normative issues about 'the virtues and vices' of a system of multiple governments (Hueglin and Fenna 2005, 31). Such problematique gave rise to the discussion of the 'kind(s) of statehood' fit for the accommodation of different identities. In particular, the instances of defunct federalism point that federal forms are characterized not only by their volatility, but also by a mode of (*sovereign*) government that contradicts both accepted norms and rules for decision-making, as well as hinders the cohabitation of distinct identity communities.

In this respect, Patrick Riley maintains that federalism has developed as 'an alternative to, and (more precisely) in opposition to' the notion and practices of national sovereignty. He identifies the hostility of federal theory to the supremacy of nation states in the works of seventeenth-century commentators such as Gottfried Leibniz and Ludolph Hugo. The paradox of contemporary federal theory and practice, therefore, is that it 'seized on the very concept (sovereignty) which it actually opposed, to defend its own position more securely'. This 'oddity' prompted the development of the theory and practice of 'national federalism', which 'defined the autonomy of its territorial units in terms of sovereignty' (Riley 1973, 87–90, emphasis in original). Such intellectual obfuscation has been reflected in the experience of defunct federalisms. Not surprisingly, the politics of sovereign statehood spurred a preoccupation with 'the national interest' which has great political consequences, especially in federal settings where 'the legitimacy given to nationalism has proven a poisoned chalice' (Webber 1997, 33–35). Such fusion of sovereignty and federalism (i) gives credence to the pursual of 'national market' and 'national security' in the state building process of federations (Ziblatt 2004, 76); and (ii) provides 'a conceptual tool for establishing unrestrained [state] control over all demands of the social body' (Bowles and Gintis 1987, 167).

The institutionalization of 'national federalism' tended to intensify the antinomy between state-centrism and devolution. In particular, it seemed to provide the nested identity groups of the federal units with (i) the institutional wherewithal (executive bodies, legislative assemblies, and judiciaries) capable of undertaking the exercise of sovereign power; and (ii) the trappings of a territorial 'homeland' (as a result of the division of the federation into sub-units) which kindled the aspiration of transforming 'these internal borders into inter-state borders' (Pavkovic and Radan 2007, 13). In the instances of defunct federalism, the prospect for secession—and, thereby, the attainment of sovereign statehood by the nested national groups—was increasingly associated with perceived weaknesses in federal arrangements. Similar to contemporary studies of state failure, these weaknesses were interpreted as the inability of federations to carry out their fundamental purpose to negotiate the contending demands of different groups. In this setting, discerning the dynamics, sources, and mechanisms generating identity affiliations and their politicization, assists in understanding the way(s) in which 'identity can and does contribute' to state in/security (Bially-Mattern 2000, 299). Identity communities and transforming perceptions of identity may produce institutional resistance and practices that 'throw off course the presumed linearity of history' (Di Palma 2004, 260). Failed federations, like failed states, are 'tense, deeply conflicted, dangerous, and contested bitterly' (Rotberg 2001, 5). Thus, for instance, Erik Nordlinger deliberately excluded federalism from his list of desirable conflict regulating practices (Nordlinger 1972; O'Leary 2001). In this respect, as Mohamed Ayoob has eloquently argued, when the existing institutions of the state 'have been rendered incapable of providing even the minimum degree of security and order … in such cases sovereignty ceases to exist' (Ayoob 2002, 82). Therefore, the erosion of the perceived capacity and legitimacy of state sovereignty preconditions the proclivity of federations to failure. As suggested, such propensity to failure has been underwritten by the exacerbation of identity-based conflicts (Gurr 2000).

More often than not, therefore, the weakening of state structures tends to be indicated by the growth in 'intercommunal enmity' (Rotberg 2003, 5). According to Robert Jackson, such conflicts reflect the features of 'quasi-states'—entities that possess the 'juridical' attributes of formal statehood, but lack its 'empirical' qualities such as the deficiency of 'political will, institutional authority, and organized power' (Jackson 1990, 21–31; Kavalski 2008). In fact, the consequences of the contestation between different identity groups tend to be aggravated by the environment of weak states (Wolff 2006, 194). The instances of defunct federalisms suggest that their citizens were required to subscribe to the dominant norms and values of sovereign states. As the case studies included in this volume attest, such allegiance to (or the construction of) a common overarching identity that can prevail among all the numerous groups was not premised on any meaningful framework for identity accommodation. The occurrences of federal failure have tended to be prompted by the securitization of very small differences between groups (Gartzke and Gleditsch 2006). Gregory Bateson has pointed out that 'the number of potential differences … is infinite but very few become effective differences … that make a difference' (Bateson 1979, 98). In this respect, the interplay between the dominant and context-specific conjectures on federal failure outline the exasperation (if not the abandonment) of federalism's capacities for accommodative cohabitation between different identity groups.

Thus, what to make of difference and diversity—whether they are securitized or engaged in a dialogue—depends on the dynamics of change and continuity characterizing the pervasive turbulence of international life. The claim here is that the identity-based conflicts that precipitated the unraveling of both failing states and federations did not occur in a vacuum. In the case of the former, the assertion is that current 'ethnic conflicts have acquired a new dimension' because of their exacerbation by weak statehood, which provides the 'conditions in which central governments are unable or unwilling to enforce law and order, and in which terrorist organizations find the freedom and infrastructure to mount their local, national, regional, and global challenges' (Wolff 2006, 189). The contention of this volume is that in the case of defunct federalisms similar dynamics have animated the genealogy of their failure. Thus, the instances of defunct federalism mirror the internal security dilemmas faced by failed states. This collection, therefore, calls for the intrication between the literatures on federal failure and weak statehood. The prospective cross-pollination of their perspectives would have important impact both on theory-building and policy-making.

Why Study Defunct Federalisms?

In lieu of a conclusion, this section (figuratively speaking) returns to the beginning of this project and revisits the objectives of its voyaging among the remnants of federal failure. The point of departure for such peregrination is the nineteenth-century statement by the French theorist Pierre-Joseph Proudhon, who declared that 'the twentieth century will open the age of federations or else humanity will undergo another purgatory of a thousand years' (Proudhon 1973 [1863], 68–69; Prichard 2007). In this respect, the beginning of the twenty-first century still seems pockmarked by the twin-prospect of increased federalization and escalating global chaos. Perhaps, not unlike the twentieth century, the two potentialities would remain in complex coexistence for a long time as their symbiosis seems ensured by the ample access to resources that both seem to exhibit. In fact, Proudhon's dichotomous bifurcation of future tendencies might be limiting and obviating a whole range of other ('fragmegrative') possible futures.

It is claimed, therefore, that the study of defunct federalisms can elicit such alternative futures. In particular, its intrication with the literature on state failure can facilitate the conceptualization of new forms of governance that can yield more convincing elaborations of the effects of identity both on federal processes and state building. In this respect, recent explorations of territorial forms of organization in a globalizing world have questioned the axiomatic hold that Westphalian statehood has had on defining patterns of governance (Kahler 2006; Kavalski and McCullock 2005; Rosenau 1988; Webber 1997). The 'unbundling of territoriality' (Ruggie 1993, 165) has spurred investigations into the emancipatory potential inherent in new forms of political organization. In this vein, Daniel Weinstock has questioned the validity of 'territoriality' as 'foundational myth' of federalism. According to him, foundational myths 'provide citizens with an account of what their political association is *about*'. They are 'persuasive fictions' aimed at convincing 'citizens of a state' that 'their political association is not simply the result of blind, contingent, or historical forces'. Foundational myths, therefore, perform both conative and epistemic functions: (i) they motivate citizens to commit to the states they live in; and (ii) they provide them with 'an important tool in the formation of their identity' (Weinstock 2005, 210–212, emphasis in original).

However, it is the preference for territoriality that seems to undermine the conviction in federalism as 'the normal condition of human interaction' (Macdonald 2005, 263). The preceding investigations of defunct federalisms seem to point to the need for a de-territorialized re-theorization of federalism. As Jean-François Gaudreault-DesBiens and Fabien Gélinas provocatively ask, 'can we imagine a reflection on federalism that would take stock of the reality of legal pluralism, and consider the state as one potential federative actor among others'?

> This question points our inquiry towards the hypothesis of 'de-statization' of the reflection on federalism, which would precisely be an attempt at taking into account the decline of the normative monopoly enjoyed by the state … and the emergence (or re-emergence) of private actors capable of enacting legal norms (Gaudreault-DesBiens and Gélinas 2005, 66).

Thus, as already suggested, the intellectual linkage between the 'reflections' on failed federations and weak statehood offer the promise for both 'imagining' and critically reengaging with the emancipatory potential underlying federal arrangements. Such reengagement should therefore begin from the underlying ideational feature of federalism—not the territorial distribution of state power between levels of government, but that states are not homogenous entities whose inhabitants have multiple bases for both shared and different identities. The inherent promise of federalism is in its emphasis on the former (i.e., facilitating cohabitation and communities of destiny) rather than the latter (securitization of difference). In this respect, federalism reminds us that the choice we have is not 'the [nation] state or barbarism' (Sur 1997, 426). As Jennifer Smith explains, 'federalism is an honorable term in political science, with positive connotations … It suggests that there is value in communities joining together for some purposes. It suggests that there can be diversity in unity. It recommends the combination of shared government and self-government'. Within this analytical framework her intuition is that the tragedy of failed federations is the tragedy of the failure of peaceful, democratic coexistence— or in Smith's own words, 'it is like the failure of a dream' (Smith 2004, 12). In this respect, the study of defunct federalisms helps to reevaluate the processes that failed many a federal dream. It has to be reiterated that each contributor to this volume rejects a simple causal path between the dominant and context-specific factors for failure and the actual collapse of federations.

Yet, without neglecting the complexity of their interaction in individual cases, the very presence of these factors should sound the warning bells for current and prospective federalizing efforts. Moreover, the experience of defunct federalisms indicates that achieving the dream of 'unity in diversity' is not always served best by federal arrangements (owing to the interactions between the factors discussed in the preceding chapters). As it was pointed out, in these instances 'a [federal] tissue of thorny texture has been woven in an atmosphere of suspicion' (Baty 2005, 315). One inference, therefore, is that intra-state relations (just as inter-state ones) tend to be concerned with managing interpretations and creating visions which go to the heart of the notion and practices of politics—i.e., it is about 'brewing the right mix of ingredients, selling it, adapting it along the way, and disposing of the mix altogether if and when necessary; all these entail the ability to interpret the mobilizing capacity of powerful identity concepts and historical myths' (Solingen 1998, 18).

It seems that it is the (perceived mis)treatment of politicized identities that is most likely to trigger the dynamics of collapse. Thus, the cases of federal failure provide relevant contexts for the parallel examination of the mobilization of different identity groups. Due to the diverse aspects of their dysfunctionality, defunct federalisms have been unable to respond to popular discontent and accommodate dissident political challenges while maintaining normative and institutional inhibitions against massive human rights violations (Rotberg 2003, 21). On the whole, the preceding analyses indicate that the success or failure of federal arrangements is dependent on the careful design of institutional arrangements for accommodating the competing claims of different identity groups. Confirming the assumptions of Yash Ghai (2000, 14–24), the contributions to this volume tend to concur that such identity accommodation is more likely to succeed if there is an independent dispute settlement mechanism, if its arrangements have been negotiated in a democratic and participatory way, and if there is agreement not only on broad political principles, but also on the technical details for their implementation.

Thus, paraphrasing Robert Dorff's oft-quoted conjecture that 'federalist structures without federalist processes' are insufficient for successful federalization (Dorff 1994, 104), this study contends that the appropriation of federalist principles without the structures and processes of federalism do not portend effective identity accommodation. Federalism, therefore, becomes a sham and a guise for the achievement of particularistic interests and not for the unprejudiced cohabitation of different identity groups. As the cases of federal failure discussed in the preceding chapters indicate, federalism is sometimes euphemistically employed to obscure unacceptable trends or changes in a political system (Stewart 1982, 14). We believe that it is in this context that one should read Rudolpho Stavenhagen's proclamation that 'federalism as such is no guarantee for ethnic harmony and accommodation in the absence of other factors' (Stavenhagen 1996, 202).

Consequently, on the background of current efforts to promote federalism as desired approach to post-conflict state building in weak states (such as in Afghanistan, Bosnia and Herzegovina, Iraq, Kosovo, Macedonia, Sudan, etc. or the now defunct union of Serbia and Montenegro), it is important to draw attention to the centrality of identity accommodation in this process. Thus, despite such resurgence of interest in federalism, there is insufficient attention to (the lessons learned from) the experience of failed federations. The absence of discussion of federal failure acts as an epistemological obstacle that prevents the promotion of intriguing heuristic devices that both challenge conventional wisdom and provoke analytical imaginations. Moreover, as Jean-François Gaudreault-DesBiens and Fabien Gélinas suggest, the multiplicity in the current forms of federalism not only complicates our appreciation of its phenomenon, but also intimates that the traditional understanding of federalism as a territorial mode of state organization is more promising than the actual elaboration of federal structures in particular socio-political contexts. In other words, neglecting the experience of defunct federalisms tends to reduce the federal phenomenon 'to only one of it incarnations. The national prism through which many observers often apprehend the phenomenon can have the effect of radically distorting their perceptions' (Gaudreault-DesBiens and Gélinas 2005, 53).

The instances of defunct federalisms point that the institutional details for successful 'unity in diversity' were afforded little attention. Such inference draws attention to the observation that federalism as values and aspirations is rarely concomitant with federalism as structures and institutions of state organization. It is in this respect that identity accommodation is critical to the state-society relations, which according to Daniel Ziblatt underscore the 'infrastructural capacity' of federal arrangements—that is (i) the degree of institutionalization of a state; and (ii) the capacity of a federal government to penetrate its territories and logistically implement decisions in consensual manner. Ziblatt's conjecture intimates that the espousal of federal principles is not the central issue. Instead, 'the issue is the extent to which the subunits of a potential federation possess both parliamentary institutions that are embedded in society, in a constitution and well-developed administrative structures … Absent state structures with high levels of institutionalization via constitutional and parliamentary legitimacy, the subunits of a potential federation will be absorbed and swell away via a unitary strategy of state formation' (Ziblatt 2004, 77–78).

The cases of failed federations included in this volume bear ample evidence in this regard. Therefore, the claim here is that the problematization of failed federal experiences would offer insights into the dynamics of state formation as well as unique glimpses into the potential pitfalls in strengthening weak states through federalization. The study of defunct federalisms is thus an important and relevant endeavor not merely because their phenomenon is under-researched, but especially because understanding exactly why and how federations slide towards failure will assist the designing of methods for its prevention, and in the cases where federal states nevertheless fail, it could provide valuable insights into how to revive them and assist in the rebuilding process (Rotberg 2003, 2; Kavalski 2006). If 'the willingness to negotiate and compromise, and the commitment to open bargaining and the desirability of accommodation are absent, it may be impossible to achieve true federalism' (Dorff 1994, 102). Paraphrasing Patrick Riley's prescient comment that reengaging with the experience of defunct federalisms illuminates the evolution of ideas and practices of state building; the assertion of this volume is that 'such knowledge will not hinder, let alone preclude, empirical federal research' (Riley 1973, 121). This suggests, perhaps more than anything else that the understanding of federal failure demands nuanced and eclectic approaches, which take into account the differences in the temporal and geo-spatial contexts of its occurrence. Venturing into the *terra incognita* of defunct federalisms, therefore, is only likely to enhance the relevance of intellectual inquiries into the federal phenomenon.

Bibliography

Abbay, A. (1998), *Identity Jilted or Re-imagining Identity? The Divergent Paths of the Eritrean and Tigrayan Nationalist Struggles* (Lawrenceville, NJ: Red Sea Press).

—— (2004), 'Diversity and State Building in Ethiopia', *African Affairs* 103:413, 593–614.

Abdullah, A. (1976), 'Land Reform and Agrarian Change in Bangladesh', *Bangladesh Development Studies* 4:1, 67–99.

Abir, M. (1970), 'Education and National Unity in Ethiopia', *African Affairs* 69:274, 44–59.

Aburish, S. (2004), *Nasser: The Last Arab* (New York, NY: St. Martin's Press).

Achary, A. and Buzan, B. (2007), 'Why Is There No Non-Western International Relations Theory', *International Relations of the Asia-Pacific* 7:3, 287–312.

Adamson, F. (2005), 'Globalization, Transnational Political Mobilization, and Networks of Violence', *Cambridge Review of International Affairs* 18:1, 31–49.

Adeney, K. (2002) 'Constitutional Centring: Nation Formation and Consociational Federalism in India and Pakistan' *Commonwealth & Comparative Politics* 40:3, 8–33.

Agnew, J. (1995), 'Federalism in the Post-Cold War Era', in Smith (ed.).

Ahmad, N. (1950), 'Industrial Development in East Bengal (East Pakistan)', *Economic Geography* 26:3, 183–95.

Ahmed, E. (1980), *Bureaucratic Elites in Segmented Economic Growth* (Dhaka: The University Press).

Ahmed, L. (1999), *A Border Passage: From Cairo to America—A Woman's Journey* (New York, NY: Farrar).

Ahmed, R. (1981), *The Bengal Muslims 1871–1906* (Delhi: Oxford University Press).

Ahmed, S. (1990), *Federalism in Pakistan* (Karachi: Pakistan Study Centre).

Al-Sayyid, M. (1998), 'The Rise and Fall of the United Arab Republic', in Hudson (ed.).

Alam, S. (1995), *The State, Class Formation and Development in Bangladesh* (New York, NY: University Press of America).

Alavi, H. (1972), 'The State in Post-Colonial Societies: Pakistan and Bangladesh', *New Left Review* 74:3, 59–80.

Albert, M., Jacobson, D. and Lapid, Y. (eds) (2001), *Identities, Borders, Orders* (Minneapolis, MN: University of Minnesota Press).

Ali, M. (1996), *Politics of Federalism in Pakistan* (Karachi: Royal Book Company).

Ali, T. (1971), 'Bangladesh: Results and Prospects', *New Left Review* 68:3, 55–79.

—— (1983), *Can Pakistan Survive?* (London: Penguin).

Althusser, L. (1971), *Lenin and Philosophy and Other Essays* (London: New Left Books).

Amalrik, A. (1970), *Will the Soviet Union Survive Until 1984?* (London: Penguin Books).

Amazee, V. (1994), 'The Role of French Cameroonians in the Unification of Cameroon 1916–1961', *Transafrican Journal of History* 22:1, 55–73.

Amery, L.S. (1953), 'The Crown and Africa', *African Affairs* 52:208, 179–85.

Amoretti, U. (2004), 'Federalism and Territorial Cleavages', in Amoretti and Bermeo (eds).

Amoretti, U. and Bermeo, N. (eds) (2004), *Federalism and Territorial Cleavages* (Baltimore, MD: Johns Hopkins University Press).

Anderson, B. (1991), *Imagined Communities* (London: Verso).

Anderson, L. (1999), 'Politics in the Middle East', in Tessler et al. (eds).

Anglin, D. (1961) 'The Political Development of the West Indies,' in Lowenthal (ed.).

Annan, K. (1999) 'Two Concepts of Sovereignty', *The Economist*, 18 September.

Ansari, H. (1984), 'The Islamic Militants in Egyptian Politics', *International Journal of Middle East Studies* 16:1, 123–44.

Ansel, C. and De Palma, G. (eds) (2004), *Restructuring Territoriality* (Cambridge: Cambridge University Press).

Araya, M. (1990), 'The Eritrean Question', *Journal of Modern African Studies* 28:1, 79–100.

Ardener, E. (1967), 'The Nature of the Reunification of Cameroon', in Hazelwood (ed.).

Ashmore, R., Jussim, L. and Wilder, D. (eds) (2001), *Social Identity, Intergroup Conflict and Conflict Resolution* (Oxford: Oxford University Press.)

Ashton, S.R. and Killingray, D. (eds) (1999), *British Documents on the End of Empire* (London: The Stationery Office).

Aspaturian, V. (1960), *The Union Republics in Soviet Diplomacy* (Geneva: Droz).

Aspinall, E. and Berger, M. (2001), 'The Breakup of Indonesia', *Third World Quarterly* 22:6, 1003–1024.

Awasom, N. (1980), *Political Problems in the Pre-Independence Southern Cameroons* (MA Thesis: The University of Yaounde).

—— (2000), 'The Reunification Question in Cameroon History', *Africa Today* 47:2, 91–119.

Ayenew, M. (2003), 'Decentralization in Ethiopia', in Zewde and Pausewang (eds).

Ayoob, M. (2002), 'Humanitarian Intervention and State Sovereignty', *International Journal of Human Rights* 6:1, 81–102.

Ba, A. and Hoffman, M. (eds) (2005), *Conflicting Perspectives on Global Governance* (London: Routledge).

Barghoorn, F. (1956), *Soviet Russian Nationalism* (Oxford: Oxford University Press).

—— (1975), 'The Post-Khrushchev Campaign to Suppress Dissent' in Tokes (ed.).

Barnett, M. (1995), 'Sovereignty, Nationalism, and Regional Order in the Arab State System', *International Organization* 49:3, 479–510.

Bartlová, A. (1995), 'Political Power-Sharing in the Interwar Period', in Musil (ed.).

Bateson, G. (1979), *Mind and Nature* (New York, NY: Dutton).

Baty, T. (2005), *International Law* (Clark, NJ: The Lawbook Exchange, Ltd.).

Bauböck, R. (2007), 'Why European Citizenship?', *Theoretical Inquiry in Law* 8:2, 451–88.

Baxter, C. (1971), 'Pakistan Votes—1970', *Asian Survey* 11:3, 197–218.

—— (1974) 'Constitution Making: The Development of Federalism in Pakistan', *Asian Survey* 14:12, 11–45.

Bayart, J. (1973), 'Review', *African Affairs* 72:289, 453–54.

Beattie, K. (2000), *Egypt during the Sadat Years* (London: PalgraveMacmillan).

Bebler, A. (1993), 'Yugoslavia's Variety of Communist Federalism and Her Demise', *Communist and Post-Communist Studies* 26:1, 72–86.

—— (2007), 'Southeast European Federalism and Contemporary Bosnia and Herzegovina', *Acta Slavica Iuponica* 24:1, 1–23.

Bedeski, R. (1977), 'The Concept of the State: Sun Yat-sen and Mao Tse-tung', *China Quarterly* 70:2, 338–54.

Behring, E., Richter, L. and Schwarz, W.F. (eds) (1999), *Geschichtliche Mythen in den Literaturen und Kulturen Ostmittel- und Südosteuropas* (Stuttgart: Franz Steiner Verlag).

Beissinger, M. (2002), *Nationalist Mobilization and the Collapse of the Soviet State* (Cambridge: Cambridge University Press).

Bell, W. (1960), 'Attitudes of Jamaican Elites Towards Federation', *Annals of the New York Academy of Sciences* 5:1, 862–77.

Bennett, C. (1995), *Yugoslavia's Bloody Collapse* (New York, NY: New York University Press).

Bermeo, N. (2002), 'A New Look at Federalism', *Journal of Democracy* 13:2, 96–110.

—— (2004), 'The Merits of Federalism', in Amoretti et al. (eds).

Bially-Mattern, J. (2000), 'Taking Identity Seriously', *Cooperation and Conflict* 35:3, 299–308.

—— (2005), *Ordering International Politics* (London: Routledge).

Biddulph, H. (1975), 'Protest Strategies of the Soviet Intellectual Opposition' in Tokes (ed.).

Birgerson, S (2002), *After the Breakup of a Mutliethnic Empire* (Westport, CT: Praeger).

Bishai, L. (2004), *Forgetting Ourselves: Secession and the (Im)possibility of Territorial Identity* (Lanham, MD: Lexington Books).

Blackburn, R. (1975), *Explosion in a Subcontinent* (Baltimore, MD: Penguin Books).

Blussé, L. (1987), *India and Indonesia from the 1920s to the 1950s* (Leiden: Brill).

Bøås, M. (2000), 'Whose Security?', *Conflict and Cooperation* 35:3, 309–19.

Boduszyński, M. (2004), 'Review of Yugoslavism', *Nationalities Papers* 32:2, 515–18.

Boettke, P. (1993), *Why Perestroika Failed* (London: Routledge).

Bol'shaya Sovetskaya Entsiklopediya (2002), CD edition (Moscow: Bol'shaya sovetskaya ehntsiklopediya-Glasnet).

Bonhoeffer, D. (1971), *Letters and Papers from Prison* (New York, NY: Touchstone).

Booth, K. (2007), *Theory of World Security* (Cambridge: Cambridge University Press).

Bošković, B. and Dašić, D. (eds) (1980), *Socialist Self-Management in Yugoslavia* (Belgrade: STP).

Bowles, S. and Gintis, H. (1987), *Democracy and Capitalism* (New York, NY: Basic Books).

Braithwaite, L. (1957a), 'Progress towards Federation, 1938–1956', *Social and Economic Studies* 6:2, 133–84.

—— (1957b), '"Federal" Associations and Institutions in the West Indies', *Social and Economic Studies* 6:2, 286–28.

Bremmer, I. (1994) 'Reassessing Soviet Nationalities Theory' in Bremmer et al (eds).

Bremmer, I. and Taras, R. (eds) (1994), *Nations and Politics in the Soviet Successor States* (Cambridge: Cambridge University Press).

Brookfield, H.C. (1957), 'Some Geographical Implications of the Apartheid and Partnership Policies in Southern Africa', *Transactions and Papers of the Institute of the British Geographers* 23:1, 225–47.

Bull, H. (1977), *The Anarchical Society* (London: Macmillan).

Bunce, V. (1999), 'Peaceful vs. Violent State Dismemberment', *Politics & Society* 27:2, 217–37.

—— (2004), 'Federalism, Nationalism and Secession' in Amoretti and Bermeo (eds).

Burg, S. (1983), *Conflict and Cohesion in Yugoslavia* (Princeton, NJ: Princeton University Press).

—— (1988), 'Political Structures' in Rusinow (ed.).

—— (1993), 'Why Yugoslavia Fell Apart', *Current History* 92:577, 357–64.

Burgess, M. (2006), *Comparative Federalism* (London: Routledge).

Burgess, M. and Gagnon, A. (eds) (1993), *Comparative Federalism and Federation* (Toronto, ON: Toronto University Press).

Burgess, M. and Pinder, J. (eds) (2007), *Multinational Federations* (London: Routledge).

Burke, E. (1998), 'Orientalism and World History' *Theory and Society* 27:4, 489–507.

Burks, A. (1954), 'Constitution-Making in Pakistan', *Political Science Quarterly* 69:4, 541–64.

Buzan, B. (1995), 'Focus On: The Present as a Historic Turning Point', *Journal of Peace Research* 30:4, 385–98.

Buzan, B. and Little, R. (2001), 'Why International Relations Theory Has Failed as an Intellectual Project and What to Do About It', *Millennium* 30:1, 19–39.

Caldwell, M. and Ultrecht, E. (1979), *Indonesia* (Sydney, NSW: Alternative Publications).

Callard, K. (1957), *Pakistan: A Political Study* (London: George Allen & Unwin).

Caplan, R. (2006), *International Governance of War-Torn Territories (Oxford: Oxford University Press).*

Carleton, W. (1949), 'Is Communism Going National', *Virginia Quarterly Review* 25:3, 321–34.

Carvalho, J. (ed.) (2006), *Religion, Ritual and Mythology* (Pisa: Pisa University Press).

Chang, C. (1952), *The Third Force in China* (New York, NY: Bookman Associates).

Chang, Y. (1956), 'The Chinese Communist State System under the Constitution of 1954', *Journal of Politics* 18:3, 520–46.

Cheah, P. (1997), 'Given Culture: Rethinking Cosmopolitan Freedom in Transnationalism', *Boundary 2* 24:2, 157–97.

Chem-Langhee, B. (1976), *The Kamerun Plebiscite, 1959–1961* (PhD Dissertation, University of British Columbia).

Chem-Langhee, B. and Njeuma, M. (1980), 'The Pan-Kamerun Movement, 1949–1961', in Kofele-Kale (ed.).

Chen, L. (1991), 'Chen Jiongming and the Chinese Federalist Movement', *Republican China* 17:1, 21–37.

Chesneaux, J. (1969), 'The Federalist Movement in China, 1920–1923' in Gray (ed.).

Choudhury, G.W. (1956), 'The Constitution of Pakistan', *Pacific Affairs* 29:3, 243–52.

—— (1969), *Constitutional Development in Pakistan* (London: Longman).

—— (1970), *Constitutional Development in Pakistan* (London: Longman).

—— (1972), 'Bangladesh: Why It Happened', *International Affairs* 48:2, 242–49.

—— (1974), *The Last Days of United Pakistan* (London: Hurst & Co.).

Clapham, C. (1975), 'Centralization and Local Response in Southern Ethiopia', *African Affairs* 74:294, 72–81.

—— (1988), *Transformation and Continuity in Revolutionary Ethiopia* (Cambridge: Cambridge University Press).

—— (1994), 'Ethnicity and the National Question in Ethiopia', in Woodward and Forsyth (eds).

Clements, F. (1969), *Rhodesia: The Road to Collision* (London: Pall Mall).

Cliffe, L. and Davidson, B. (eds) (1988), *The Long Struggle of Eritrea for Independence and Constructive Peace* (Nottingham: Spokesman).

Cmnd6607 (1945), *Report of the West India Royal Commission* (London: HMSO).

Cmnd7291 (1948), *Conference on the Closer Association of the British West Indian Colonies* (London: HMSO).

Cohen, A. (1985), *The Symbolic Construction of Community* (London: Routledge).

—— (2000), *Signifying Identities* (London: Routledge).

Cohen, J. (1987), *Integrated Rural Development: The Ethiopian Case* (Uppsala: Scandinavian Institute for African Studies).

Cohen, P. (2003), 'Reflections on a Watershed Date' in Wassenstrom (ed.).

Col218 (1948), *Conference on the Closer Association of the British West Indian Colonies* (London: HMSO).

Cole, J. (ed.) (1992), *Comparing Muslim Societies* (Ann Arbor, MI: University of Michigan Press).

Coleman, J. (1955), 'The Problem of Political Integration in Emergent Africa', *Western Political Quarterly* 8:1, 44–57.

Colović, I. (2004), 'On Models and Batons' in Leposavić (ed.).

Connor W. (1984), *The National Question in Marxist–Leninist Theory and Strategy* (Princeton, NJ: Princeton University Press).

Conversi, D. (ed.) (2004), *Ethnonationalism in the Contemporary World* (London: Routledge).

Coore, D. (1999), 'The Role of the Internal Dynamics of Jamaican Politics on the Collapse of Federation', *Social and Economic Studies*, 48:4, 65–82.

Cornwall, M. and Evans, R.J.W. (2007), *Czechoslovakia in a Nationalist and Fascist Europe* (Oxford: Oxford University Press).

Coury, R. (1982), 'Who "Invented" Egyptian Arab Nationalism', *International Journal of Middle East Studies* 14:3, 249–81.

Cox, R. and Frankland, E. (1995), 'The Federal State and the Breakup of Czechoslovakia', *Publius* 25:1, 71–88.

Crawford, B. (1998), 'Explaining Cultural Conflict in Ex-Yugoslavia' in Crawford, B. and Lipschutz, R. (eds).

Crawford, B. and Lipschutz, R. (eds) (1998), *The Myth of 'Ethnic Conflict'* (Berkeley, CA: University of California Press).

Critchley, W. (1993), 'The Failure of Federalism in Yugoslavia', *International Journal* 48:3, 434–47.

Cummings, D. (1954), 'The UN Disposal of Eritrea', *African Affairs* 52:207, 127–36.

Daniels, R. (1993), *The End of the Communist Revolution* (London: Routledge).

Davis, M. (1999), 'The Case for Chinese Federalism', *Journal of Democracy* 10:2, 124–37.

Davis, R. (1978), *The Federal Principle* (Berkeley, CA: University of California Press).

Dawisha, A. (2000), 'Arab Nationalism and Islamism', *International Studies Review* 2:3, 79–90.

de Villiers, B. (ed.) (1994), *Evaluating Federal Systems* (Dordrecht: Martinus Nijhoff Publishers).

Decalo, S. (1998), *Civil-Military Relations in Africa* (Gainesville, FL: Florida Academic Press).

DeLancey, M. (1989), *Cameroon and Independence* (Boulder, CO: Westview Press).

Delaney, E. and Barani, L. (2003) 'The Promotion of "Symmetrical" European Citizenship', *Journal of European Integration*, 25:2, 95–114.

Denber, R. (ed.) (1992), *The Soviet Nationality Reader* (Boulder, CO: Westview Press).

Denitch, B. (1990). *Limits and Possibilities: The Crisis of Yugoslav Socialism and State Socialist Systems* (Minneapolis: University of Minnesota Press).

—— (1993), 'Unmaking Multi-Ethnicity in Yugoslavia', *Anthropology of East Europe Review*, 11:1/2, 43–54.

Derrick, J. (1990), 'Review', *African Affairs* 89:357, 606–608.

Di Palma, G. (2004), 'What Inefficient History and Malleable Practices Say About Nation-States and Supranational Democracy When Territoriality Is No Longer Exclusive', in Ansell et al. (eds).

Diehl, P. (ed.) (1999), *A Roadmap to War* (Nashville, TN: Vanderbilt University Press).

Dimitrijević, V. (1994), *The 1974 Constitution* (Florence: European University Institute).

Djilas, A. (1991), *The Contested Country* (Cambridge, MA: Harvard University Press).

Djokić, D. (ed.) (2003), *Yugoslavism: Histories of a Failed Idea 1918–1992* (London: Hurst).

Djordjević, J. (1975), 'Remarks on the Yugoslav Model of Federalism', *Publius* 5:2, 77–88.

Domingo, W. (1973) 'British West Indian Federation)' in Lowenthal et al. (eds).

Dorff, R. (1994), 'Federalism in Eastern Europe', *Publius* 24:2, 99–114.

Dowlah, A. and Elliott, J. (1997), *The Life and Times of Soviet Socialism* (Westport, CT: Greenwood Press).

Drakeley, S. (2005), *The History of Indonesia* (Westport, CT: Greenwood Press).

Duara, P. (1995), *Rescuing History from the Nation* (Chicago, IL: University of Chicago Press).

Duchachek, I. (1988), 'Dyadic Federations and Confederations', *Publius* 18:2, 5–31.

'Duiyu bensheng difang zizhi de jidian yijian' (Some Opinions about This Province's Local Self-Government), *Gonglunbao*, 20 July 1949, 2.

Dunlop, J. (1993), *The Rise of Russia and the Fall of the Soviet Empire* (Princeton, NJ: Princeton University Press).

Dunn, C. (1959), *Central African Witness* (London: Victor Gollancz).

Dunn, W. (1975), 'Communal Federalism', *Publius* 5:2, 127–50.

Dvorin, E. (1954), 'Central Africa's First Federal Election', *Western Political Quarterly* 7:3, 369–90.

Economic Survey of East Pakistan (1970) (Dacca: East Pakistan Government Press).

Eko, L. (2003), 'The English-Language Press and the "Anglophone Problem" in Cameroon', *Journal of Third World Studies* 20:1, 79–102.

Elazar, D. (1985), 'Federalism and Consociational Regimes', *Publius* 15:2, 17–34.

—— (1991), *Federal Systems of the World* (London: Longman).

Ellingson, L. (1977), 'The Emergence of Political Parties in Eritrea', *Journal of African History* 18:2, 261–81.

Enský, J. (1978), 'O Slovákoch a Čechoch-Historicky', *Svědectví* 15:57, 85–104.

Ereli, E. (1956), 'The Bat Galim Case before the Security Council', *Middle Eastern Affairs* 6:4, 61–109.

Eriksen, T. (2001), 'Ethnic Identity, National Identity and Intergroup Conflict' in Ashmore et al (eds).

Esberey, J. and Johnston, L. (1994), *Democracy and the State* (Peterborough, ON: Broadview Press).

Eyinga, A. (1978), 'Government by State of Emergency' in Joseph (ed.).

Faist, T. (2001), 'Social Citizenship in the European Union', *Journal of Common Market Studies* 39:1, 37–58;

Falk, R. (1978), 'Anarchism and World Order' in Pennock and Chapman (eds).

Feifer, G. (1975), 'No Protest: The Case of Passive Minority' in Tokes (ed.).

Fernandez, J. (2001), 'Peripheral Wisdom' in Ashmore et al (eds).

Ferrazzi, G. (2000), 'Using the "F" Word: Federalism in Indonesia's Decentralization Discourse', *Publius* 30:2, 63–85.

Finkelstein, L. (1951), 'The Indonesian Federal Problem', *Pacific Affairs* 24:3, 284–95.

Fisiyu, C. and Geschiere, P. (1996), 'Witchcraft, Violence, and Identity', in Werbner et al. (eds).

Fonchingong, C. (2005), 'Exploring the Politics of Identity and Ethnicity in State Reconstruction in Cameroon', *Social Identities* 11:4, 363–80.

Forsyth, M. (1989), 'Introduction', in Forsyth (ed.).

—— (ed.) (1989), *Federalism and Nationalism* (Leicester: Leicester University Press).

Fossungu, P. (1999), *Understanding Confusion: A Historical and Critical Essay on the Constitution of Cameroon* (PhD Thesis: The University of Montreal).

Frankland, M. (1966), *Khruschev* (Harmondsworth: Penguin).

Friedrich, C. (1968), *Trends in Federalism in Theory and Practice* (New York, NY: Praeger).

Franck, T. (1968), 'Why Federations Fail' in Franck (ed.).

—— (ed.) (1968), *Why Federations Fail* (New York: New York University Press).

Frankel, J. (1955), 'Federalism in Yugoslavia', *American Political Science Review*, 49:2, 416–30.

Frey, M. (2003), 'The Indonesian Revolution and the Fall of the Dutch Empire', in Frey et al. (eds).

Frey, M., Pruessen, R. and Yong, T. (eds) (2003), *The Transformation of Southeast Asia* (Armonk, NY: M.E. Sharpe).

Friend, T. (2003), *Indonesian Destinies* (Cambridge, MA: Harvard University Press).

Gagnon, A. and Tully, C. (eds) (2001), *Multinational Democracies* (Cambridge: Cambridge University Press).

Gagnon, V. (1991), 'Yugoslavia: Prospects for Stability', *Foreign Affairs* 70:3, 17–35.

—— (2004), *The Myth of Ethnic War* (Ithaca, NY: Cornell University Press).

Gallie, W. (1964), *Philosophy and the Historical Understanding* (London: Chatto & Windus).

Gann, L. and Gelfand, M. (1966), *Huggins of Rhodesia* (London: Allen & Unwin).

Gartzke, E. and Gleditsch, S. (2006), 'Identity and Conflict', *European Journal of International Relations* 12:1, 53–87.

Garver, E. (1990), 'Essentially Contested Concepts', *Philosophy and Rhetoric* 23:4, 251–70.

Gaudreault-DesBiens, J. and Gélinas, F. (2005), 'Opening New Perspectives on Federalism' in Gaudreault-DesBiens et al. (eds).

—— (eds) (2005), *The State and the Mood of Federalism* (Brussels: Bruylant).

Gebre-Medhin, J. (1989), *Peasants and Nationalism in Eritrea* (Trenton, NJ: Red Sea Press).

Gee, J., Vitalis, R. and Levin, S. (1988), 'Letters: The Uprising: The Next Phase', *Middle East Report* 154:4, 2–3.

Geertz, C. (1993), *The Interpretation of Cultures* (London: Fontana).

Gerber, H. (2004), 'The Limits of Constructedness', *Nations and Nationalism* 10:3, 251–68.

Gershoni, I. and Janowski, J. (eds) (1997), *Rethinking Nationalism in the Arab Middle East* (New York, NY: Columbia University Press).

Ghai, Y. (1998), 'Decentralization and the Accommodation of Ethnicity' in Young (ed.).

—— (ed.) (2000), *Autonomy and Ethnicity: Negotiating Competing Claims in Multi-Ethnic States* (Cambridge: Cambridge University Press).

Ghebre-Ab, H. (1993), *Ethiopia and Eritrea* (Trenton, NJ: Red Sea Press).

Gibson, E. (ed.) (2004), *Federalism and Democracy in Latin America* (Baltimore, MD: Johns Hopkins University Press).

Gibson, E. and Falleti, T. (2004), 'Unity by the Stick: Regional Conflict and the Origins of Argentine Federalism' in Gibson (ed.).

Gill, G. (1996), *The League of Nations from 1929–1946* (Knoxville, TN: Avery Publishing Group).

Ginat, R. (2003), 'The Egyptian Left and the Roots of Neutralism in the Pre-Nasserite Era', *British Journal of Middle Eastern Studies* 30:1, 5–24.

Godina, V. (1998), 'The Outbreak of Nationalism on Former Yugoslav Territories', *Nations and Nationalisms* 4:3, 409–422.

Goertz, G. (1994), *Contexts of International Politics* (Cambridge: Cambridge University Press).

Gonsalves, R. (1998), 'Our Caribbean Civilization', *Caribbean Quarterly* 44:1, 131–150.

Gow, J. (1997), *Triumph of the Lack of Will* (London: Hurst).

Gow, J. and Michalski, M. (2005), 'The Impact of the War on Serbia' in Ramet et al. (eds).

Gramsci, A. (1971), *Prison Notebooks* (London: Lawrence and Wishart).

Gran, P., Vitalis, R. and Binder, L. (1998), 'Essays on Middle East Exceptionalism', *Arab Studies Journal* 6:1, 6–59.

Gray, G. (ed.) (1969), *Modern China's Search for a Political Form* (Oxford: Oxford University Press).

Greenfeld, L. (1992), *Nationalism* (Cambridge, MA: Harvard University Press).

Grigorov, D. (2006), 'Druže Tito, mi ti se kunemo'! Ritual and Political Power in Yugoslavia: Tito's Birthday Celebrations (1945–1987)' in Carvalho (ed.).

Gripp, R. (1960), 'Eastern Europe's Ten Years of National Communism', *Western Political Quarterly*, 13:4, 934–49.

Gurr, T. (2000), *Peoples versus States* (Washington, DC: United States Institute of Peace).

Haddad, M. (1994), 'The Rise of Arab Nationalism Reconsidered', *International Journal of Middle East Studies* 26:2, 201–222.

Haile, S. (1988), 'Historical Background to the Ethiopia–Eritrea Conflict', in Cliffe and Davidson (eds).

Hale, H. (2004), 'Divided We Stand: Institutional Sources of Ethnofederal State Survival and Collapse', *World Politics* 56:2, 165–93.

Hamza, A. (1963), *Post-Revolution Pakistani Themes* (Lahore: Progressive Papers).

Harris, E. (2002), *Nationalism and Democratization* (Aldershot: Ashgate).

Hart, R. (2004), *Time for a Change* (Kingston: Arawak).

Hasani, E. (2003), *Self-Determination, Territorial Integrity, and International Stability* (Vienna: Austrian National Defence Academy).

Hazelwood, A. (ed.) (1967), *African Integration and Disintegration* (Oxford: Oxford University Press).

Hechter, M. (2000), *Containing Nationalism* (Oxford: Oxford University Press).

Heim, S. (1955), 'Islam and the Theory of Arab Nationalism', *Die Welt Des Islams* 4:2/3, 124–49.

Heinemann-Grüder, A. (ed.) (2002), *Federalism Doomed?* (New York, NY: Berghahn Books).

Hellman, J. (2003), *Cultural Politics in New Order Indonesia* (Copenhagen: NIAS).

Hensel, P. (1999), 'Charting a Course to Conflict' in Diehl (ed.).

Heraclides, A. (1991), *The Self-Determination of Minorities in International Politics* (London: Frank Cass).

Hesse, J. and Wright, V. (eds) (1996), *Federalizing Europe?* (Oxford: Oxford University Press).

Heuglin, T.O. and Fenna, A. (2006), *Comparative Federalism* (Toronto, ON: Broadview Press).

Heywood, A. (2000), *Key Concepts in Politics* (New York, NY: St. Martin's Press).

Hickey, J. and Ugrinsky, A. (eds) (1996), *Government Structures in the USA and the Former USSR* (Westport, CT: Greenwood Press).

Hicks, U. (1978), *Federalism: Failure and Success* (London: Macmillan).

Holderness, H. (1985), *Lost Chance: Southern Rhodesia 1945–58* (Harare: Zimbabwe Publishing House).

Holland, R. (1985), *European Decolonization* (London: Macmillan).

Horowitz, D. (1980), *Coup Theories and Officers' Motives* (Princeton, NJ: Princeton University Press).

—— (ed.) (1985), *Ethnic Groups in Conflict* (Los Angeles, CA: University of California Press).

Hosking, G. (1991), *The Awakening of the Soviet Union* (Cambridge, MA: Harvard University Press).

Hou K. (1995), 'You jisi dao baodong: minguo sanshisannian sichuan jiangyouxian zhongjuzhen 'sanerba' shijian' (From Investigating Smugglers to Uprising: The March 28 Incident of Zhongju Village, Jiangyou District, Sichuan, 1944) draft.

Howarth, D. (2000), *Discourse* (Buckingham: Open University Press).

Howarth, D. and Stavrakakis, Y. (2000), 'Introducing Discourse Theory and Political Analysis' in Howarth et al. (eds).

Howarth, D., Norval, A. and Stavrakakis, Y. (eds), *Discourse Theory and Political Analysis* (Manchester: Manchester University Press).

Hoyos, F. (1974), *Grantley Adams and the Social Revolution* (London: Macmillan).

Hu, C. (1984), *Minchu de difang zhuyi yu liansheng zizhi* (Localism and Federal Self-Government During the Early Republican Era) (Taibei: Zhengzhong shuju).

Hudson, M. (ed.) (1998), *The Middle East Dilemma* (New York, NY: Columbia University Press).

Hueglin, T. and Fenna, A. (2006), *Comparative Federalism* (Peterborough, ON: Broadview Press).

Huntington, S. (1957), *The Soldier and the State* (Cambridge, MA: Belknap Press).

—— (1968), *Political Order in Changing Societies* (New Haven, CT: Yale University Press).

—— (1991/1992), 'How Countries Democratize', *Political Science Quarterly* 106:4, 579–616,

Huth, P. (1996), *Standing Your Ground: Territorial Disputes and International Conflict* (Ann Arbor, MI: University of Michigan Press).

—— (1999), 'Enduring Rivalries and Territorial Disputes, 1950–1990' in Diehl (ed.).

Huth, P. and Allee, T. (2003), *The Democratic Peace and Territorial Conflict in the Twentieth Century* (Cambridge: Cambridge University Press).

Horton, J. and Mendus, S. (eds) (1999), *Toleration, Identity and Difference* (Basingstoke: Macmillan).

Íñigo-Mora, I. (2004) 'On the Use of the Personal Pronoun *We* in Communities', *Journal of Language and Politics* 3:1, 27–52.

Innes, A. (1997), 'The Breakup of Czechoslovakia', *East European Politics and Societies* 11:3, 393–435.

—— (2001), *Czechoslovakia: The Short Goodbye* (New Haven, NJ: Yale University Press).

Isaacs, H. (1975), *Idols of the Tribe: Group Identity and Political Change.* (Cambridge, MA: Harvard University Press).

Ismael, T. (1971), *The UAR in Africa* (Evanston, IL: Northwestern University Press).

Iyob, R. (1995), *The Eritrean Struggle for Independence* (Cambridge: Cambridge University Press).

Jackson, R. (1975), *South Asian Crisis* (London: Chatto and Windus).

—— (1990), *Quasi-States* (Cambridge: Cambridge University Press).

Jackson, R. and James, A. (1993), 'The Character of Independent Statehood' in Jackson et al. (eds).

—— (eds) (1993), *States in a Changing World* (Oxford: Oxford University Press).

Jalal, A. (1990), *The State of Martial Rule: The Origins of Pakistan's Political Economy of Defence* (Cambridge: Cambridge University Press).

James, C. (1961), *Federalism We Failed Miserably* (Trinidad: Tunapuna).

Janowitz, M. (1960), *The Professional Soldier* (New York, NY: The Free Press).

Jankowski, J. (1991), 'Egypt and Early Arab Nationalism, 1908–1922', in Kakhlidi (ed.).

—— (1997), 'Arab Nationalism and Nasserism in Egyptian State Policy', in Gershoni et al. (eds).

—— (2001), *Nasser's Egypt, Arab Nationalism, and the United Arab Republic* (Boulder, CO: Lynne Rienner).

Jansen, M. (1954), *The Japanese and Sun Yat-sen* (Cambridge, MA: Harvard University Press).

Johnson, W. (1965), 'The Cameroon Federation', in Lewis (ed.).

—— (1970), *The Cameroon Federation* (Princeton, NJ: Princeton University Press).

Joseph, R. (1977), *Radical Nationalism in Cameroon* (Oxford: Oxford University Press).

—— (ed.) (1978), *Gaullist Africa* (Enugu: Fourth Dimension Publishers).

Jin, T. (1950), *Taiwan de difang zizhi* (Taiwan's Local Self-Government) (Taibei: Zhengzhong shuju).

Johnson, G. (1973), *Our English Heritage* (Westport, CT: Greenwood Press).

Johnson, M. (1999), 'The Beginning and the End', *Social and Economic Studies* 48:4, 117–49.

Jović, D. (2003), 'Yugoslavism and Yugoslav Communism' in Djokić (ed.).

Judah, T. (2000), *The Serbs: History, Myth, and the Destruction of Yugoslavia* (New Heaven, NJ: Yale University Press).

Judt, T. (2005), *Postwar: A History of Europe since 1945* (New York, NY: The Penguin Press).

Kazowicz, A. (1994), *Peaceful Territorial Change* (Columbia, SC: University of South Carolina Press).

Kagarlitsky, B. (1996), *Farewell Perestroika: A Soviet Chronicle* (London: Verso).

Kahin, A. (1985), 'Introduction', in Kahin (ed.).

—— (ed.) (1985), *Regional Dynamics of the Indonesian Revolution* (Honolulu, HI: University of Hawaii Press).

Kahin, G. (1947), 'Government in Indonesia', *Far Eastern Survey* 16:4, 37–41.

—— (1949), 'Indirect Rule in East Indonesia', *Pacific Affairs* 22:3, 227–38.

—— (2003), *Nationalism and Revolution in Indonesia* (Ithaca, NY: Cornell University Southeast Asia Program Publications).

Kahler, M. (2006), 'Territoriality and Conflict in an Era of Globalization' in Kahler et al. (eds).

Kahler, M. and Walter, B. (eds) (2006), *Territoriality and Conflict in an Era of Globalization* (Cambridge: Cambridge University Press).

Kakhlidi, R. (ed.) (1991), *Origins of Arab Nationalism* (New York, NY: Columbia University Press).

Kamenec, I. (1992), *Slovenský štát 1939-1945* (Prague: Anomal).

Kaplan, K. (1989), *Mocní a bezmocní* (Toronto, ON: Sixty-Eight Publishers).

Kardelj, E. (1977). 'Excerpts from the Keynote Address by Edvard Kardelj Delivered at the Thirtieth Session of the Presidency of the CC LCY' in Bošković et al. (eds).

—— (1975), 'The System of Socialist Self-Management in Yugoslavia' in Bošković et al. (eds).

—— (1980), *Self-Management and the Political System* (Belgrade: STP).

Katzenstein, P. (ed.) (1996), *The Culture of National Security* (New York, NY: Columbia University Press).

Kavalski, E. (2005), '"All o' we is one": Imaginary Federation and the Federation of the Imagination of the West Indies', *Journal of West Indian Literature* 13:1/2, 28–56.

—— (2006), 'From the Western Balkans to the Greater Balkans Area: The External Conditioning of "Awkward" and "Integrated" States', *Mediterranean Quarterly* 17:3, 86–100.

—— (2007), 'The Fifth Debate and the Emergence of Complex International Relations Theory: Notes on the Application of Complexity Theory to the Study of International Life', *Cambridge Review of International Affairs* 20:3, 435–54.

—— (2008), *Extending the European Security Community: Constructing Peace in the Balkans* (London: I.B. Tauris).

Kavalski, E. and McCullock, M. (2005), 'Back to Althusius: Pre-Westphalian Suggestions for a Post-Westphalian World', *Atlantic Journal of World Affairs* 1:1, 106–127.

Keatley, P. (1963), *The Politics of Partnership* (Harmondsworth: Penguin).

Keddie, N. (1992), 'Material Culture, Technology, and Geography: Toward a Holistic Comparative Study of the Middle East', in Cole (ed.).

Kemp, W. (1999), *Nationalism and Communism in Eastern Europe and the Soviet Union* (New York, NY: St. Martin's Press).

Kempton, D. and Clark, T. (eds). (2002), *Unity or Separation* (Westport, CT: Praeger).

Kenez, P. (2006), *A History of the Soviet Union from the Beginning to the End* (Cambridge: Cambridge University Press).

Kennedy, M. (1991), 'Dilemmas in Middle Eastern Social Sciences', in Sullivan et al. (eds).

Keohane, R. (2002), *Power and Governance in a Partially Globalized World* (London: Routledge).

Khadduri, M. (1946), 'Towards and Arab Union', *American Political Science Review* 40:1, 90–100.

Khalidi, R. (1991), 'Arab Nationalism: Historical Problems in the Literature', *American Historical Review* 96:5, 1363–1373.

Khalil, N. (2002), 'The Forgotten President', *Al-Ahram Weekly* 595, 18–24 July.

Khan, M. (1967), *Friends Not Masters* (Oxford: Oxford University Press).

Khan, A. (2005), *Politics of Identity* (New Delhi: Sage Publications).

Kienle, E. (1995), 'Arab Unity Schemes Revisited: Interests, Identity, and Policy in Syria and Egypt', *International Journal of Middle East Studies* 27:1, 53–71.

Killion, T. (1998), *Historical Dictionary of Eritrea* (Lanham, MD: Scarecrow Press).

Kim, M. (1972), *Sovetskiy narod—novaya istoricheskaya obshchnost* (Moscow: Politizdat).

Kincaid, J. (1995), 'Values and Value Tradeoffs in Federalism', *Publius* 25:2, 29–44.

Kincaid, J. and Tarr, G. (eds) (2005), *Constitutional Origins, Structure, and Change in Federal Countries* (Montreal, QC: McGill-Queen's University Press).

King, A. (2001), *Identity and Decolonisation: The Policy of Partnership in Southern Rhodesia 1945–1962* (DPhil Thesis: Oxford University).

King, G., Keohane, R. and Verba, S. (1994), *Designing Social Inquiry* (Princeton, NJ: Princeton University Press).

Kingsbury, D. (1998), *The Politics of Indonesia* (Oxford: Oxford University Press).

Kirkwood, K. (1955), 'British Central Africa', *Annals of the American Academy of Political and Social Sciences* 298:1, 130–41.

Klaus, V. (2006), 'Co prezident nikdy neřekl o Visegrádské čtyřce—dementi č. 17' <http://www.hrad.cz/cms/cz/prezident_cr/co_prezident_nerekl/3859.shtml>, accessed 22 September 2006.

Kleis, G. (1980), 'Confrontation and Incorporation: Igbo Ethnicity in Cameroon', *African Studies Review* 23:3, 89–100.

Knop, K., Ostry, S., Simeon, R. and Swinton, K. (eds) (1995), *Rethinking Federalism* (Vancouver, BC: University of British Columbia Press).

Kofele-Kale, N. (ed.) (1980), *An African Experiment in Nation Building: The Bilingual Cameroon Republic* (Boulder, CO: Westview Press).

Konings, P. (2000), *The Anglophone Struggle for Federalism in Cameroon* (Leiden: African Studies Center).

—— (2005), 'The Anglophone Cameroon-Nigeria Boundary', *African Affairs* 104:415, 275–301.

Konings, P. and Nyamnjoh, F. (1997), 'The Anglophone Problem in Cameroon', *Journal of Modern African Studies* 35:2, 207–229.

—— (2000), 'Construction and Deconstruction: Anglophones or Autochthons', *African Anthropologist* 7:1, 5–35.

Kowalski, R. (1997), *The Russian Revolution, 1917–1921* (London: Routledge).

Kower, P. and Legro, J. (1996), 'Norms, Identity, and Their Limits', in Katzenstein (ed.).

Kozlova, N. (1996), *Gorizonty povsednevnosti sovetskoy ehpokhi. Golosa iz khora* (Moscow: Russian Academy of Sciences).

Krahman, E. (2005), 'American Hegemony or Global Governance', *International Studies Review* 7:4, 531–45.

Krasner, S. (1999), *Sovereignty: Organized Hypocrysy* (Princeton, NJ: Princeton University Press).

Kraus, M. and Stanger, A. (eds) (2000), *Irreconcilable Differences?* (Lanham, MD: Rowman & Littlefield).

—— (2000), 'The Past as Prologue', in Kraus and Stanger (eds).

Krejci, J. and Machonin, P. (1996), *Czechoslovakia, 1918–1992* (New York, NY: St. Martin's Press).

Kroupa, D. (2000), 'A Comment on Čarnogurský and Pithart', in Kraus and Stanger (eds).

Kučera, M. and Pavlík, Z. (1995), 'Czech and Slovak Demography', in Musil (ed.).

Kukushkin, Y. and Kuznetsov, O. (1987), *Ocherk istorii sovetskoy konstitutsii* (Moscow: Politizdat).

Kull, A. (1992), *The Color-Blind Constitution* (Cambridge: Cambridge University Press).

Kuhn, P. (1975), 'Local Self-Government under the Republic' in Wakerman et al. (eds).

Kusý, M. (2004), 'My Reflections on the Czechoslovak Split', *The New Presence: The Prague Journal of Central European Affairs*, 6:3, 18.

Kux, S. (1990), *Soviet Federalism* (Boulder, CO: Westview Press).

—— (1996), 'From USSR to the Commonwealth of Independent States' in Hesse et al (eds).

Kymlicka, W. (1996), *Multicultural Citizenship* (New York, NY: Oxford University Press).

—— (1997), *States, Nations and Cultures* (Assen: Van Gorcum).

—— (1998), 'Is Federalism a Viable Alternative to Secession' in Lehning (ed.).

—— (2001), *Politics in the Vernacular* (Oxford: Oxford University Press).

—— (2007), *Minority Rights and the New International Politics of Diversity* (Toronto, ON: University of Toronto Press).

Kymlicka, W. and Norman, W. (eds) (2000), *Citizenship in Diverse Societies* (Oxford: Oxford University Press).

Laclau, E. (1979), *Politics and Ideology in Marxist Theory* (London: Verso).

—— (1990), *New Reflections on the Revolution of Our Time* (London: Verso).

Laclau, E. and Mouffe, C. (1985), *Hegemony and Socialist Strategy* (London: Verso).

Lake, D. and Morgan, P. (eds) (1997), *Regional Orders* (University Park, PA: Pennsylvania State University Press).

Lambert, R. (1959), 'Factors in Bengali Regionalism in Pakistan', *Far Eastern Survey* 28:4, 49–58.

Lampe, J. (1996), *Yugoslavia as History* (Cambridge: Cambridge University Press).

Lapidus, G. (1992), *From Union to Commonwealth* (Cambridge: Cambridge University Press).

LaPorte, R. (1975), *Power and Privilege: Influence and Decision-Making in Pakistan* (Berkeley, CA: University of California Press).

Larner, W. and Walters, W. (eds) (2004), *Global Governmentality* (London: Routledge).

Lary, D. (1997), 'Regions and Nation', *Pacific Affairs* 70:2, 181–94.

Lee, T. (2004), 'Democracy and Federalism in Greater China', *Orbis* 48:2, 275–83.

Lehning, P. (ed.) (1998), *Theories of Secession* (London: Routledge).

Leff, C. (1988), *National Conflict in Czechoslovakia* (Princeton, NJ: Princeton University Press).

—— (1996), *The Czech and Slovak Republics* (Boulder, CO: Westview Press).

Legge, J. (1961), *Central Authority and Regional Autonomy in Indonesia* (Ithaca, NY: Cornell University Press).

Lenin, V. (1964), *Collected Works*, Vol. 20 (Moscow: Progress).

—— (1965), *Collected Works*, Vol. 31 (Moscow: Progress)

Leposavić, R. (ed.) (2004), *Samizdat* (Belgrade: B92).

Lev, D. and McVey, R. (eds) (1996), *Making Indonesia* (Ithaca, NY: Cornell University Press).

Levich, E. (1993), *The Kwangsi Way in Kuomintang China, 1931–1939* (Armonk, NY: M.E.Sharpe).

LeVine, V. (1964), *The Cameroons* (Berkeley, CA: University of California Press).

—— (1971), *The Cameroon Federal Republic* (Ithaca, NY: Cornell University Press).

—— (1986), 'Leadership and Regime Changes in Perspective', in Schatzberg et al. (eds).

Lewis, W. (ed.) (1965), *French Speaking Africa* (New York, NY: Walker).

Leys, C. (1958), *European Politics in Southern Rhodesia* (Oxford: Oxford University Press).

Li Z. (1948), 'Ping xianfazhong de difang zhidu' (Criticizing the Local System Contained in the Constitution), *Xinshengbao*, 9 May 1948, 2.

—— (1951), *Taiwan difang zizhi xinlun* (A New Discussion of Taiwan's Local Self-Government) (Taibei: Zhongyang wenwu gongyingshe yinhang).

—— (1954), *Zhongguo difang zizhi zonglun* (A General Discussion of China's Local Self-Government) (Taibei: Zhongguo difang zizhi xuehui).

—— (1972), *Li Zonghuang huiyilu: bashisan nian fendou shi* (The Memoirs of Li Zonghuang: Eighty-three Years of Struggle) (Taibei: Zhongguo difang zizhi xuehui).

Liddle, R. (1970), *Ethnicity, Party and National Integration* (New Haven, NJ: Yale University Press).

Lincoln, W. (1999), *Red Victory: A History of the Russian Civil War* (Jackson, TN: De Capo Press).

Lindebarger, P. (1937), *The Political Doctrines of Sun Yat-sen* (Baltimore, MD: Johns Hopkins University Press).

Lipták, L. (1999), *Storočie dlhšie ako sto rokov* (Bratislava: Kalligram).

Longrigg, S. (1974), *A Short History of Eritrea* (Westport, CT: Greenwood Press).

Lowenthal, D. (1960), 'The Range and Variation of Caribbean Societies', *Annals of the New York Academy of Sciences* 5:1, 786–95.

—— (1961) 'The Social Background of West Indian Federation' in Lowenthal (ed.).

—— (ed.) (1961), *The West Indies Federation* (New York, NY: Columbia University Press).

Lowenthal, D. and Comitas, L. (eds) (1973), *The Aftermath of Sovereignty: West Indian Perspectives* (New York, NY: Anchor Press/Doubleday).

Lyons, T. (2006), 'Diasporas and Homeland Conflict' in Kahler et al. (eds).

Lukic, R. and Lynch, A. (1996), *Europe from the Balkans to the Urals* (Oxford: Oxford University Press).

Macdonald, R. (2005), 'Kaleidoscopic Federalism', in Gaudreault-DesBiens et al. (eds).

Macek, M. (2000), 'Fragments from the Dividing of Czechoslovakia', in Kraus and Stanger (eds).

MacFarquhar, R. (ed.) (1993), *The Politics of China: The Eras of Mao and Deng* (Cambridge: Cambridge University Press).

MacGregor-Hastie, R. (1959), *The Life and Times of Nikita Kruschev* (London: Hamilton).

Mackie, J. (1980), 'Integrating and Centrifugal Factors in Indonesian Politics', in Mackie (ed.).

—— (ed.) (1980), *Indonesia: The Making of a Nation* (Canberra, ACT: Australian National University Press).

Máiz, R. and Requejo, R. (eds) (2005), *Democracy, Nationalism and Multiculturalism* (London: Frank Cass).

Makropoulou, I. (2007), *Pan-Arabism* (Athens: Hellenic Center for European Studies).

Malesevic, S. (2000), 'Ethnicity and Federalism in Communist Yugoslavia and Its Successor States' in Ghai, Y. (ed.).

Maluka, Z.K. (1995), *The Myth of Constitutionalism in Pakistan* (Karachi: Oxford University Press).

Mann, M. (1993), 'Nation State in Europe and Other Continents', *Daedalus* 122:3, 115–40.

Mansoor, A.K. (2002), 'Federalism in Pakistan' *Asian and African Studies* 11:1, 37–48.

Mao Zedong (1942), 'Rectify the Party's Style of Work' in *The Selected Works of Mao Tse-tung*, <http://www.marxists.org/reference/archive/mao/selected-works/volume-3/mswv3_06.htm#bm5>, accessed on 10 December 2007.

—— (1956), 'On the Ten Major Relationships' in *The Selected Works of Mao Tse-tung*, <http://www.marxists.org/reference/archive/mao/selected-works/volume-5/mswv5_51.htm>, accessed on 10 December 2007.

Marcus, H. (1994), *A History of Ethiopia* (Berkeley, CA: University of California Press).

Marein, N. (1954), *The Ethiopian Empire* (Rotterdam: Royal Netherlands Print and Lithographing Co.).

Margalit, A. (2002), *The Ethics of Memory* (Cambridge, MA: Harvard University Press).

Markakis, J. (1988), 'The Nationalist Revolution in Eritrea', *Journal of Modern African Studies* 26:1, 51–70.

Markovic, M. (1995), 'The Federal Experience in Yugoslavia' in Knop et al. (ed.).

Martin, T. (2001), *The Affirmative Action Empire* (Ithaca, NY: Cornell University Press).

Marx, K. and Engels, F. (1970), *The German Ideology* (London: Lawrence and Wishart).

Mason, A. (2000), *Community, Solidarity and Belonging* (Cambridge: Cambridge University Press).

Mason, P. (1957), 'Partnership in Central Africa', *International Affairs* 33:2, 154–64.

Mastny, V. (1996), *The Cold War and Soviet Insecurity* (Oxford: Oxford University Press).

—— (2000), 'The Historical Experience of Federalism in East Central Europe', *East European Politics and Societies*, 14:1, 64–96.

Maxwell, A. (2002), 'Hungaro-Slavism: Territorial and National Identity in Nineteenth-Century Slovakia', *East Central Europe* 29:1, 45–58.

—— (2005), 'Multiple Nationalism', *Nationalism and Ethnic Politics* 11:3, 385–414.

Mbaku, M. and Ihonvbere, J. (eds) (1998), *The Transition to Democratic Governance in Africa* (Westport, CT: Praeger).

Mbiakop, J. (1996), *E.M.L. Endeley and His Quest for Southern Cameroon's Integration with Nigeria, 1955–1961* (Long Essay, University of Buea).

Mbuagbo, O. (2002), 'Cameroon: Exploring Anglophone Identity in State Deconstruction', *Social Identities* 8:3, 431–38.

McAdam, D., Tarrow, S. and Tilly, C. (2001), *Dynamics of Contention* (Cambridge: Cambridge University Press).

McAuley, A. (1991), *Soviet Federalism* (Leicester: Leicester University Press).

McClellan, W. (1969), 'Postwar Political Evolution' in Vucinich, W. (ed.).

McCullock, M. (2006), 'Johanes Althusius' *Politica*: The Culmination of Calvin's Right to Resistance', *European Legacy* 11:5, 485–99.

McGarry, J. and O'Leary, B. (1993), *The Politics of Ethnic Conflict Regulation* (London: Routledge).

—— (1994), 'The Political Regulation of National and Ethnic Conflict', *Parliamentary Affairs* 47:1, 94–115.

—— (2007), 'Federation and Managing Nations', in Burgess et al. (eds).

McKay, D. (1999), *Federalism and European Union* (Oxford: Oxford University Press).

McLean, H. and Vickery W. (eds) (1961), *1956: The Year of Protest 1956* (New York, NY: Vintage Books).

McMahon, R.J. (1981), *Colonialism and Cold War* (Ithaca, NY: Cornell University Press).

McVey, R. (1996), 'Building Behemoth: Indonesian Constructions of the Nation State', in Lev and McVey (eds).

Meehan, D. (1980), 'Yugoslavia After Tito: Powder Keg of the Balkans', *Air University Review* 31:6, 114–17.

Mengisteab, K. (1997), 'New Approaches to State Building in Africa', *African Studies Review* 40:3, 111–132.

Merill, G. (1961), 'The Survival of the Past in the West Indies' in Lowenthal (ed.).

Milanovic, B. (1994), 'Why Have Communist Federations Collapsed', *Challenge* 37:2, 61–5.

Miller, D. (1999), 'Group Identities, National Identities and Democratic Politics', in Horton et al. (eds).

—— (2001), 'Nationality in Divided Societies', in Gagnon et al. (eds).

Miller, R. (1981), *Federalism as a Safety Valve* (Canberra, ACT: Australian National University Press).

Mirsepassi, A., Basu, A. and Weaver, F. (eds) (2003), *Localizing Knowledge in a Globalizing World* (Syracuse, NY: Syracuse University Press).

Mitchell, T. (2003), 'Deterritorialization and the Crisis of Social Science', in Mirsepassi et al. (eds).

Mkwi, P. and Nyamnjoh, F. (1997), *Regional Balance and National Integration* (Yaoundé: ICASSRST Monograph).

Monga, Y. (2001), 'The Politics of Identity Negotiation in Cameroon', *International Negotiation* 6:1, 199–228.

Mordecai, J. (1968), *The West Indies: The Federal Negotiations* (London: Allen and Unwin).

Morris-Jones, W. (1972), 'Pakistan: Post-Mortem and the Roots of Bangladesh', *Political Quarterly* 43:2, 187–200.

Munroe, T. (1984), *The Politics of Constitutional Decolonization* (Kingston: University of the West Indies Press).

Murphy, P. (1995), *Party Politics and Decolonization* (Oxford: Clarendon Press).

Musil, J. (ed.) (1995), *The End of Czechoslovakia* (Budapest: Central European University Press).

Namier, L. (1917), *The Czecho-Slovaks: An Oppressed Nationality* (London: Hodder and Stoughton).

Negash, T. (1987), *Italian Colonialism in Eritrea, 1882–1941* (Stockholm: Almqvist and Wiksell).

—— (1997), *Eritrea and Ethiopia: The Federal Experience* (New Brunswick, NJ: Transaction Publishers).

Ngoh, V. (1999), 'The Origins of the Marginalization of Former Southern Camcroonians', *Journal of Third World Studies* 16:1, 162–85.

—— (2000), *Southern Cameroons, 1922–1961* (Aldershot: Ashgate).

Nice, D. (1987), *Federalism: The Politics of Intergovernmental Relations* (New York, NY: St. Martin's Press).

Njeuma, M. (1995), 'Reunification and Political Opportunity in the Making of Cameroon's Independence', *Paideuma* 41:1, 27–37.

Nordlinger, E. (1972), *Conflict Regulation in Divided Societies* (Cambridge, MA: Harvard University Press).

—— (1977), *Soldiers in Politics* (Upper Saddle River, NJ: Prentice-Hall).

Nyamnjoh, F. (1999), 'Cameroon: A Country United by Ethnic Ambition and Difference', *African Affairs* 98:390, 101–18.

Nyamnjoh, F. and Rowlands, M. (1998), 'Elite Associations and the Politics of Belonging in Cameroon', *Africa* 68:3, 309–319.

Ó Tuathail, G. and Dahlman, C. (2004), 'The Clash of Governmentalities: Displacement and Return in Bosnia', in Larner et al. (eds).

O'Brien, R. (2005), 'Global Civil Society and Global Governance', in Ba et al. (eds).

Ocić, Č. (1998), 'The Regional Problem and the Breakup of the State', *Acta Slavica Iaponica* 16:1, 74–110.

O'Leary, B. (2001), 'An Iron Law of Nationalism and Federation', *Nations and Nationalism* 7:3, 273–96.

—— (2004), 'Federations and the Management of Nations', in Conversi (ed.).

Olynyk, S. (1965), *Soviet Federalism in Theory and Practice* (Washington, DC: Georgetown University Press).

O'Riordan, T. (ed.) (2001), *Globalism, Localism, Identity* (London: Earthscan).

O'Riordan, T. and Church, C. (2001), 'Synthesis and Content', in O'Riordan (ed.).

Osaghae, E. (2004), 'Federalism and the Management of Diversity in Africa', *Identity, Culture and Politics* 5:1/2, 162–78.

Ozughen, J. (1997), *The Origins and Development of the Reunification Movement in the British Southern Cameroons* (Long Essay, University of Buea).

Osiander, A. (2001), 'Before Sovereignty', *Review of International Studies* 21:1, 119–45.

Ostrovidova, H. (1996), 'A Comparative Analysis of Theories of Sovereignty' in Hiceky and Ugrinsky (eds).

Padmore, O. (1999), 'Federation: The Demise of an Idea', *Social and Economic Studies* 48:4, 21–63.

Parfitt, T. (2006), 'Hylomorphism, Complexity and Development', *Third World Quarterly* 27:3, 421–41.

Park, R. (1954), 'East Bengal: Pakistan's Troubled Province', *Far Eastern Survey* 23:5, 70–74.

Park, R. and Wheeler, R. (1954), 'East Bengal Under Governor's Rule', *Far Eastern Survey* 23:9, 129–34.

Paul, J. (2000), 'Ethnicity and the New Constitutional Orders of Ethiopia and Eritrea' in Ghai (ed.).

Pavkovic, A. and Radan, P. (2007), *Creating New States* (Aldershot: Ashgate).

Pavlowitch, S. (1992), *Tito: Yugoslavia's Great Dictator* (Columbus, OH: Ohio State University Press).

—— (2002), *Serbia: The History Behind the Name* (London: Hurst and Company).

Pennock, J. and Chapman, J. (eds) (1978), *Anarchism* (New York, NY: New York University Press).

Pepper, S. (1978), *Civil War in China* (Berkeley, CA: University of California Press).

Perica, V. (2002), *Balkan Idols* (Oxford: Oxford University Press).

Perlmutter, A. (1969), 'The Praetorian State and the Praetorian Army', *Comparative Politics* 1:3, 382–404

Pfabian, A. (1991), 'The Political Feasibility of the Austro-Marxist Proposal for the Solution of the Nationality Problem of the Danubian Monarchy' in Ra'anan et al. (eds).

Pfaff, R. (1970), 'The Function of Arab Nationalism', *Comparative Politics* 2:2, 147–67.

Phillips. F. (1977), *Freedom in the Caribbean* (New York, NY: Oceana Publications).

Pilkington, H. (1998), *Migration, Displacement and Identity in Post-Soviet Russia* (London: Routledge).

Pinder, J. (2007), 'Multinational Federations: Introduction' in Burgess, M. and Pinder, J. (eds).

Pithart, P. (1990), *Osmašedesátý* (Praha: Rozmluvy).

—— (1995), 'The Division of Czechoslovakia', *Canadian Slavonic Papers* 38:3/4, 321–38.

—— (2000), 'The Division/Dissolution of Czechoslovakia', in Kraus and Stanger (eds).

Pittsburská dohoda (1918), <http://www.pef.zcu.cz/pef/khi/pittsb.htm>, accessed 30 September 2006.

Pomerance, M. (1976), 'The United States and Self-Determination', *American Journal of International Law* 70:1, 1–27.

Popovski, V. (1995), 'Yugoslavia: Politics, Federation, Nation' in Smith (ed.).

Příbram, J. (1976), 'Slováci českýma očima', *Svědectví* 13:52, 637–53.

Prichard, A. (2007), 'Justice, Order, and Anarchy: The International Political Theory of Pierre-Joseph Proudhon (1809-1865)', *Millennium* 35:3, 623–45.

Prigogine, I. and Stengers, I. (1985), *Order Out of Chaos* (London: Fontana).

Příhoda, P. (1995), 'Mutual Perceptions in Czech-Slovak Relationships', in Musil (ed.).

Proudhon, P.-J. (1973 [1863]), *The Principle of Federation* (Toronto, ON: University of Toronto Press).

Prouty, C. and Rosenfeld, E. (1994), *Historical Dictionary of Ethiopia and Eritrea* (Metuchen, NJ: Scarecrow Press).

Putnam, R. (1973), *The Beliefs of Politicians* (New Heaven, NJ: Yale University Press).

Pynsent, R. (1994), *Questions of Identity: Czech and Slovak Ideas of Nationality and Personality* (Budapest: Central European University Press).

Quinlivan, J. (1999), 'Coup-Proofing: Its Practice and Consequences in the Middle East', *International Security* 24:2, 131–65.

Ra'anan, U., Mesner, M., Armes., K. and Martin, K. (eds) (1991), *State and Nation in Multiethnic Societies* (Manchester: Manchester University Press).

Raeff, M. (1990), *Russia Abroad* (Oxford: Oxford University Press).

Ramet, P. (1984), *Nationalism and Federalism in Yugoslavia* (Bloomington, IN: Indiana University Press).

Ramet, S. (1992), *Nationalism and Federalism in Yugoslavia, 1962–1991* (Bloomington, IN: Indiana University Press).

—— (2005), *Thinking about Yugoslavia* (Cambridge: Cambridge University Press).

—— (2006), *The Three Yugoslavias* (Washington, DC: Woodrow Wilson Center Press).

Ramet, S. and Pavlakovic, V. (eds) (2005), *Serbia since 1989: Politics and Society under Milosevic and After* (Seattle, WA: Washington University Press).

Raßloff, U. (1999), 'Gründungsmythen in der tschechischen Literatur', in Behring et al. (eds).

Reid, A. (1973), *The Indonesian National Revolution 1945–1950* (Melbourne, VIC: Longman).

Requejo, F. (1999), 'Cultural Pluralism, Nationalism and Federalism', *European Journal of Political Research* 32:5, 255–86.

—— (ed.) (2001), *Democracy and National Pluralism* (London: Routledge).

—— (2001), 'Democratic Legitimiacy and National Pluralism' in Requejo, F. (ed.) *Democracy and National Pluralism* (London: Routledge).

—— (2004), 'Federalism and the Quality of Democracy in Multinational Contexts', in Amoretti and Bermeo (eds).

Rhodesia and Nyasaland (1953), *The Federation of Rhodesia and Nyasaland* (Salisbury: Government Printer).

Rich Dorman, S. (2005), 'Narratives of Nationalism in Eritrea', *Nations and Nationalism* 11:2, 203–22.

Ricklefs, M. (1993), *A History of Modern Indonesia* (Stanford, CA: Stanford University Press).

—— (2001), *A History of Modern Indonesia since c. 1200* (London: Palgrave).

Riley, P. (1973), 'The Origins of Federal Theory in International Relations Ideas', *Polity* 6:1, 87–121.

Rizvi, H. (2000), *Military, State and Society in Pakistan* (Basingstoke: Macmillan).

Roeder, P. (1991), 'Soviet Federalism and Ethnic Mobilization', *World Politics* 43:2, 196–232.

—— (1998), 'Liberalization and Ethnic Entrepreneurs in the Soviet Successor States' in Crawford et al (eds).

Ronen, D. (1979), *The Quest for Self-Determination* (New Haven, NJ: Yale University Press).

Rosberg, C.G. (1956), 'The Federation of Rhodesia and Nyasaland', *Annals of the American Academy of Political and Social Sciences* 306:1, 98–105.

Rosenau, J. (1988), 'The State in an Era of Cascading Politics', *Comparative Political Studies* 21:1, 13–44.

—— (2003), *Distant Proximities* (Princeton, NJ: Princeton University Press).

Rosenau, J., Der Derian, J., Elshtain, J, Smith, S. and Sylvester, C. (1993), *Global Voices: Dialogues in International Relations* (Boulder, CO: Westview Press).

Rotberg, R. (1988), *The Founder: Cecil Rhodes and the Pursuit of Power* (Oxford: Oxford University Press).

—— (2003), 'Failed States, Collapsed States, Weak States: Causes and Indicators' in Rotberg (ed.).

—— (ed.) (2003), *State Failure and State Weakness in Time of Terror* (Washington, DC: Brookings Institution Press).

Roy, O. (2004), *Globalized Islam* (New York, NY: Columbia University Press).

Rubin, B. (1991), 'Pan-Arab Nationalism', *Journal of Contemporary History* 26:3/4, 535–51.

Ruggie, J. (1993), 'Territoriality and Beyond', *International Organization* 47:1, 139–74.

Rupnik, J. (1995), 'The International Context', in Musil (ed.).

Rusinow, D. (1977), *The Yugoslav Experiment* (London: Hurst).

—— (ed.) (1988), *Yugoslavia: A Fractured Experiment* (Washington, DC: Wilson Center Press).

—— (1991), 'Yugoslavia: Balkan Breakup?', *Foreign Policy* 83:1, 143–59.

—— (1995), 'The Yugoslav People' in Sugar (ed.).

Ryan, S. (1997), 'Nationalism and Ethnic Conflict' in White et al. (eds).

Rychlík, J. (1995), 'From Autonomy to Federation, 1938–1968', in Musil (ed.).

—— (2000), 'The Possibilities for Czech-Slovak Compromise, 1989–1992', in Kraus and Stanger (eds).

—— (2007), 'Czech-Slovak Relations in Czechoslovakia, 1918–1939', in Cornwall and Evans (eds).

Sakwa, R. (1996), *Russian Politics and Society* (London: Routledge).

Samad, D. (1990), 'Arise the West Indian', *Journal of West Indian Literature* 4:1, 66–79.

Sarup, M. (1996), *Identity, Culture and the Postmodern World* (Edinburgh: Edinburgh University Press).

Sattar, A. (2007), Pakistan's Foreign Policy (Oxford: Oxford University Press).

Sayeed, K. (1954), 'Federalism and Pakistan', *Far Eastern Survey* 23:9, 139–43.

—— (1967), *The Political System of Pakistan* (Boston, MA: Houghton Mifflin).

Schapiro, L. (1960), *The Communist Party of the Soviet Union* (London: Random House).

Schatzberg, M. and Zartman, I. (eds) (1986), *The Political Economy of Cameroon* (New York, NY: Praeger).

Schiller, A.A. (1955), *The Formation of Federal Indonesia* (The Hague: W. Van Hoeve).

Schoppa, R. (1977), 'Province and Nation', *Journal of Asian Studies* 36:4, 661–74.

Schram, S. (1985), *The Scope of State Power in China* (London: School of Oriental and African Studies).

Sekulic, D. (1997), 'The Creation and Dissolution of the Multinational State', *Nations and Nationalism* 3:2, 165–79.

Sekulic, D., Massey, G. and Hodson, R. (1994), 'Who Were the Yugoslavs?', *American Sociological Review* 59:1, 83–97.

Seers, D. (1957), 'Federation of the British West Indies', *Social and Economic Studies* 6:2, 197–214

Selassie, B. (1989), *Eritrea and the United Nations* (Trenton, NJ: Red Sea Press).

Seliktar, O. (2004), *Politics, Paradigms and Intelligence Failures* (Armonk: M.E. Sharpe).

Sergeevitch, V. (1982), *The State and Nations in the USSR* (Moscow: Progress Publishers).

Seroka J. (1978), 'Prospects for Stability in Post-Tito Yugoslavia', *Slavic Review* 37:2, 268–82.

—— (1993), 'Variation in the Evolution of the Yugoslav Communist Parties' in Seroka et al. (eds).

—— (1994), 'The Dissolution of Federalism in East and Central Europe' in de Villiers (ed.).

—— (2002), 'The Demise of Socialist Federations' in Heinemann-Grüder (ed.).

Seroka, J. and Pavlović, V. (eds) (1993), *The Tragedy of Yugoslavia* (London: M.E. Sharpe).

Sisson, R. and Rose, L.E. (1990), *War and Secession: Pakistan, India, and the Creation of Bangladesh* (Karachi: Oxford University Press).

Shah, S. (1994), *Federalism in Pakistan* (Islamabad: National Institute of Pakistan Studies).

Sheehan, M. (2005), *International Security: An Analytical Survey* (Boulder, CO: Lynne Rienner).

Shen Z. and Zhang J. (1993), *Gu Zhenfu zhuan* (Biography of Gu Zhenfu) (Taibeixian: Shuhua chuban, 1993).

Sherlock, P. (1980), *Norman Manley: A Biography* (London: Macmillan).

Shi Y. (1946), *Zhongguo sheng xingzheng zhidu yice* (A Volume on China's Provincial Administration) (Chongqing: Shangwu yinshuguan).

Shoup, P. (1968), *Communism and the Yugoslav National Question* (New York, NY: Columbia University Press).

—— (1992), 'Titoism and the National Question in Yugoslavia' in van den Heuvel et al. (eds).

Shugarman, D. and Whitaker, R. (eds) (1989), *Federalism and Political Community* (Peterborough, ON: Broadview Press).

Siddiqi, F. (2000), 'The State, Relative Deprivation, and War', *Pakistan Perspectives* 5:3, 95–114.

Sidgwick, H. (1903), *The Development of European Polity* (London: Macmillan).

Simeon, R. and Conway, D. (2001), 'Federalism and the Management of Conflict in Multinational Societies', in Gagnon et al. (eds).

Simic, P. (1992), 'Civil War in Yugoslavia' in van den Heuvel et al (eds).

Simonovic, I. (1988), 'Socialism, Federalism, and Ethnic Identity' in Rusinow (ed.).

Singh, T. (1982), *The Soviet Federal State* (New Delhi: Sterling).

Singhal, D. (1962), 'The New Constitution of Pakistan', *Asian Survey* 2:6, 15–23.

Sirc, L. (1979), *The Yugoslav Economy under Self-Management* (London: Macmillan).

Smiley, D. (1972), *Canada in Question* (Toronto, ON: McGraw-Hill).

Smith, G. (1995), 'Mapping the Federal Condition', in Smith (ed.).

—— (ed.) (1995), *Federalism: The Multiethnic Challenge* (London: Longman).

Smith, J. (2004), *Federalism* (Vancouver, BC: University of British Columbia Press).

Soekarno (1952), *Lahirnja Pantjasila: An Outline of the Five Principles of the Indonesian State* (Djakarta: Ministry of Information).

Solingen, E. (1998), *Regional Orders* (Princeton, NJ: Princeton University Press).

Solinger, D. (1977), *Regional Government and Political Integration in Southwest China, 1949–1954* (Berkeley, CA: University of California).

Sorenson, J. (1991), 'Discourses on Eritrean Nationalism and Identity', *Journal of Modern African Studies* 29:2, 301–17.

Springer, H. (1953), 'On Being a West Indian', *Caribbean Quarterly* 3:1, 181–83.

—— (1962), *Reflections on the Failure of the First West Indian Federation* (Cambridge, MA: Harvard University Press).

Stalin, J. (1949), *Sochineniya,* Vol. 11 (Moscow: Gosudarstvennoe izdatel'stvo politicheskoy literatury).

Stanger, A. (1996), 'Czechoslovakia's Dissolution as an Unintended Consequence of the Velvet Constitutional Revolution', *East European Constitutional Review* 5:4, 40–46.

—— (2000), 'The Price of Velvet: Constitutional Politics and the Demise of the Czechoslovak Federation', in Kraus and Stanger (eds).

Stanković, S. (1981), *The End of the Tito Era* (Stanford, CA: California University Press).

Stanovcic, V. (1988), 'History and Status of Ethnic Conflicts' in Rusinow (ed.).

Stark, F. (1976), 'Federalism in Cameroon', *Canadian Journal of African Studies* 10:3, 423–42.

—— (1986), 'Theories of Contemporary State Formation in Africa', *Journal of Modern African Studies* 24:2, 335–347.

Stavenhagen, R. (1996), *Ethnic Conflicts and the Nation State* (Basingstoke: Macmillan).

Stayer, R. (1998), *Why Did the Soviet Union Collapse* (London: M.E. Sharpe).

Steiner, E. (1973), *The Slovak Dilemma* (Cambridge: Cambridge University Press).

Stepan, A. (2001), 'Toward a New Comparative Politics of Federalism', in Stepan (ed.).

—— (ed.) (2001), *Arguing Comparative Politics* (Oxford: Oxford University Press).

Stepanovitch, S. (1978), 'Yugoslavia After Tito: Certain Uncertainty', *Parameters* 8:2, 80–92.

Sterling-Folker, J. (2005), 'Realist Global Governance', in Ba et al. (eds).

Stern, R. (2001), *Democracy and Dictatorship in South Asia* (New Delhi: India Research Press).

Stewart, W. (1982), 'Metaphors, Models, and the Development of Federal Theory', *Publius* 12:2, 5–24.

Stojanović, S. (2000), 'On the Sinking of the Titonik', *Peace Review* 12:1, 51–8.

Suda, Z. (1996), 'Slovakia in Czech National Consciousness, in Musil (ed.).

Sugar, P. (ed.) (1995), *Eastern European Nationalism* (Washington, DC: American University Press).

Sullivan, E. and Ismael, J. (eds) (1991), *The Contemporary Study of the Arab World* (Edmonton, AB: University of Alberta Press).

Sun Yat-sen (1928), *San Min Chu I: The Three Principles of the People* (Shanghai: Commercial Press).

Sur, S. (1997), 'The State Between Fragmentation and Globalization', *European Journal of International Law* 8:3, 421–34.

'Taiji zhanzui qisushu quanwen' (Taiwan War Criminals: Complete Text of the Indictment), *Guoshengbao*, 29 June 1947, 3.

Takougang, J. (2003), 'Nationalism, Democratization and Political Opportunism in Cameroon', *Journal of Contemporary African Studies* 21:3, 427–45.

Tarlton, C. (1965), 'Symmetry and Asymmetry as Elements of Federalism', *Journal of Politics* 27:4, 861–74.

—— (1967) 'Federalism, Political Energy, and Entropy', *Western Political Quarterly* 20:4, 866–76.

Taylor, B. (2003), *Politics and the Russian Army* (Cambridge: Cambridge University Press).

Teiwes, F. (1993), 'The Establishment and Consolidation of the New Regime' in MacFarquhar (ed.).

Tepper, E. (1972/1973), 'Pakistan and the Consequences of Bangladesh', *Pacific Affairs* 45:4, 573–81.

Tessler, M., Nachtwey, J. and Banda, A. (eds) (1999), *Area Studies and Social Science* (Bloomington, IN: Indiana University Press).

Thomas, S. (1955), *Government and Administration in Communist China* (Westport, CT: Greenwood Press).

Thomas-Wooley, B. and Keller, E. (1994), 'Majority Rule and Minority Rights: American Federalism and African Experience', *Journal of Modern African Studies* 32:3, 411–27.

Thompson, R. (1995), *China's Local Councils in the Age of Constitutional Reform* (Cambridge, MA: Harvard University Press).

Thornhill, M. (2004), 'Britain, the United States and the Rise of an Egyptian Leader', *English Historical Review* 119:483, 892–921.

Tilly, C. (2003), *The Politics of Collective Violence* (Cambridge: Cambridge University Press).

Tir, J. and Diehl, P. (1998), 'Demographic Pressure and Interstate Conflict', *Journal of Peace Research* 35:3, 319–339.

Todorović, M. (1974), 'Yugoslavia's New Constitution', *Review of International Affairs* 25:574, 1–4.

Toft, M. (2003), *The Geography of Ethnic Violence* (Princeton, NJ: Princeton University Press).

Tokes, R. (ed.) (1975), *Dissent in the USSR* (Baltimore, MD: Johns Hopkins University Press).

Tomc, G. (1988), 'Classes, Party Elites, and Ethnic Groups' in Rusinow (ed.).

Tønnesson, S. and Antlöv, H. (2001), 'Why Federalism Failed in Indonesia and Indochina but Triumphed in Malaya, 1945–1950', Paper presented at the workshop 'Decolonization and Transformation in Southeast Asia', Singapore, 19–21 February.

Trevaskis, G. (1960), *Eritrea: A Colony in Transition* (Oxford: Oxford University Press).

Tummala, K.K. (1996) 'The Indian Union and Emergency Powers', *International Political Science Review* 17:4, 373–84.

Tung, W. (1964), *The Political Institutions of Modern China* (The Hague: Martinus Mijhoff).

United Nations Review (1959) 'The UN Charts Course for the Cameroons', April/ New York.

van den Heuvel, M. and Siccama, J. (eds) (1992), *The Disintegration of Yugoslavia* (Amsterdam: Rodopi).

van der Linden, M. (2008), *Marxism and the Soviet Union* (Leiden: Brill).

van der Kroef, J. (1954), 'Pantjasila: The National Ideology of New Indonesia', *Philosophy East and West* 4:3, 225–51.

Varma, S. and Narain, V. (eds) (1972), *Pakistan's Political System in Crisis* (Jaipur: University of Rajasthan Press).

Vasiliev, V. (1995), 'Questions of Citizenship After the Breakup of the USSR' in Knop et al. (ed.).

Verdery, K. (1993), 'Nationalism and Nationalist Sentiments in Post-Socialist Romania', *Slavic Review* 52:2, 179–203.

Vershave, F.-X. (1999), *La Francafrique: Le Plus Long Scandale de la République* (Paris: Stock).

Vickers, A. (2003), *A History of Modern Indonesia* (Cambridge: Cambridge University Press).

von Beyme, K. (2005), 'Asymmetric Federalism between Globalization and Regionalization', *Journal of European Public Policy* 12:3, 432–47.

Vucinich, W. (1969), 'The Yugoslav Variation on Marx', in Vucinich (ed.).

—— (ed.) (1969), *Contemporary Yugoslavia* (Berkeley, CA: University of California Press).

Vucković, G. (1997), *Ethnic Cleavages and Conflict* (Aldershot: Ashgate).

Vujacic, V. (1996), 'Institutional Origins of Contemporary Serbian Nationalism', *East European Constitutional Review* 5:4, 51–61.

Wachtel, A. (1998), *Making a Nation, Breaking a Nation* (Stanford, CA: Stanford University Press).

Wade, R. (2005), *The Russian Revolution, 1917* (Cambridge: Cambridge University Press).

Wakeman, F. and Grant, C. (eds) (1975), *Conflict and Control in Late Imperial China* (Berkeley, CA: University of California Press).

Waldron, A. (1990), 'Warlordism versus Federalism', *China Quarterly* 121:2, 116–28.

Walker, E. (1953), 'The Franchise in Central Africa', *Cambridge Historical Journal* 1:1, 93–113.

—— (2003), *Dissolution: Sovereignty and the Breakup of the Soviet Union* (Lanham, MD: Rowman and Littlefield).

Walker, R. (1989), 'Marxism-Leninism as Discourse', *British Journal of Political Science* 19:1, 161–89.

Wasserstrom, J. (ed.) (2003), *Twentieth-Century China* (London: Routledge).

Watts, R. (1966), *New Federations* (Oxford: Clarendon Press).

—— (1989), 'Executive Federalism: The Comparative Context', in Shugarman et al. (eds).

—— (1998), 'Federalism, Federal Political Systems and Federations', *Annual Review of Political Science* 1:1, 117–37.

—— (1999), *Comparing Federal Systems* (Montreal, QC: McGill-Queen's University Press).

—— (2007), 'Multinational Federations in Comparative Perspective', in Burgess and Pinder (eds).

Webber, M. (1997), 'States and Statehood' in White et al. (eds).

—— (2002), 'A Confederation in the Making? Means, Ends, and Prospects of the Commonwealth of Independent States' in Heinemann-Grüder (ed.).

Weinstock, D. (2001), 'Towards a Normative Theory of Federalism', *International Social Science Journal* 53:167, 75–83.

—— (2005), 'The Moral Psychology of Federalism', in Gaudreault-DesBiens et al. (eds).

Welch, C. (1966), *Dream of Unity: Pan-Africanism and Political Unification in West Africa* (Ithaca, NY: Cornell University Press).

Welensky, R. (1952), 'Towards Federation in Central Africa', *Foreign Affairs* 31:2, 141–149.

Wenger, E. (1998), *Communities of Practice: Learning, Meaning and Identity* (Cambridge: Cambridge University Press)

Werbner, R. and Ranger, T. (eds) (1996), *Postcolonial Identities in Africa* (London: Zed Books).

West, R. (1995), *Tito: And the Rise and Fall of Yugoslavia* (New York, NY: Carroll and Graf).

Westfall, G. (1992), *French Colonial Africa* (Lochcarron: Hans Zell Publishers).

Wheeler, R. (1970), *The Politics of Pakistan* (Ithaca, NY: Cornell University Press).

White, B., Little, R. and Smith, M. (eds) (1997), *Issues in World Politics* (New York, NY: St. Martin's Press).

Wilcox, W. (1968), 'Political Change in Pakistan: Structures, Functions, Constraints and Goals', *Pacific Affairs* 41:3, 341–54.

Windrich, E. (1975), *The Rhodesian Problem* (London: Routledge and Kegan Paul).

Winks, R. (1971), *Failed Federations: Decolonization and the British Empire* (Nottingham: University of Nottingham Press).

Wodak, R. and Chilton, P. (eds) (2005), *A New Agenda in (Critical) Discourse Analysis* (Philadelphia, NJ: Benjamins).

Wolchik, S. (1995), 'The Politics of Transition and the Breakup of Czechoslovakia', in Musil (ed.).

Wolf, C. (1948), *The Indonesian Story* (New York, NY: John Day).

Wolff, S. (2006), *Ethnic Conflict* (Oxford: Oxford University Press).

Woodward, P. and Forsyth, M. (eds) (1994), *Conflict and Peace in the Horn of Africa* (Aldershot: Dartmouth).

Woodward, S. (1995), *Balkan Tragedy* (Washington, DC: The Brookings Institution Press).

Wynbrandt, J. (2007), *A Brief History of Pakistan* (New York, NY: Facts on File).

Xenakis, C. (2002), *What Happened to the Soviet Union* (Westport, CT: Praeger).

Xu L. (1974), *Zhongguo xiandaishi* (A history of modern China) (Taibei: Zhengzhong shuju).

Yan, J. (1992), *Lianbang Zhongguo gouxiang* (The concept of federalism in China) (Hong Kong: Minbao chubanshe).

'Yanchang gongshan' (Extension Granted in Public Trial), *Guoshengbao,* 27 June 1947, 3.

Young, C. (ed.) (1993), *The Rising Tide of Cultural Pluralism* (Madison, WN: University of Wisconsin Press).

—— (ed.) (1998), *Ethnic Diversity and Public Policy* (Basingstoke: Macmillan).

Zaidi, A.S. (1995), *Issues in Pakistan's Economy* (Oxford: Oxford University Press).

Žák, V. (1995), 'The Velvet Divorce—Institutional Foundations', in Musil (ed.).

Zewde, B. (1991), *A History of Ethiopia, 1855–1974* (London: James Currey).

Zewde, B. and Pausewang, S. (eds) (2003), *Ethiopia* (Uppsala: Nordiska Afrikainstitutet).

Zheng Y. (1948), 'Sheng zizhi de yiyi ye tezhi' (The Special Qualities and Meaning of Provincial Self-Government), *Xinshengbao*, 7 June 1948, 2.

Ziblatt, D. (2004), 'Rethinking the Origins of Federalism', *World Politics* 57:1, 70–98.

Ziring, L. (1980), *Pakistan: The Enigma of Political Development* (Boulder, CO: Westview Press).

—— (2003), *Pakistan: At the Crosscurrent of History* (Oxford: Oneworld).

'Zizhi juefei tuoyi' (Self-government is Absolutely Not Severing), *Quanmin ribao*, 25 April 1948, 3.

Zubaida, S. (2004), 'Islam and Nationalism: Continuities and Contradictions', *Nations and Nationalism* 10:4, 407–420.

Index

accommodation 3, 6–8, 10, 14, 17, 34, 68, 79, 83, 110, 126, 165, 170
  identity 5, 8, 9, 14, 16, 24, 34, 38, 42, 68, 83, 101, 122, 130, 161–164, 166, 170
  of diversity 7–8, 9, 14, 25, 35, 80–83, 161, 171 *see* identity
Adams, Grantley 19, 21, 22, 26, 29
Afghanistan 170
African nationalism 12, 47, 49, 51–52, 55–56, 58
'African Unity' 60
Ahidjo, Ahmadou 60, 62–65, 68
Albania 117
Amhara 32, 34, 36, 42
Antigua 17, 18, 19, 22
apartheid 49, 50 *see* racial discrimination
Arab federalism 13, 103–104, 108, 110, 112, 164
Arab nationalism 13, 103–104, 107, 109, 112, 159
asymmetric federalism *see* federalism
Australia 3, 24
Austro-Hungarian Empire 130, 134, 137, 139
autonomy 13, 18, 22, 27, 40, 43, 55, 64, 74, 78, 87, 93, 100, 118, 131, 148, 166
Awami League 76, 78, 82
awkward state *see* state

Bangladesh 71, 78, 83
Barbados 17, 18, 19, 22
Basque country 83
Beijing 89–91, 99, 101
Bengali 13, 71, 74, 75, 78–79, 82, 84
  ethnonationalism 72–78, 80, 160–161
  language 74–75, 82
Bolshevik 147, 150, 151, 152 *see* USSR
Bosnia and Herzegovina 3, 115–117, 170
border/boundary 4, 16, 38, 43–44, 61, 62, 65, 80, 99, 105, 141, 150, 167
British Colonial Office 12, 17, 33, 48, 54, 65, 73

British Empire 11, 20, 23, 32, 47, 49, 51, 53, 55, 58, 60, 62, 71, 81, 83
British government 11, 17, 21, 26–28, 32, 37, 48, 51, 54, 57, 109
Bulgaria 117
Bustamante, Alexander 22, 23, 29

Cameroon 12, 59–70, 161
  Anglophone elites 12, 60, 63–66, 68–69
  Eastern 59, 62, 65
  federalism 12, 59–70
  Francophone elites 12, 60, 62, 65, 67–68
  Northern 59
  Southern 59–60, 62–63, 65, 67
  united 62, 64
  West 64
Canada 3, 83
Caribbean 18–20, 23, 26–27, 29
Chiang Kai-shek 13, 87–88, 91–96, 98, 100, 102
China 13, 87–102
  1947 Constitution 88, 93–95, 96
  1954 Constitution 99–100
  feudalism 13, 40, 87, 89, 91, 99
  'Free China' 95–98, 102
  'Third Force' 89, 92–93, 97, 100
Chinese Nationalist Party 87–91, 95–97, 99, 102 *see* Chiang Kai-shek, Sun Yat-sen
Chinese Communist Party 91, 94, 98, 102 *see* Mao Zedong
citizenship 4, 51, 53, 97, 111, 112
civil-military relations 13, 103, 104–106
coercion 10, 109, 121 *see* imposed federalism
cognitive liberation 155
Cold War 2, 48, 98, 100, 102, 109, 115, 126, 151, 165
colonialism 12, 40, 44, 106
communism 96, 99, 118, 119, 136, 151, 153–155 *see* Marxism

comparative study 1, 6, 11, 15, 23, 31, 44, 72–73, 120, 157, 164, 170
complexity 2, 5, 60, 68, 103, 106, 110, 124, 127, 158, 166, 185
compromise 10, 24, 33, 37, 39, 55, 72–74, 90, 126, 136, 141, 171
confederation 2, 9, 15, 18, 88, 101, 103, 107, 124
control 3, 17, 22, 25, 31, 34, 36, 39, 42, 45, 50, 63, 75, 80, 91, 96, 109, 121, 134, 137, 142, 148, 166 *see* power
counter-revolution 40, 147, 154 *see* revolution
coup d'état 41, 104–110
critical assessment 1, 6–8, 11, 14, 61, 84, 137, 163, 169
Croatia 115–117, 124, 126,
culture 7, 24, 35, 36, 40, 43, 60, 63, 69, 78, 101, 110, 138, 156
Czech Republic 129, 131, 134
Czechs 129, 136, 138–141
Czechoslovakia 14, 85, 109, 129–143, 160, 164
  federalism 14, 129–143, 161, 164
Czechoslovakness/Czechoslovak identity 129–130, 134, 139–141
Czechoslovak Communist Party 131–132, 135

decolonization 12, 18, 22, 24, 38, 45, 48, 58, 60, 67, 93
defunct federalism *see* federalism
democracy 8, 42, 52, 71, 73, 77, 79, 82, 89, 93, 96, 100, 102, 113, 141, 154, 160
  constitutional 8, 72, 101, 118
  liberal democracy 8, 17, 22, 35, 40, 47, 50, 62, 68, 79, 101, 121, 130, 140, 159, 161
difference 3, 5, 9, 14–16, 23, 29, 35, 40, 59, 61, 72, 80, 83, 99, 109, 117, 120, 123, 129, 132, 139, 147, 149, 151, 155, 165, 167, 169, 171
discourse theory 14, 149–150, 164
discursive moment 14
disparity 35, 78, 84
'divide and rule' 31, 41
Djilas, Milovan 117, 121
Dominica 17, 18, 22, 26
Dubček, Alexander 135
Dutch colonial rule 31–42, 44–45, 160

East Timor 32, 43
Egypt 13, 32, 103–104, 106–112
elites *see* state elites
emancipation 15, 33, 134, 168 *see* freedom
Endeley, Emmanuel 65, 66
Engels, Friedrich 146, 152,
Eritrea 31, 32–38, 45, 161
  identity 31–33, 37–38, 161
Ethiopia 11, 32–38, 45, 159, 161
  identity 34
Ethiopia-Eritrea federation 12, 32–35, 45, 182
ethnicity 3, 7, 12, 14, 31, 42, 69, 72, 115, 148, 154
ethnonationalism 72, 85, 160
exclusion 6, 15, 33, 40, 42, 52, 71, 74, 81, 102, 111, 134, 141, 153 *see* inclusion
executive federalism *see* federalism

failed state *see* state
federal failure 5, 8, 26, 31, 34, 44, 66, 69, 82, 85, 87, 91, 103, 124, 140, 168
federal identity *see* identity
federal institutions 5, 17, 35, 52–53, 58, 63, 83, 136, 148, 162 *see* federal failure, federalism, state
federal narrative *see* narrative
federal process *see* process
federal state *see* federation, state
federal theory 15, 166 *see* federalism
federalism 1, 2–4, 6, 10–15, 26, 36, 43, 47, 59, 64, 66, 73, 88–90, 100, 103, 117, 130, 145, 156, 158, 160
  asymmetric 9, 12, 35, 38, 41, 52, 79–81, 131, 136, 140–141, 161
  civic 13, 14, 119, 122, 135, 162
  defunct 1, 4, 5, 7, 8–11, 15, 34–37, 39–44, 60, 82, 85, 101–102, 104, 123, 129, 140, 145, 157, 158–171
  degree of 9–10, 67, 73, 105, 131, 140, 148, 161, 171
  domestically-imposed 37, 40, 82, 137, 162, 166
  'essentially contested concept' 1, 180
  executive 9, 25, 77, 81, 94
  externally-imposed 26, 37, 40, 51, 82, 142, 161, 166
  ideological 14, 40, 51, 62, 87, 122, 145, 148, 153, 156, 160, 164
  instrumental 36, 64–67, 76, 130, 134–137, 140, 148, 162

multinational 2, 108, 127, 134
national 166–167
organic 13–14, 119–120
plural 2, 79
successful 7, 10, 14, 24, 67, 73, 82, 83,
 130, 138, 140, 142, 171
territorial 2–4, 10, 44, 118, 166, 168, 171
federalizing 2, 39, 45, 67, 113, 135, 164,
 169 *see* federal process
federation 3, 7, 12, 14, 17, 19–20, 24, 30,
 34, 85, 88, 118, 132, 137, 147, 158,
 164, 167, 171
 domestically-imposed 37, 40, 82, 137,
 162, 166
Federation of Rhodesia and Nyasaland 12,
 47–58, 159, 161, 164
foundational myths 36, 53, 130, 137–140,
 143, 147, 164, 168–169
 aspirational 137–140, 164
 nostalgic 61, 137–140, 164
fragmegration 3, 115, 156, 158, 168
France 59, 61–62, 67–69, 109
franchise 47, 50–51, 53, 55, 57, 65
'Free China' *see* China
freedom 1, 21, 33, 121, 130, 142, 151,
 168 *see* emancipation

Gao Gang 99
Gaullism 60, 62–64, 68
Germany 59, 61, 117, 131, 134
glasnost 154–155
godfather state *see* state
governance 4, 14, 22, 36, 38, 71, 73, 76,
 81, 83, 91, 98, 104, 107, 109–110, 112,
 158, 164, 168
 shared 2, 18, 82, 93, 104, 169
Greece 117
Grenada 17, 18
Guangxi 92
 'Guangxi Clique' 92

Havel, Václav 136
human rights 8, 10, 33, 35, 37, 53, 104,
 112, 119, 122, 170
Hungary 131, 139

identity 1, 4, 6, 9, 14, 20, 24, 28, 36, 43,
 60, 64, 68, 82, 105, 108, 110, 116, 119,
 122, 125, 134, 138, 141, 146, 150, 153,
 155, 159, 163, 166, 170
 ethnic 12, 24, 28, 32, 42, 47, 52, 72

federal 4, 5–6, 12, 14, 53, 55, 81, 103,
 116, 120, 122, 132, 137, 140, 145, 152,
 155, 161
 'identities-within-a-federation' 5
 inherent 4
 national 3, 4, 5–6, 10, 26, 32, 38, 40, 58,
 72, 81, 103, 112, 124, 126, 132, 145,
 148, 158
 natural 4
 regional 24, 26, 28, 30
 socialist 119–121, 122, 124
 tensions 3, 5, 7–8, 16, 34, 38, 42, 44, 60,
 69, 79, 107, 160
 territorial 3, 175
identity accommodation *see* accommodation
identity community 3, 5–6, 12, 63, 126,
 165, 167
identity narrative *see* narrative
ideological federalism *see* federalism
imagined community 5
imposed federalism *see* federalism
inclusion 9, 23, 36, 42–43, 54, 63, 67, 72,
 79, 81, 108, 130, 138, 140, 152 *see*
 exclusion
India 12, 48, 71, 73, 75, 83
Indonesia 12, 32, 38–44, 45, 159, 163
 federalism 12, 31, 38–44, 160, 164
instrumental federalism *see* federalism
Iraq 3, 104, 107, 170
insecurity 67, 166, 189 *see* security
Islamic fundamentalism 103, 112
Israel 104, 108, 109, 111
Italy 32, 37, 83

Jamaica 17, 19–28, 30, 161
Japan 91, 93–95, 102
Jerusalem 104
Jinnah, Mohammed Ali 74
Jordan 104, 107, 110

Kardelj, Edvard 13, 117, 118, 120, 121,
 123–125, 160
Khan, Ayub 73, 76–77, 160
Kosovo 115, 116, 124, 170
Kurds 83

LCY (League of Communists of
 Yugoslavia) 117, 119, 121, 123
Lebanon 104
Lenin, Vladimir 91, 100, 102, 147, 148,
 150, 152, 155, 160

Li Zonghuang 95, 96, 97
Libya 103, 107

Macedonia 115, 120, 170
Manchu rule 89
Manley, Norman 25, 26, 28, 29
Mao Zedong 13, 87, 98–100, 102
Marx, Karl 146, 147, 152
Marxism 14, 43, 62, 108, 111, 124, 146,
    150, 152, 155, Soviet 146, 148, 150,
    152, 154 *see* communism
Middle East 13, 103, 105–107, 109–113
military rule 103, 107, 111, 112
minority group 6, 7, 8, 12, 34, 47, 49, 76,
    79, 100, 141
Montego Bay Conference 20–23, 26, 27
Montenegro 116, 117, 170
Montserrat 17, 18, 22
Moscow 91, 99, 148,
multinational federalism *see* federalism
multiracial partnership 47–49, 53, 57, 58
Muna, Salomon 63, 66
mutuality 8

Nanjing 91–92, 94
narrative 36, 43, 87, 93, 98, 107, 131, 145,
    150, 164
    federal 151, 154, 164
    identity 107, 116, 119, 137, 164
    national 38, 42, 87, 107, 148, 151, 154
    Westphalian 115, 150
nascent state *see* state
Nasser, Gamal Abd al- 13, 103, 106–112
nationalism 4, 12, 13, 14, 39, 45, 58, 60, 85,
    87, 108, 111, 130, 139, 148, 154, 166
    nested 4, 167
    populist 122 *see* patriotism
nation state *see* state
national federalism *see* federalism
Nigeria 61, 65, 67, 83
Northern Expedition 91, 92 *see* China
Northern Ireland 53, 83

October Revolution 14, 147, 150, 152,
    155 *see* revolution, USSR
One Unit *see* Pakistan
oppression 5, 13, 36, 99, 151, 161 *see*
    subordination
order 2, 4, 12, 21, 24, 31, 94, 97, 99, 111,
    113, 121, 125, 146, 150, 152, 154, 165,
    167

organic federalism *see* federalism
Ottoman Empire 32, 104, 111, 116

Pakistan 13, 71–86, 160, 163
    1956 Constitution 74, 76–78, 82
    1962 Constitution 73, 77–78, 160
    East 71, 74–75, 78, 82, 84
    federalism 12, 71–86, 159, 161
    language controversy 74–75
    One Unit 12, 76, 80, 82
    West 12, 71–72, 76, 79, 81
Palestine 104, 111, 112
Pancasila 40, 43, 44
parallel examination 6, 15, 23, 157, 164,
    170 *see* comparative study
patriotism 102, 120, 125 *see* nationalism
People's National Party 25, 26
People's National Movement 25, 28
perestroika 154, 155
Poland 131
police state *see* state
political extremism 104, 108, 112
political system 40, 54, 62, 68, 79–82, 98,
    102, 121, 126, 170
polity 7, 43, 83, 92, 102, 140, 160 *see* state
power 2, 4, 9, 10, 12, 17, 22, 24, 29, 32, 62,
    71, 74, 81, 87, 99, 109, 122, 134, 148,
    155, 163, 167
    balance of 22, 25, 63
    diffuse 2, 10, 25, 35, 49, 72, 80, 89, 95,
        133, 137, 158, 161
    discursive 151, 155
    executive 22, 76–77, 84, 92, 106, 109,
        121
    territorial 3, 13, 34, 105, 169 *see* control
Prague Spring 134, 135
process 1, 3, 9, 17, 20, 23, 26, 28, 30, 34,
    39, 44, 60, 64, 72, 84, 90, 102, 118,
    121, 126, 131, 135, 146, 150, 153, 155,
    158, 164, 169
    constitutional 62–63, 71, 84, 120, 122,
        124
    democratic 25, 27, 33, 41, 53, 79, 101,
        133, 155, 159, 170
    economic 22, 26, 29, 171
    federal 2, 5, 14, 17, 21, 23, 27, 30, 34,
        39, 67, 78, 119, 143, 145, 164, 166,
        168, 170
    political 2, 5, 16, 21, 24, 26, 29, 32, 45,
        53, 79, 84, 113, 119, 132, 149, 154, 165
plural federalism *see* federalism

pluralism 8, 37, 63, 121, 169
public debate 41, 43, 129, 140, 153

quasi-state *see* state
Quebec 83

racial discrimination 48, 51, 56–58 *see*
    apartheid
reciprocity 8
region 3, 13, 17–19, 24, 26–27, 29, 32, 36,
    39, 52, 61, 63, 65, 67, 78, 82, 83, 93,
    99, 103, 105, 107, 110, 158, 161, 164
regional identity *see* identity
regionalism 19, 158
representation 8, 47, 50, 52, 58, 72, 74, 76,
    79, 82, 84, 107, 118, 121, 146, 155
responsibility 9, 23, 28, 35, 52, 65, 68, 84,
    89, 95, 104, 108
revolution 14, 38, 60, 90, 91, 107, 111, 121,
    147, 150, 155 *see* counter-revolution

sacralization 155
safe haven 63
secession 6, 32, 55, 65, 71, 78, 82, 84, 107,
    121, 167
security 56, 67, 74, 92, 113, 142, 156, 167
  global 113
  national 160, 166, 168 *see* insecurity
securitization 15, 16, 147, 161, 167–169
self-determination 37, 79, 121, 137, 143,
    148, 151, 154, 160
self-government 2, 10, 17, 19–24, 28, 49,
    52, 54, 58, 62, 74, 79, 88, 90–98
self-management 13, 116, 118–125, 162
Serbia 115, 116, 124, 170,
shared governance *see* governance
Slovakia 129–131, 133, 135, 137, 139
Slovaks 14, 129–131, 134, 136, 139, 141
Slovenia 115, 116, 117, 120
socialist state *see* state
South Africa 48–49, 51, 53, 57
sovereignty 1, 13, 15, 33, 39, 49, 67, 88, 92,
    95, 97, 100, 105, 111, 113, 118, 133,
    150, 166
  dual 38, 87, 99
  national 12, 61, 78, 106, 166
  popular 40
  post-colonial 11
  shared 2, 35, 38, 87, 89, 91, 93, 98, 100,
    102
  'Westphalian straitjacket' 15

Soviet Union *see* USSR
Spain 83
St Kitts-Nevis-Anguilla 17, 18, 22
St Lucia 17, 18
St Vincent and the Grenadines 17, 18, 22
state 1, 7–9, 12, 39, 42, 47, 63, 66, 71,
    74–75, 79, 81, 88, 96, 100, 105–106,
    113, 118, 123, 129, 132, 134, 136, 147,
    154, 159, 164
  autocratic 39, 123
  awkward 12, 165, 185
  failed 15, 98, 110, 113
  federal 5, 7, 12, 31, 39, 41, 44, 54, 58,
    63, 66, 68, 83, 101, 111, 113, 115, 117,
    122, 131, 155
  godfather 59
  multinational 3, 10, 45, 72, 84, 118, 133,
    148
  nascent 60, 155
  nation 3, 9, 71, 73, 79, 98, 129, 134, 165,
    169
  police 56, 96, 123
  quasi 48, 64, 96, 116, 134, 165, 167
  socialist 132, 147, 150–151, 155, 160
  unitary 3, 12, 31–32, 36, 40–45, 58,
    59–60, 101, 117
  weak 15, 110, 113, 167–168, 170 *see*
    federation, polity, sovereignty
state building 3, 5, 12, 15, 31, 72, 79, 88,
    90, 98, 104, 107, 110, 112, 116, 117,
    125, 131, 158
state collapse 3, 6, 15, 29, 34, 42, 116, 123,
    145, 147, 160, 165, 169 *see* failed
    state, federal failure
state elites 11, 13, 31, 34, 36, 39, 44, 53, 60,
    67, 73, 81, 84, 89, 137, 160, 164
statehood *see* state
Standing Closer Association Committee 21,
    22
strategic identity *see* identity
strategy 3, 9, 13, 27, 48, 60, 64, 93, 98, 106,
    108, 110, 119, 125, 148, 155, 162, 165,
    171
subordination 2, 5, 23, 29, 33, 36, 87,
    99 *see* oppression
successful federalism *see* federalism
Sudan 33, 170
Suez crisis 107–109, 111
Sukarno 12, 31, 40, 41, 42
Sun Chuanfang 92
Sun Yat-sen 87, 90–91, 95

Switzerland 3
Syria 103, 104, 107, 110–112

Taiwan 13, 87, 89, 92, 94–98, 101
territorial federalism *see* federalism
territory 2, 10, 18, 20, 27, 31, 39, 43, 47,
      51, 59, 72, 78, 90, 116, 125, 131, 147,
      158, 163, 166, 168, 171
'Third Force' *see* China
Tibetans 100
Tito, Josip Broz 13, 115, 117, 119–123,
      125–126, 130, 160
tolerance 8
Trinidad and Tobago 19, 21–23, 25–28
turbulence 15, 116, 126, 168
Turkey 83

Uighurs 100
unitary state *see* state
United Arab Republic 103, 107, 109, 110
United Arab State 103, 107
United Kingdom 27, 59, 61, 67, 69, 109
United Nations 16, 31, 33, 39, 60, 61, 62, 67
United States of America 3, 33, 37, 39, 78,
      109, 116
Urdu 74–75, 79, 81
USSR (Union of Soviet Socialist
      Republics) 3, 49, 91, 96, 99–100, 117,
      131, 136, 145–156, 160
   federalism 14, 145–156, 159, 162
   identity 147, 151, 152–153
   society 150–151, 153

Velvet Revolution 14, 130, 142 *see*
      revolution

violence 3, 7, 44, 84, 94, 105, 113, 115,
      117, 165
Vojvodina 116

warlords 88–91, 94, 96, 98
weak state *see* state
West Indies 11, 17–21, 73, 159
   federalism 11, 17–21, 159, 161
   identity 20, 24, 25, 26, 29, 161
West Indies Federal Labour Party 25
West Indies Royal Commission 18–19
westernization 106
'Westphalian straitjacket' *see* sovereignty
Williams, Eric 21
wisdom 2, 157, 170
working class 14, 121, 146, 150

Xie Xuehong 94
Xikang 93
Xinjiang 93

Yemen 103, 107
Yugoslavia 3, 13, 115–128, 142, 160, 161,
      163
   1974 Constitution 116, 118–119, 123, 125
   'brotherhood and unity' 120, 126
   self-management 13, 116, 118–119, 121,
      123, 125, 162
Yugoslavism (Jugoslovenstvo) 116–117,
      120, 122, 125, 162

Zhejiang 92